RESEARCH IN EDUCATION

RESEARCH IN EDUCATION

Dr. M.S. Talawar
M.A., M.Ed., Ph.D.
Professor in Education &
Director –UGC-Academic Staff College,
Bangalore University, Bangalore

Dr. V.A. Benakanal
M.A., M.Ed., M.Phil., Ph.D.

CENTRUM PRESS
NEW DELHI-110002 (INDIA)

CENTRUM PRESS
H.O.: 4360/4, Ansari Road, Daryaganj,
New Delhi-110 002 (India)
Ph.: 23278000, 23261597

B.O.: No. 1015, Ist Main Road, BSK IIIrd Stage
IIIrd Phase, IIIrd Block,
Bangalore - 560 085 (India)
Tel.: 080-41723429
Visit us at: www.centrumpress.com

Research in Education

First Edition, 2009

PRINTED IN INDIA

Printed at Balaji Offset, Delhi

Contents

Preface

Education in its broadest sense is any act or experience that has a formative effect on the mind, character, or physical ability of an individual (e.g., the consciousness of an infant is educated by its environment through its interaction with its environment); and in its technical sense education is the process by which society deliberately transmits its accumulated knowledge, values, and skills from one generation to another through institutions.

Teachers in such institutions direct the education of students and might draw on many subjects, including reading, writing, mathematics, science and history.

This technical process is sometimes called schooling when referring to the compulsory education of youth. Teachers in specialized professions such as astrophysics, law, or zoology may teach only a certain subject, usually as professors at institutions of higher learning.

There is also instruction in fields for those who want specific vocational skills, such as those required to be a pilot. In addition there is an array of education possible at the informal level, e.g., at museums and libraries, with the Internet, and in life experience.

Teachers need to understand a subject enough to convey its essence to students.

The goal is to establish a sound knowledge base on which students will be able to build as they are exposed to different life experiences. The passing of knowledge from generation to generation allows students to grow into useful members of society.

Good teachers can translate information, good judgment, experience and wisdom into relevant knowledge that a student can understand, retain and pass to others. Studies from the US suggest that the quality of teachers is the single most important factor affecting student performance, and that countries which score highly on international tests have multiple policies in place to ensure that the teachers they employ are as effective as possible.

Author

Unit I

Scope and Need for Educational Research

PROBLEMS FACED IN EDUCATIONAL RESEARCH

Universities have traditionally accepted the fact that new faculty members require help and guidance in developing their research programs, in developing their teaching skills and in developing a role in the academic administration of the institution. However, many faculty members at other stages of their academic careers also require help and guidance in order to remain productive and enthusiastic members of the university which is necessary if they are to continue serving the institution to their full potential.

Few universities provide such help and guidance and, as a result, the quality of the education they provide, the quality of their academic administrative systems and the quality of their research programs often suffer. In considering the problems and needs of the faculty it is important to realize that these problems and needs are dependent upon academic discipline, upon gender, upon the personality of the faculty member and upon whether a faculty member chooses to follow a career path involving major administrative appointments.

However, it appears that there are certain common requirements that emerge when the problems and needs of faculty members are considered and it is these common requirements that will be considered here. The problems and needs of faculty members are also, of course, dependent upon age and length of service and this effect must, it appears, be taken into account. A typical academic career has a length of thirty to forty years and in order to account for the effects of age and length of service upon faculty problems and needs, it is common to split an academic career into three phases, these being:

- The Early Years: This phase is usually taken to cover the period between first appointment and the granting of tenure and the promotion from Assistant to Associate Professor. It includes the period during which a research programme is being developed and a good research funding base is being established and when a teaching style and role is being developed. This stage typically covers approximately the first six to ten years of an academic career.
- The Mid-Career Years: This phase is usually taken to cover the period that includes promotion to the rank of Full Professor, completion of the development of a mature and well recognized research programme supported by significant research funding, the taking on of a significant teaching load and the assumption of an increased role in academic administration. This phase ends when retirement begins to be considered and typically covers the middle twenty to twenty-five years of an academic career.
- The Late Years: This phase is usually taken to cover the period from the time retirement is first seriously considered to the time when retirement actually occurs. This phase typically covers the last five to ten years of an academic career and is often characterized by a decreasing involvement in research and in academic administration, this often not being at the choice of the academic.

Each of these three phases tends to involve different faculty needs and problems, those in the second two phases often being just as difficult as those in the first phase. The nature of the problems and difficulties that arise in each of the three phases will now be separately and briefly discussed. It must again be stressed that these problems and difficulties faced by academics at various stages in their careers do tend to vary with discipline and with the individual and that each particular case needs some degree of individual attention.

THE EARLY YEARS

New academics face intense pressure to develop a good teaching record and to build a strong funding and publication record in the first three to five years of their academic careers. This can lead to high stress levels in these new academics and confusion as to exactly what is being required of them. They often respond by spending their time inappropriately and may end up feeling very frustrated.

Studies of faculty members in their first 3-4 years of an academic career suggest that the problems encountered by new faculty members often result from the fact that they: spent less time on the development of their research programs than was needed in order to produce a programme capable of generating the results needed to meet the promotion and tenure criteria of their institutions.

- Admitted going to class over-prepared (with more material than they could reasonably cover in the allotted time) and rushing to complete everything, often at the expense of student understanding and participation.
- Taught defensively, doing whatever they could to avoid student complaints.
- Received student evaluations that fell well below their expectations but blamed these results on external factors (invalid rating systems, poor students, unfavorable class times and sizes).
- Experienced a sense of loneliness and lack of collegial acceptance, and had difficulty establishing productive contacts with colleagues who could provide guidance and support.

Of course, not all new faculty members showed these characteristics. Some of the new faculty successfully developed more than adequate research records for promotion and tenure and scored in the top quartile of student ratings of teaching.

Compared to the majority of their colleagues, these successful new "quick starter" academics:

- Spent, on average, more time on their research
- did not spend major amounts of time on course preparation averaging about 1 to 1.5 hours of preparation per lecture hour after their first semester
- Lectured at a pace that allowed for student understanding and participation
- Regularly sought advice from colleagues on research and teaching.

The main differences between typical new faculty and these successful "quick starters" were the latter group's abilities to balance conflicting demands on their time and to quickly establish productive networking with colleagues.

The above, and other observations, indicate that the problems encountered by academics in the early stages of their careers can largely be alleviated by:

- Ensuring that new faculty members receive adequate and frequent feedback concerning their progress towards meeting institutional expectations. A useful practice is a meeting each semester between the chair and new faculty member, discussing what the new faculty member has accomplished, what is currently underway, and what is planned in research, teaching, and service. Feedback to new faculty members can also come from a committee made up of senior colleagues some of whom will eventually be involved in making tenure and promotion decisions. The committee and the new faculty member should meet at least once each semester in order to discuss past, current, and planned activities, and the committee should provide affirmation and guidance when each is appropriate.
- Ensuring that an adequate and formal mentoring system is in place, one or two mentors for each new faculty member usually being required. Despite the criticism that has been leveled at it, mentoring has a long history as a technique for teaching new

practitioners their craft and, when done properly, can be of great benefit to a new faculty member. A mentor can help a new faculty member integrate into the academic community, offer guidance about getting started in research and teaching, and serve as an advocate in the tenure and promotion process.

- Ensuring that a new faculty member is provided with adequate resources including financial support in order to allow them to develop their research and teaching programs.

THE MID-CAREER YEARS

Faculty members face many challenges during the mid-career years. Sometimes they realize that it is necessary for them to change the focus of their research but to do so often involves the risk of losing research funding and of not being able to make a significant contribution in the new research area. Sometimes mid-career academics begin to lose some of their enthusiasm for research and want to concentrate more on teaching and service to the university but find that for a variety of reasons, this is not allowed by the institution. Some mid- career academics who are competent but not highly successful researchers or teachers develop the feeling that they are unappreciated and marginalized and as a result, they grow resentful and withdraw to some extent from their colleagues.

Events such as being passed over for a leadership opportunity or discovering that their accomplishments are ignored by their colleagues Andlor chair tend to lead to the feelings of resentment that characterize some mid-career academics. Depression and stress are all too often features of the mid-career years. Despite the fact that mid-career academics do the majority of the teaching in many universities and bring in relatively large amounts of research money to the institution, their needs and problems are very often completely ignored by the institution. It appears, however, that encouraging mid-career professional development is as equally important as supporting early career faculty.

Unfortunately, this need is often not well addressed.

Although very few mid- career faculty development programs exist, there are steps that can be taken even at the departmental level to help. Most of the ideas for encouraging faculty mid-career development relate to sharing resources, giving these faculty members some extra attention and allowing them to modify the balance between research and teaching as long as the result is beneficial to both the university and the academic.

Some of the ways in which mid-career academics can be assisted are:

- Encourage Creativity and Provide the Means to Change their Research Focus: To encourage creativity, a department may need to make some small, but worthwhile investments in a faculty member's career. Providing some bridge money or seed money to encourage risk can give faculty the opportunity to transform their focus. Sometimes a small investment, such as seed money, can reap larger rewards later as the stalled faculty member now has some resources to invest. Stalled faculty may need to be taught how to be competitive with organizations other than their standard funding agencies. Department chairs could consider giving stalled faculty an internal sabbatical. Having more time may be all that is needed in order to boost their research efforts. Or, the faculty member may wish to focus temporarily on a new area such as education or leadership development. If they become energized in one area, they often can transfer that energy to their research interests. Success begets success.
- Mentoring: Many mid-career faculties also need mentoring. A department chair might work with this faculty on the presentation of their ideas, serving as a sounding board or offering extra guidance on communicating ideas. Matching the stalled faculty with research-active faculty both within and outside the department creates another mentoring forum. People who may in the past have been stalled in their development but who are currently experiencing

success may also be good mentors. For example, they may have failed several times to obtain funding from a granting agency before finding multiple successes at the very same agency. Talking with someone who has overcome a similar challenge can be inspiring. By finding ways to help create opportunities to achieve some level of success, chairs can help mid-career faculty to become productive (and satisfied) again.

- Nominating Mid-Career Academics for Awards: Faculty at all levels appreciates being recognized for their contributions. Department chairs should be encouraged to actively nominate their mid-career faculty for awards and recognition. National and university awards are excellent professional development opportunities. Department chairs should work closely with their entire faculty to identify potential opportunities and to create strong nomination packets.
- Faculty Development Programs: Universities should institute development programs for faculty at all levels. It is important that such programs aimed at mid-career academics not be condescending or trivial.
- Allowing an Adjustment in the Balance between Teaching and Research: Although it is not easy to do in many institutions, attempts should be made to accommodate the changes that occur during mid-career by allowing academics in this stage to take on heavier teaching loads to compensate for reduced research productivity. This assumes that the faculty member has a good teaching record.

THE LATE YEARS

The problems and challenges faced by faculty members in the last period of their academic career tend to be even more dependent upon the individual than those encountered in the earlier periods and it is, as a result, difficult to categorize these difficulties of the later years. However, the problems and challenges faced by academics in this later year period tend to include the following:

- They have relatively little interaction with their younger colleagues and are excluded from the informal discussions that so often are the foundation upon which academic decisions are made.
- They are not considered when the formation of new research groups is being considered.
- Although they are often willing to increase their contributions in the service area, they are overlooked by nominating committees who often assume that they have long since retired or assume that they will resist change and should not therefore be considered.
- They are not given any clear indication of whether or not they will be allocated the space to continue their research after retirement and consequently are not sure whether to seek new research funding or develop new research areas.
- Even when they know that the decision as to when to retire is a personal one, many academics in this stage of their career dread retirement fearing that they will no longer be able to in any way undertake the research, teaching and service work that they really enjoy.
- Academics at this career stage often suffer from bouts of depression and feelings of resentment for reasons that are frequently not clearly understood.

This list is meant to illustrate the difficulties faced by this academic group and is not meant to be comprehensive. Some of the ways that can be considered to assist academics in the late-year period are:

- Chairs should actively try to ensure that late-year academics are kept involved in the operation of the department and the faculty.
- Some form of mentoring for these academics should be considered if this seems appropriate and if a suitable person to undertake the mentoring is available.

- An attempt should be made well in advance of retirement to give the academic a clear indication of what support and facilities they can expect for their research after they have retired.
- The possibilities for teaching on a very limited scale as an adjunct after retirement should be openly discussed.
- Phased retirement schemes should be put in place. In such schemes, if an academic so chooses, retirement is allowed to be phased in over a period of say three years, the teaching and service workload decreasing in steps over this period with the salary decreasing in steps and the pension benefits increasing in steps over this period.

KARPIAAK'S RECOMMENDATIONS

In "Ghosts in a Wilderness: Problems and Priorities of Faculty at Mid-Career and Mid- Life," Karpiak (1996) presents a study of mid-career and some late year problems.

Among the recommendations made as a result of this study were:

- Humanize the institution through more realistic expectations of faculty, and recognition and support of the different efforts and contributions that they bring,
- Provide academic support and resources for research, including space to carry out research, and time, through lower teaching loads, reduced administrative duties, and mini- sabbaticals,
- Promote among faculty a sense that they are involved in a joint enterprise, and that they are members of a team,
- Foster an environment in which colleagues stimulate each other's intellectual interests and help each other to develop and grow as intellectuals,
- Develop support networks so that faculty know they are not alone
- Acknowledge the particular circumstances of women

faculty, e.g., child bearing and be flexible about the personal demands that women have,

- Help faculty fulfill their potential for the last 10 or 15 years of their academic lives by providing resources, such as career counseling, for people in mid-career. These recommendations will be seen to be, for the most part, similar to those presented above.

Problems and difficulties arise at all stages of an academic career, the nature of these problems and difficulties varying however with the career stage. Universities would benefit by acknowledging that such problems exists and by trying to adopt measures that will assist academics to deal with these problems at all stages of their careers. More attention should be given to the adoption of procedures that allow more flexibility in what is deemed to be a successful academic career.

Unit II

Major Steps in Research

DEFINING A RESEARCH PROBLEM

Defining a research problem is the fuel that drives the scientific process, and is the foundation of any research method and experimental design, from true experiment to case study. It is one of the first statements made in any research paper and, as well as defining the research area, should include a quick synopsis of how the hypothesis was arrived at. Operationalization is then used to give some indication of the exact definitions of the variables, and the type of scientific measurements used. This will lead to the proposal of a viable hypothesis. As an aside, when scientists are putting forward proposals for research funds, the quality of their research problem often makes the difference between success and failure.

STRUCTURING THE RESEARCH PROBLEM

Look at any scientific paper, and you will see the research problem, written almost like a statement of intent. Defining a research problem is crucial in defining the quality of the answers, and determines the exact research method used. A quantitative experimental design uses deductive reasoning to arrive at a testable hypothesis. Qualitative research designs use inductive reasoning to propose a research statement.

DEFINING A RESEARCH PROBLEM

Formulating the research problem begins during the first steps of the scientific process. As an example, a literature review and a study of previous experiments, and research, might throw up some vague areas of interest. Many scientific researchers look at an area where a previous researcher generated some interesting results, but never followed up. It could be an interesting area of research, which nobody else has fully explored. A scientist may even review a successful experiment, disagree with the results, the tests used, or the methodology, and decide to refine the research process, retesting the hypothesis. This is called the conceptual definition, and is an overall view of the problem. A science report will generally begin with an overview of the previous research and real-world observations. The researcher will then state how this led to defining a research problem.

THE OPERATIONAL DEFINITIONS

The operational definition is the determining the scalar properties of the variables. For example, temperature, weight and time are usually well known and defined, with only the exact scale used needing definition. If a researcher is measuring abstract concepts, such as intelligence, emotions, and subjective responses, then a system of measuring numerically needs to be established, allowing statistical analysis and replication.

For example, intelligence may be measured with IQ and human responses could be measured with a questionnaire from '1- strongly disagree', to '5 – strongly agree'. Behavioral biologists and social scientists might design an ordinal scale for measuring and rating behaviour. These measurements are always subjective, but allow statistics and replication of the whole research method. This is all an essential part of defining a research problem.

EXAMPLES OF DEFINING A RESEARCH PROBLEM

An anthropologist might find references to a relatively unknown tribe in Papua New Guinea. Through inductive reasoning, she arrives at the research problem and asks, 'How do these people live and how does their culture relate to nearby tribes?' She has found a gap in knowledge, and she seeks to fill it, using a qualitative case study, without a hypothesis.

The Bandura Bobo Doll Experiment is a good example of using deductive reasoning to arrive at a research problem and hypothesis. Anecdotal evidence showed that violent behaviour amongst children was increasing. Bandura believed that higher levels of violent adult role models on television, was a contributor to this rise. This was expanded into a hypothesis, and operationalization of the variables, and scientific measurement scale, led to a robust experimental design.

Research forms a cycle. It starts with a problem and ends with a solution to the problem. The problem statement is therefore the axis which the whole research revolves around, because it explains in short the aim of the research.

A research problem is the situation that causes the researcher to feel apprehensive, confused and ill at ease. It is the demarcation of a problem area within a certain context involving the WHO or WHAT, the WHERE, the WHEN and the WHY of the problem situation. There are many problem situations that may give rise to research. Three sources usually contribute to problem identification. Own experience or the experience of others may be a source of problem supply. A second source could be scientific literature.

You may read about certain findings and notice that a certain field was not covered. This could lead to a research problem. Theories could be a third source. Shortcomings in theories could be researched. Research can thus be aimed at clarifying or substantiating an existing theory, at clarifying contradictory findings, at correcting a faulty methodology, at correcting the inadequate or unsuitable use of statistical techniques, at reconciling conflicting opinions, or at solving existing practical problems.

IDENTIFICATION OF THE PROBLEM

The prospective researcher should think on what caused the need to do the research (problem identification). The question that he/she should ask is: Are there questions about this problem to which answers have not been found up to the present? Research originates from a need that arises. A clear distinction between the PROBLEM and the PURPOSE should be made. The problem is the aspect the researcher worries about, thinks about, wants to find a solution for. The purpose is to solve the problem, i.e. find answers to the question(s). If there is no clear problem formulation, the purpose and methods are meaningless.

Keep the following in mind:

- Outline the general context of the problem area.
- Highlight key theories, concepts and ideas current in this area.
- What appear to be some of the underlying assumptions of this area?
- Why are these issues identified important?
- What needs to be solved?
- Read round the area (subject) to get to know the background and to identify unanswered questions or controversies, and/or to identify the most significant issues for further exploration.

The research problem should be stated in such a way that it would lead to analytical thinking on the part of the researcher with the aim of possible concluding solutions to the stated problem. Research problems can be stated in the form of either questions or statements.

- The research problem should always be formulated grammatically correct and as completely as possible. You should bear in mind the wording (expressions) you use. Avoid meaningless words. There should be no doubt in the mind of the reader what your intentions are.
- Demarcating the research field into manageable parts by dividing the main problem into sub-problems is of the utmost importance.

SUB-PROBLEM(S)

Sub-problems are problems related to the main problem identified. Sub-problems flow from the main problem and make up the main problem. It is the means to reach the set goal in a manageable way and contribute to solving the problem.

STATEMENT OF THE PROBLEM

The statement of the problem involves the demarcation and formulation of the problem, i.e. the WHO/WHAT, WHERE, WHEN, WHY. It usually includes the statement of the hypothesis.

SOURCES FOR RESEARCH PROBLEM

Problems can be conceptualized at a number of levels. At one level we are all searching for the answer to the question "why do organisms behave the way they do?" Questions with more specificity could proceed from; why do humans behave the way they do, to how does reinforcement affect behaviour, to how does reinforcement affect studying, to how does reinforcement affect studying for tests in university males. Beginners tend to start with relatively specific research problems focused on the face value of the question, but eventually develop a broad research question with great generality.

For example, what started as "how can I help my roommate study more?" evolves into "what controls studying in people?" At the beginning, the roommate's behaviour is at issue for itself. Later the person and the behaviour are seen as arbitrary instances of a much more important and challenging question. Career long research problems tend to emerge following several years of specific research topics, and require many specific research studies to solve. This section details some of the sources for an initial, relatively specific, research problem. It is intended to help you come up with research which is manageable, enjoyable, and productive.

A very serious impediment facing new researchers is well illustrated by trying to use a foreign language dictionary to learn what foreign words mean. Until you know "enough" of a language, you cannot find out what the words mean. Until you know "enough" of a paradigm, you do not know what unresolved questions remain, or when the paradigm is wrong. "A" below is generally a person's first exposure to a research project for that reason. In addition to not knowing what unresolved problems remain, is missing the more fundamental broader issue underlying any specific behaviour change. When looking at the world, try to see each functional relationship as only an instance of a more general class of relationships.

RESEARCH PROBLEM FROM EXPERT

The simplest source of a problem to solve is to have it given to you as a class assignment, as a directed research project, or as a task while you are an apprentice in someone's lab. You are told what problem to research and how to do it. This is probably an ideal way to assure that your first research topic is a good one.

Example: Students in Experimental Psychology were assigned the task of finding out if social attention made their roommate study more.

They were told to measure the amount of time their roommate studied on days during which they expressed interest in their roommate's course material as compared to days when they refrained from talking about academic topics.

RESEARCH PROBLEM FROM FOLKLORE

Common beliefs, common sense, or proverbs could be right but on the other hand, they could also be wrong. You must verify that they are true before considering them as a source of knowledge. It is possible that some unverified beliefs have the roots of a better idea and therefore would be a worthy research topic. It is critical to note, however, that the task of research is not to simply validate or invalidate common sense but rather to come to understand nature.

Example: It's commonly believed that studying within the two hours preceding a test will decrease test scores. To research this belief a randomly selected half of a class was told to study immediately before taking a test while the other half was prohibited from studying before the test. This research was intended to determine whether or not studying immediately before a test decreased the points earned.

RESEARCH PROBLEM FROM INSIGHT

Sometimes people research an issue simply because it occurred to them and it seemed important. The systematic development of the idea is lacking. This is "intuitive" or good guess research. It is risky because you may not be able to get other researchers to understand why the research is important. It is fun because you get to do what interests you at the moment. Alternatively, it could be the application of a general rule of thumb or guessing that a new problem is actually a well-understood function in disguise.

Example: While feeling especially competent after explaining course material to three friends you realize that orally presenting material may help test performance. You conducted a study in which material was orally presented before the test on a random half of the occasions. The research was based on your insightful realization that oral presentation may increase test performance.

RESEARCH PROBLEM FROM INFORMAL DISCUSSION

This is a research problem that some discussion group feels is interesting. Discussion among friends can often spark our interest in a problem or provides us with the reinforcers for pursuing a question.

Example: After telling a group of friends about your success with oral presentations on test taking, the group talks about it for awhile and becomes interested in the possibility of the subject becoming confused as well as doing better as a result of feedback from the listeners. The group provides you with the idea and the excitement to do research on how students can affect the accuracy of a teacher's understanding.

RESEARCH PROBLEM FROM KNOWLEDGE OF TECHNIQUES AND APPARATUS

This is the selection of a research topic based on your special knowledge outside the field. A technique or apparatus with which you are familiar can offer the potential for a major advance in the field of psychology. Sometimes we realize that we can apply a new technique or apparatus to an area to which it has not yet been applied. Because we are specially qualified to succeed, solving the problem can be especially gratifying.

Example: You may know about microelectronics and be good at detailed work. You find out that many researchers are anxious to discover the migration patterns of butterflies so you mount an integrated circuit transmitter on a butterfly and thereby trace the behaviour of the free ranging butterfly.

RESEARCH PROBLEM FROM READING THE LITERATURE

These are research problems which capture your interest while reading. While reading you will often wonder why, or will disagree, or will realize that you have a better idea than the original author.

Example: While you were reading about jet lag and its effects on sleep the first night, you realize that the author failed to control for light cycle. You try stretching either the light period or stretching the dark period to make up the phase shift. You implement this by changing the cabin illumination period on various trans-Atlantic flights, and monitoring the passengers sleep for the next three days.

SOURCES OF RESEARCH LITERATURE

Initially, it may be hard to know where to start reading on your quest for knowledge. Consider starting at a very broad general level and working your way to the more recondite. A good place to start is several Introductory Psychology textbooks. Understand the basic area, what it is, how it fits in Psychology, and why it is important.

Then look through several middle level textbooks which cover that particular area.

Understanding the structure of the area by reading the table of contexts, then read the specific section relevant to your research topic. Read the table of contents and sections relevant to your paper in several more textbooks, paying particular attention to the original research which led to the general paradigm and conclusions. Pay attention to the theoretical significance of various types of results and to the functional relationship depicted in the figures.

Note the authors, titles, dates, volume, and pages of the journals and books which are referred to. Then consult Psychological Abstracts. This is a publication that organizes and provides short abstracts of the mass of knowledge provided in journals. The Psychological Abstracts are available in the library. Locate key papers in the Abstracts.

Introductory texts
Second-level or area texts
Annual Review / review articles
Special topic text / symposium reports
Journal articles

- How to Find Additional Sources:

Web
Psych Info
Dictionary of Psychology
Card catalog
Psychological Abstracts
Current Contents
Citation Index (find subsequently-published related articles)
Reference sections of relevant papers (find previously-published related articles)
Knowledgeable people

Actively participate while you are reading. At first it will keep you from falling asleep, later it will keep you from thinking about other things, and eventually it will make it a lot of fun. Underline, write questions and answers in the margins, and keep an idea log. Draw a diagram of the procedure. Consider how the research bears on your interests. Look for what's important.

- What was the research problem and why must it be answered?
- What subjects were used and why?
- What apparatus or setting was used and why?
- What general procedure was used and why?
- Was the procedure applicable and the best available?

- What was the independent variable, how was it measured, and what was it inferred to be doing (its interpretation) (e.g., did shock produce fear or something else)?
- What were potential confounds and how were they controlled?
- What was the dependent variable, how was it measured, and what was it inferred to be the result of, or what did it represent (its interpretation)?
- What were the actual results, what were they interpreted to mean, and to what extent is it likely they would happen again if the experiment were replicated (their reliability)?
- How sensitive was the dependent measure? To what degree would small changes in the independent variable be expected to change the dependent variable?
- How much of the variability obtained could be accounted for?
- To what extent will the findings apply to other subjects, situations, and procedures? Was there generality?
- What was gained by the research ("so what")? How has the paradigm been extended by this finding?

RESEARCH PROBLEM FROM A PARADOXICAL INCIDENT OR CONFLICTING RESULTS

If the world is perfectly understood, then there can be no surprises. Contrariwise, if something surprises you, then your theoretical framework is inadequate and needs development.

If two seemingly similar procedures produce different results, then something is wrong with your understanding of the procedures.

They are not actually similar in the important respect of how they affect the dependent variable. Given that an error has been made, something is not correctly understood and must be resolved.

RESEARCH PROBLEM DEDUCED FROM PARADIGMS OR THEORIES

Researchers who propose theoretical accounts for phenomena cannot think through every possible ramification. As you come to understand a theory, potential errors or extensions become apparent. This type of research tests the implications of theories to confirm or reject them.

This is classic deductive "normal" science. Using the object in the lake from the first chapter as an example — this would be deducing "if it is an steam shovel under there, then we should find a long row of high spots coming out of one end." You then test that prediction by probing around trying to find a boom. If response strength approaches asymptotic response strength on each reinforced trial, then presenting a compound stimulus of asymptotically conditioned stimuli should result in a response decrement on subsequent tests with isolated stimuli.

STUDY OF RELATED LITERATURE

In writing a research paper, the review of related literature is considered a difficult task but plays an essential part in the completion of the study. Review of related literature involves the systematic identification, location and analysis of documents containing information related to the research problem. Conducting a review of literature will require you to have enough patience, persistence and industry know-how. Your knowledge of techniques and tools in using library resources or internet searching is badly needed to make this part.

Here are reasons that make the review of literature important in a research paper:

Through the review of related literature, researcher was provided the knowledge and background on the topic or subject being studied. Reading these literatures will help you determine what has been done in the past and will give you pointers on how to develop or make some progress on its status. Remember that in a research study, since you are dealing with factual information, it is therefore necessary to acquire the most recent update of the subject under study or investigation.

It will also refrain the researcher from doing a duplicate research study. It will be a waste of effort and time to do a research study that has been done before. Unless if you wish to improve or make further analysis on the subject matter that will result to a much updated outcome.

The review of related literature will also provides the researcher some information about some parts of the problem which were left uninvestigated before. With this information, it will give you a chance to explore new aspects of the problem or try new methods that will result to a much improved research findings.

It will also be a good source of ideas or information in developing various parts of the study such as the problem and terms definition, research design, data gathering techniques and instruments, form and style of report presentation. By means of review, whatever weaknesses, ethical issues and problems encountered in the previous studies can be avoided in your own study. It will also serves as the guide as to how to proceed with the research.

An idea on who are the people involved, what information needed to consult, and what boundaries to cover. The review will also serves as your comparative basis of findings and conclusions. It will also provide the relationship of the variables used in the study and will make it easy for you to analyse and process. ALL cited literature was written and published in the past, so use past tense to refer to the findings of these studies. An article published in 1995 was written in 1994 or even earlier. The authors may have changed their minds.

Do not use first names when referring to the authors of studies you cite. People who use them rarely are consistent in their use of such names. Use only last names in the body of the manuscript. In the references list, use last names and initials. This approach reduces attention to the gender of the author, thereby attenuating discrimination on irrelevant dimensions. You are required to have at least 25 references somewhere in your final research paper, (at least 15 in the proposal).

In most cases, at least two-thirds of these should be from empirical research, studies published in a manner similar to your masters research. Most recent journal articles have an abstract at the beginning of the article. Research the literature on both your independent and dependent variables.

Go up and down in the hierarchy in terms of generalizing your terms. Consider dogs as a topic or category. Going up in the hierarchy labels them as four-legged mammals. Going down in the hierarchy gives you the various breeds: German Shepherd, Cocker Spaniel, Beagle, etc. Suppose you have chosen to study whether 360° feedback has less influence if given anonymously than if the receiver knows who gave the feedback. Because this is an unusual approach to 360° feedback, there may be little or no empirical research in the literature on this exact topic. There is a great deal of research on feedback per se (not all of it on human subjects) and such topics as the timeliness of such feedback.

There is also literature on interpersonal communication which is what personalized feedback becomes. Many of you will have to "pad" your research citations by analyzing the ingredients. Even though this approach is more difficult in terms of key word searches, it may provide you with a more balanced and conceptually-sound basis for evaluating the variables you wish to study. Review some literature comparing how the methodology used affects the results. In many cases, is a quick summary of the findings of the study cited. Because different methodology often leads to different results, and because you always have to choose your method for measuring your variables, you should spend some time discussing the various ways cited studies made their variables operational. It can be interesting, at least informative.

Where is the best place to start? A recent refereed empirical study on the topic you have chosen. With such an article, you have that study's references, those authors who typically have published other articles in the area, and that journal which probably has similar articles. You also get to analyse that study's methodology (and the methodology of the studies those authors cited).

CRITERIA FOR SELECTING A PROBLEM

- A question raised for inquiry, consideration or solution
- An intricate unsettled question

What do we do with Problems?

- Ignore them
- Talk about them
- Try to solve them

What is a Research Problem?

- It is a problem that someone would like to investigate.
- It is considered a situation that needs to be changed or addressed.
- These problems consist of:
  - Areas of concern
  - Conditions to be improved
  - Difficulties to be eliminated
  - Questions seeking answers

The Research Problem:

- In educational research, the research problem is typically posed as a question.

Factors to consider in Selecting a Research Problem:

- The topic should be important (significant)
- Writing a thesis or dissertation is an exercise to learn how to conduct research.
- However, graduate students can learn the research process on an important topic just as easy as learning the research process on a piddle topic!

More Factors to Consider:

- Consider the feasibility of the project.
- How much time do you have available
- Do you really want to do a longitudinal study that will take 3 years to complete for a MS thesis?
- How difficult is it. Are data available?
- How much will it cost?

More Factors:

- Make sure the topic is ethical to study.

Factors to Consider in Selecting a Research Problem

- You should have a personal interest in the topic.
- By the time you are done, you may really be tired of the topic

More Factors to Consider:

- The "newness" of the topic may hold you interest longer, however there is some value in repeating previous research

More Factors:

- Make sure the research question is clear.

Researchable vs. Non-researchable Questions

Writing Clear Questions:

- Don't use words open to interpretation
- Humanistic, teacher centered classroom
- Be very specific
- 4-H agents, not extension agents
- It is measurable
- End of Course Test Scores, not learning

Defining Terms:

- There are 3 ways to clarify important terms or meaning in a research question: 1) use of constitutive definition (the dictionary approach) 2) use of proper example(s) 3) use of operational definition (specifying operations used to measure or identify examples of the term), "Key Terms to Define in a Research Study"

When Operational Definitions would be Helpful How does one find topics to research?

- Become a scholar in an area of specialization
- Read, listen, discuss and think critically
- Follow up on ideas that stem from present research
- Explore areas of dissatisfaction Steps in "Zeroing In" on a Problem
- Identify a broad area that interests you
- Read the literature
- Narrow the area to 2 or 3 topics

- Thoroughly examine the literature on the 2-3 topics
- Select a single problem from 2-3 topics Refining the Topic
- The topic has to be "sized"!
- Generally this means reducing the scope of the topic, occasionally it might be expanded.
- Graduate students often select topics that are too broad I want to research the effect of providing immediate feedback to university students! Way too general and broad!

Refining the Topic:

- The topic has to be "clarified"!
- The topic needs to reworded so that it states clearly and unambiguously the matter to be investigated, the variables to be investigated, and participants, if any, that will be involved. I want to research the impact of providing immediate feedback via e-Instruction responders in AEE graduate classes! Much Better!

Refining the Topic:

- A series of research questions or one or more hypotheses, or both, should be stated.
- Such questions and hypotheses orient the study, add cohesiveness, and are essential in helping solve the problem.

Does the use of e-Information responders to provide immediate feedback to graduate students in AEE classes:

- Increase student learning?
- Improve student evaluations of classes?

It is hypothesized that:

- Graduate students in AEE classes who use the e-Instruction responders will score higher on mid-term and final exams than graduate students in AEE classes who do not use the e-Instruction responders.

It is further hypothesized that:

- Graduate AEE classes in which e-Instruction responders are used will have higher course evaluations than will graduate AEE classes in which the e-Instruction responders were not used.

The Research Process:

- Select and define the problem
- Accumulated pertinent knowledge and information
- Develop specific objectives
- Design the study, the collect and analyse data
- Interpret data
- Prepare the research report

The Research Proposal/Report:

- For graduate students, the research proposal is presented to your committee for their approval before you conduct the research or
- For others, the research proposal is typically presented to a funding agency, school board or extension administration for approval/funding

The Research Proposal/Report:

- A research proposal is future tense, a research report is past tense
- A research report may be longer (as in the case of a thesis or dissertation) or it may be shorter (as is the case in a journal article or research paper presented at a conference)

What should be in a research proposal/report?

- Typically a thesis or dissertation in AEE has five chapters/sections.
- Introduction
- Review of the Literature
- Methodology
- Findings
- Conclusions/Implications

Research proposal/report:

- The length of a thesis or dissertation will be from 50-150 pages.
- A journal article or research paper will contain the same content in the same sequence as listed in the previous slide but will be greatly abbreviated.
- A research proposal will contain the first 3 chapters listed in the previous slide. Introduction Section or Chapter.

- The introductory section introduces the problem to be studied and could range from 3 or so paragraphs to several pages
- This is often followed by a section titled "Need for the Study". This is 1- 3 paragraphs in length. Here you make the case for studying the problem you have selected.

Introduction Section:

- Statement of the Problem is next. This is one or two sentences clearly stating what it is being study. If often starts with "The purpose..."

The purpose of this study is to determine if immediate feedback in AEE graduate classes improves student learning and course evaluations.

Introduction Section:

- Research questions and/or hypothesis follow.
- Descriptive research often uses just research questions. It is permissible to have a hypothesis.
- In experimental, quasi-experimental, correlational or ex post facto research a hypothesis is generally expected. You can also have research questions if desired.

Research Question(s):

- Sample Research Questions
- Does the use of e-Information responders to provide immediate feedback to graduate students in AEE classes increase student learning?
- Does the use of e-Information responders to provide immediate feedback to graduate students in AEE classes improve student evaluations of classes?

Research Question(s):

- One may have several research question
- For data analysis avoid research questions with an "and"
- Does the use of e-Information responders to provide immediate feedback to graduate students in AEE classes increase student learning and improve student evaluations of classes?

One part of the question may be yes and the other no. It is best to compartmentalize everything.

The Hypothesis:

- In proposing or reporting research, two types of hypotheses are normally stated:
- Directional
- AEE graduate students will learn more in classes in which e-Instruction responders are used than in classes where they are not used.
- Null
- There will be no difference in AEE graduate student learning in classes in which e-Instruction responders are used and in classes in which they are not used.

The Hypothesis:

- It is possible to have a nondirectional hypothesis. This is stated the same as a null hypothesis.
- When one performs a statistical test, they are actually testing the Null hypothesis Introduction continued...

The introductory section generally contains:

- *Assumptions:* You think people will answer honestly, they have knowledge of the subject, they are representative, etc. Typically this is included in a proposal and in theses and dissertations but is not reported in journal articles or research presentations.
- The introductory section generally contains:
- *Limitations:* Things that happened during the study they may impact on your findings or the generalizability of the research

Typically this is included in a proposal and in theses and dissertations but is not reported in journal articles or research presentations unless there is a glaring problem.

- *Definitions:* Define the terms in your research that the average person might not know
- Typically this is included in a proposal and in theses and dissertations but is not reported in journal articles or research presentations. It is assumed your audience will know the words.
- By the time you finish your research, you should

know more about the topic than anyone else, including members of your committee. You accomplish this by a thorough review of existing research regarding the problem.

- In a thesis or dissertation, this section may be 10-50 pages.
- In a journal article it may only be 2-3 pages at the most. You have to prove you know the research but can't go overboard because of page limitations on manuscripts.
- It is generally best to start globally and then narrow it down to the specific research question you have.
- Next week's class focuses on how to conduct a literature review.
- You want to synthesize and merge what others had done, not just string a bunch of quotes together!!!!
- Moving around the classroom helps to maintain student interest
- Banks (2001) says it is important to move around in the classroom.
- Carpenter (1996) believes movement in the classroom helps students to focus on the teacher.
- James (1998) says teachers should change their position every 3-4 minutes in order to keep student attention. YES! NO!

Methods:

- Describe the research methodology (correlational, descriptive, etc.) you are used (or plan to use) and why.
- Describe the population you are studying and how it is described.
- If a sample is used, tell how big the sample is, why that sample size was chosen, and the sample was selected (i.e. stratified random sample, cluster sample, etc.)
- If the research is experimental, describe the research design and what was done to control extraneous variables.

- If the research is historical discuss sources of data.
- Describe the research instrument used.
- How many sections and items or on it and how do people respond.
- What is the rating scale? What is a high score? What is a low score?
- How was it developed.
- Was it field tested?
- How do you know it is valid.
- How do you know it is reliable
- Describe how the data were collected (Personal interview, Mail survey, etc.)
- When and where were the data collected
- What was done about non-respondents?
- How were the data coded
- Describe the statistical process used in analyzing the data. Why did you use the statistics you did.
- Report the data you have collected.
- Follow the same sequence in presenting the data so that is corresponds with your research questions or hypotheses.
- Data should be reported both in writing and in graphic form (tables, graphs, etc.)
- Report any statistical tests.
- Just report the facts, don't make any interpretations.
- Based upon the findings section, what can be concluded?
- What are the implications of this research for practice?
- What recommendations do have for further research?

One of the most significant problems in business decision-making is the selection of a new product, which usually has to be performed on the basis of a larger number of criteria. That is why various multi-criteria analysis methods are frequently applied (AHP, PROMETHEE, and others). Selecting a new product is not only important for the survival and future of every company, but it also presents an extremely complex task because of the range of this problem area and a large number of influential values which are of a prevailingly stochastic character.

Complexity and subjectivity are particularly prominent in the procedure of assigning relative values to criteria when selecting a new product. Existing research of the criteria for selecting a new product (indices of the future success of a product) mainly deals with singling out several such indices and deter- mining the intensity of their influence. Then potentially new products are compared with these indices, and the product with the best assessments is adopted.

This is the basic idea in much important research which has been carried out in this way, for example. However, it is very difficult, almost impossible, to make a universal model (a model which could be suitable for a large number of companies) for defining the relative importance of criteria when selecting a new product. In the research carried out in, the initial hypothesis was that every company is a multi-dimensional system, with its specificities and characteristics which have direct influence on assigning certain levels of importance to individual criteria.

As a consequence of this, there is the question of variability of the importance of individual criteria that depend on numerous characteristic features of the company, and above all, the company's degree of success. Furthermore, if one takes into account the fact that a company is a dynamic system in which there are constant numerous changes, as well as changes in its setting, then there is the question of variability of importance of some criteria in time, for one and the same company. Furthermore, it must not be overlooked that the existing research, for example, mainly refers to countries with developed economies.

Hence, it follows that the results of this research especially favour the indices related to the originality and attractiveness of a product, user's needs and the like, whereas indices related to the very capacities of the company, above all financial, are largely ignored. As a consequence of this, similar research in the countries in transition must take into account more seriously the financial capacities of both the company and the market. Because of all this, a special research methodology has been developed to research the relative importance of the criteria for selecting a new product, taking into account the above-mentioned difficulties.

This methodology is essentially based on expert methods and fuzzy sets theory. Alternative research methodology of criteria for selecting a new product The main difference between this methodology and some existing research, for example, is that the methodology proposed here highlights the importance of defining precisely at the start the criteria for selecting a new product, and that they are fixed.

Therefore, the objective of the research is not to determine which criteria are important and to what level they are important, but to research the importance of predetermined criteria depending on the characteristics of a company and its setting. What has contributed to such formulation is the concept that the criteria are generally the same and that they can be defined on the grounds of existing knowledge, and that a more significant problem is that these criteria do not have the same importance for all companies and in all conditions. So, the stress is laid on establishing the dependence of importance of criteria for selecting a new product on the company's degree of success and the conditions in its setting.

What characterizes the proposed methodology is that the research can be repeated and realized for different groups of criteria when it is necessary, or in the case of a different approach. The ultimate objective is to determine the recommendations on the basis of which every company could define the importance (relative weights) of the criteria according to its own characteristics at a given point of time. The proposed research methodology of the criteria for selecting a new product foresees an eight-step procedure. Detailed descriptions of each step follow.

Step One: Selection of criteria and sub-criteria for selecting a new product. In this step, the criteria for selecting a new product are defined. These criteria are researched in the further procedure. The methodology that is presented here also foresees defining the sub-criteria for each criterion (one can also work without any sub-criteria). Step Two: Selection of parameters which influence the selected criteria and sub-criteria.

In step two the parameters which have influence on the selected criteria and sub-criteria for selecting a new product are identified.These parameters are in reality the characteristics of companies influencing the importance of a particular criterion. Certain parameters can simultaneously influence a larger number of the selected criteria. The parameters have the greatest importance in the last step, step eight, as well as when applying the results of the research, which will also be discussed in a further presentation. Each criterion is described with a certain number of influential parameters. However, the importance of these parameters (within each criterion) does not have to be the same and it is usually not the same: some parameters have a greater influence, and some less.

For this reason, it is necessary to determine relative weights of the selected parameters within the framework of each criterion separately. These weights are used in step eight when determining the similarity value of the companies which belong to the same classes, as when applying the models. Relative weights of the selected parameters which influence the criteria and the sub-criteria for selecting a new product are determined on the basis of the opinion given by the experts in the field of product development. The necessary opinions are collected through the survey. The polled are asked to evaluate each parameter with an assessment in the intervals between 0 and 10.

This assessment should represent the quantitatively expressed strength of influence of a particular parameter on the importance of the observed criterion for selecting a new product. In view of the fact that some parameters can have influence on more criteria, such parameters ought to be assessed more than once. In other words, the same parameter can have a different influence on the importance of different criteria.

The research related to determining the relative weights of the parameters for each criterion should be entrusted to experts from scientific institutions and to experts from the companies who deal with the problems of company development, and especially product development. Those polled should be organization engineers, managers, mechanical engineers, economists, technichians, etc. Step Four: Determining relative weights of the selected parameters for each criterion. In this step, processing of the data provided in the previous step is carried out.

All the parameter assessments (given by the experts) are translated into fuzzy assessments, or the interval [0, 1], through the function y = x / 10, where: x " [0, 10]. Fuzzy assessments of each parameter for a particular criterion are observed. A set is formed from these fuzzy assessments, and processing is performed with this set by determining the average value of the set. The obtained average values represent the final fuzzy assessments of all the parameters for each criterion. The final fuzzy assessment of the parameters within one criterion represents the input data for determining the relative weights of the parameters for that criterion. In the process, one of numerous procedures can be applied; like, for example and others.

An original approach is applied in, which is also presented in. In this way relative weights of parameters within each criterion are obtained separately. These are values w ij – relative weight of the j-th parameter for the i-th criterion (item 2.1.). They are applied in step eight, and also when applying the research results (item 3.).

Step Five: Polling company managers (Survey 2) This is the step in which polling of company managers in certain companies is carried out (Survey 2). The basic characteristics of polling in this case are:

- Company Type. In order to focus on the problem, it is necessary to select the subject of the research in the form of the type of company which will be researched. In, a research which applied the proposed methodology was carried out for the companies in the food processing industry. The rationale is that food industry is the most vital part of the economy of Serbia and Montenegro, in addition to being the part of economy with the greatest potential.

- The Polled. The polled must be at high-level leading positions in companies so that they can have insight in the company's business results, its development strategy, and the like. It is assumed that they are university-educated, and are by vocation economists, managers, mechanical engineers, technologists and similar. In a further text, those polled who answer questions in Survey 2 will be called 'managers'.
- Number of Managers. For the scope of getting reliable and relevant data, it is foreseen that it is necessary to poll N = 150 - 200 managers.
- Research Domain in Geographical Terms. Research must also include the plan of the area in which the research would be carried out.

The research requires asking two groups of questions:

- Questions that can provide the data about all the identified parameters (characteristics) of the company describing the selected criteria. Those polled will be required to quantitatively assess the required parameters in the assessment range between 0 and 10. It is very important that those polled assess the parameters according to the current state of the company.
- Questions which provide the data on all the selected criteria and sub-criteria. Those polled will be asked to quantitatively assess the importance of the criteria and sub-criteria with one single assessment in the range between 0 and 10.

It is also very important that the subjects assess the criteria and sub-criteria according to the current state in that company and its setting. The primary objective of this survey is to establish the mutual dependence between parameters and criteria. That is why stress is laid on the subjective opinion of an individual (manager), and the company is in the background serving as the framework in which an individual forms his/her opinion.

Step Six: Ranking of companies into classes according to the relative importance of the criteria Ranking of companies into classes is carried out at the level of a single criterion, i.e., for each criterion separately. It is essential that the ranking be carried out according to the size of the relative importance of the observed criterion in relation to other criteria. The managers, according to their opinion, quantitatively assess the importance of the criteria with one assessment ranging from 0 to 10 (step five). This is repeated for every polled manager separately.

Then, companies (managers' opinions) are ranked according to the size of the relative importance of the observed criterion, starting from the highest to the lowest. The total number of companies is divided by the desired number of classes and the number of companies in one class is obtained. For example, if 150 managers were surveyed in companies, and we want to rank them into three classes, then the number of companies in each class is 50. The first 50 companies make up the first class, the second 50 companies the second, and the third 50 companies make up the third class for the observed criterion. This procedure is carried out for each criterion separately.

The companies are thus divided into three classes according to each criterion separately: Class I – Companies whose managers assigned a high fuzzy assessment to the observed criterion in relation to the other criteria, as a result of which the relative importance of the observed criterion is great (for these man- agers, the observed criterion has a great importance in relation to the other ones), Class II – Companies whose managers assigned an average fuzzy assessment to the observed criterion in relation to other criteria, as a result of which the relative importance of the observed criterion is average (for these managers, the observed criterion has an average importance in relation to the other ones), Class III – Companies whose managers assigned a low fuzzy assessment to the observed criterion in relation to other criteria, as a result of which the relative importance of the observed criterion is low (for these managers, the observed criterion has an average importance in relation to the other ones). The classification is carried out according to the relative weights of the criteria, and not according to the fuzzy assessments of the criteria because the managers can use different parts of the 0–10 scale. Therefore, what is important is the position of the observed criterion in relation to other criteria, and not only its initial fuzzy assessment.

The columns with values w Ci are ranked according to the size for each criterion separately. It is proposed here that the number of classes be S = 3.

When determining the number of classes it was certain that the number of classes ought to be an odd one in order to have the category "average" and several qualitative values on both sides of the average. Seven classes would be far too many, so that the main dilemma was whether the number of classes ought to be three or five.

Considering the fact that the planned number of polled managers was N = 150–200, the number of classes S = 3 is more appropriate, since there would be 50 to 60 companies within one class, which represent a sufficient number for drawing certain conclusions. It would require considerably more managers to form five classes.

Since managers form their opinions on the basis of the characteristics and potentials of their respective companies, the next conclusion is that the companies in one class must have significant mutual similarities. For groups of similar companies within one criterion, it is possible to carry out objective statistical processing of the data obtained. Step Seven: Statistical processing of the data within each class for each criterion separately statistical processing of the data provided by polling company managers (Survey 2) is carried out in this step.

All the assessments obtained by Survey 2 are translated into fuzzy assessments, that is, the interval [0, 1]. Processing is carried out within each class for each criterion separately. Data processing is carried out in two segments: 1. Determining the criteria fuzzy assessments Values from one w ci column are ranked according to their size and are divided into the desired number of classes (it is proposed that S = 3 classes), as with dividing into classes (step six). For each class the average of values, w ci, in that class (values w Ci,av,cl) is found. The ranking is carried out for each criterion separately, and the average of respective values, w ci, is found for each class within each criterion. It is obvious that in the first class there will always be the highest average, and in the third the lowest. Then follows the fuzzification of these average relative weights for every class of every single criterion.

The value in relation to which fuzzification is carried out is labelled as w Ci,av, max, and it indicates the criterion's maximum average relative weight, for all the criteria average relative weights in all the classes (values w Ci,av,cl). Fuzzification is carried out for every average of every class. For example: if there are 12 criteria in a model, and within each criterion the companies are divided into 3 classes, then it is necessary to carry out fuzzification of 36 values.

These fuzzy assessments represent the fuzzy assessments of each class of a single criterion, and they are used in the application of the model (described in item 3). Determining the sub-criteria relative weights for each criterion separately Managers follow their opinion when they quantitatively evaluate the importance of the sub-criteria with one of the assessments from the 0–10 range (step five). These assessments are translated into the [0,1] interval by means of the function y = x / 10, where: x " [0, 10]. The sub-criteria relative weights are determined for each criterion separately, that is, for each class of companies within each criterion separately.

An example of the s-th class of the C i criterion is given. The assessments given by the managers from the s-th class to the sub-criteria of the i-th criterion are entered first. After that, the average value of the fuzzy assessment for each sub-criterion is determined. The sub-criteria relative weights are calculated on the basis of fuzzy assessments of these sub-criteria for each class of that criterion separately.

STATEMENT OF RESEARCH PROBLEM

As human beings, we are curious about the unknowns.

We ask many questions and try to find out answers to them. When you hear a person speaking a different dialect, you may ask which country the person initially came from. When you see an unusual colour a local lake has, you may ask what type of pollution has caused it. However, not every question can become a research problem. A research problem has to indicate the possibility of empirical investigation—that is, of data collection and analysis. In order to make your research problem appropriate, we need to follow some guidelines, which is the objective of this session.

FUNCTIONS OF PROBLEM STATEMENT

In order to demonstrate that your problem is researchable, the statement of research problem should perform the following functions:

- The context of research.
- The focus of research.
- The significance of research.
- The framework for results and conclusions.

PROBLEM STATEMENT IN QUANTITATIVE RESEARCH

Types of Research Questions

Quantitative research questions usually include:

- Descriptive research questions.
- Relational research questions.
- Difference research questions.

Logic of Quantitative Problems

The quantitative research problems are formulated through a deductive logic, that is starting with a general construct or theory, then identifying some operational variables to quantify the general construct or theory, and finally deciding on which variables to be observed.

- Review of the construct.
- Identification of variables.
- Operational definitions of variables.

Research Hypothesis

For quantitative research, the framework of results and conclusions is presented in the format of hypothesis. In order to make a hypothesis useful in a research, research hypothesis has to meet the following criteria:

- A hypothesis should state the expected pattern, relationship or difference between two or more variables.
- A hypothesis should be testable.
- A hypothesis should offer a tentative explanation based on theories or previous research.
- A hypothesis should be concise and lucid.

PROBLEM FORMULATION IN QUALITATIVE RESEARCH

Problem formulation in qualitative research begins with selecting a general topic and methodology (ethnographic research or an analysis of historical/legal documents). The topic and methodology are interrelated and are selected interactively rather than in separate steps. Most qualitative research interests come from personal experiences and a long interest in a topic developed from accidents of current biography and personal history. The researcher begins by narrowing a general topic to a more definitive topic.

Types of Qualitative Questions:

- Ethnographic Questions.
- Historical Questions.
- Legal Questions.

LOGIC OF QUALITATIVE PROBLEMS

Qualitative research, in contrast to quantitative research, employs primarily inductive reasoning. Qualitative research problems are reformulated several times after the researcher has begun data collection. In contrast, quantitative research problems are stated before data collection. The research problem is stated initially in planning for the study, reformulated during beginning data collection, and reformulated as necessary throughout data collection. The continuing reformulation of the research problem reflects an emergent design.

This emergent design allows qualitative research to build the findings from the data by analyzing and presenting data in increasingly abstract and synthesized forms. Reformulation of a research problem relates t o changing data collection strategies to acquire the "totality" of the phenomena and then to study some aspect in greater depth.

The specific research problem emerges and is condensed toward the end of data collection.

The condensed version of the research problem in most publications often is not the èxact same problem statement which initiated the research.

- Foreshadowed problems;
- Condensed problems.

STANDARDS OF ADEQUACY FOR PROBLEM STATEMENTS

General Research Problem

- Does the statement of the general research problem imply the possibility of empirical investigation?
- Does the problem statement restrict the scope of the study?
- Does the problem statement give the educational context in which the problem lies?

Significance of Problem

Is the significance of the problem discussed in terms of one or more of the following criteria?

- Develops knowledge of an enduring practice;
- Develops theory;
- Generalizable—that is, expands knowledge or theory;
- Provides extension of understandings;
- Advances methodology;
- Is related to a current social or political issue;
- Evaluates a specific practice at a given site;
- Is exploratory research.

SPECIFIC RESEARCH QUESTIONS OR HYPOTHESIS

Quantitative

- Does the specific research purpose, question, or hypothesis state concisely what is to be determined?
- Does the level of specificity indicate that the question or hypothesis is researchable? Or do the variables seem amenable to operational definitions?
- Is the deductive logic of a research question, or the hypothesis with variables, precise? Are the independent and dependent variables identified?
- Does the research question or hypothesis indicate the framework for reporting the results?

Qualitative

- Do the foreshadowed problems or the condensed problem statement indicate the particular case of some phenomena to be examined?
- Is the qualitative methodology appropriate for description of present or past events?
- Is the inductive logic of the research reasonably explicit?
- Does the research purpose (understanding of a social situation or grounded theory) indicate the framework for reporting the findings?

DETERMINING FEASIBILITY OF THE STUDY

If a project is seen to be feasible from the results of the study, the next logical step is to proceed with it. The research and information uncovered in the feasibility study will support the detailed planning and reduce the research time.

TYPES OF FEASIBILITY STUDIES (FS)

The following sections describe various types of feasibility studies.

Market and Real Estate Feasibility

Market Feasibility Study typically involves testing geographic locations for a real estate development project, and usually involves parcels of real estate land. Developers often conduct market studies to determine the best location within a jurisdiction, and to test alternative land uses for a given parcels.

Jurisdictions often require developers to complete feasibility studies before they will approve a permit application for retail, commercial, industrial, manufacturing, housing, office or mixed-use project. Market Feasibility take into account the importance of the business in the selected area.

Technology and System Feasibility

This involves questions such as whether the technology needed for the system exists, how difficult it will be to build, and whether the firm has enough experience using that technology.

The assessment is based on an outline design of system requirements in terms of Input, Processes, Output, Fields, Programs, and Procedures.

This can be quantified in terms of volumes of data, trends, frequency of updating, etc in order to estimate if the new system will perform adequately or not.

Resource Feasibility

This involves questions such as how much time is available to build the new system, when it can be built, whether it interferes with normal business operations, type and amount of resources required, dependencies, etc. Contingency and mitigation plans should also be stated here so.

Cultural Feasibility

In this stage, the project's alternatives are evaluated for their impact on the local and general culture. For example, environmental factors need to be considered and these factors are to be well known. Further an enterprise's own culture can clash with the results of the project.

OPERATIONAL FEASIBILITY

Operational feasibility is dependent upon the human resources available for the project. It also concerns itself with whether or not the system will operate and work once it is implemented. Do the current work practices and procedures support a new system? Also social factors i.e. how the organizational changes will affect the working lives of those affected by the system.

Determines whether the proposed system conflicts with legal requirements, e.g. a Data Processing system must comply with the local Data Protection Acts.

When an organization has either internal or external legal counsel, such reviews are typically standard. However, a project may face legal issues after completion if this factor is not considered at this stage.

A project will fail if it takes too long to be completed before it is useful. Typically this means estimating how long the system will take to develop, and if it can be completed in a given time period using some methods like payback period.

Economic analysis is the most frequently used method for evaluating the effectiveness of a candidate system. More commonly known as cost/benefit analysis, the procedure is to determine the benefits and savings that are expected from a candidate system and compare them with costs. If benefits outweigh costs, then the decision is made to design and implement the system.

HYPOTHESIS: MEANING, TYPES AND FORMULATION

In the history of human civilization, man was encountered with many perplexing problems in making life more comfortable and resolved such problems through a kind of systematic inquiry into phenomena. This tendency of systematic inquiry resulted in rapid advancement in science and technology, wherein the barriers of time and space were conquered. The method that facilitated the scientists for their remarkable achievements is the scientific method. It is necessary to understand the concept of scientific method, as it is the base for any experimental research/action research. Scientific method is a systematic approach to verify ones assumptions emerged out of observation of phenomena. The essential components in the process of scientific method are:

- Observation
- Formulation of assumptions
- Deduction of consequences and
- Verification and proof

OBSERVATION

This is the first step in scientific method. There are two types of observations, namely, common and scientific. In scientific observation several doubts and assumptions are formulated, whereas in common observation such doubts would not arise.

Though two persons observe a same phenomenon, for one it may be common but for the other it may be scientific. For example, observing an apple falling from a tree is scientific observation for Newton but for others it is common observation. Scientific observation alone can help a researcher to proceed to the second step of scientific method.

FORMULATION OF ASSUMPTIONS

Scientific observation produces certain doubts. Basing on these doubts one would arrive at some assumptions. These assumptions are called as hypotheses. So all hypotheses are assumptions but not vice versa.

In Newton's observation, the doubts emerged out are – why had the apple fallen down? Why had it not gone up? These doubts result in formulation of a hypothesis that earth must have some magnetic attraction.

Deduction of Consequences

In the third step, the consequences are deduced. If the assumption were true, what would be the consequences? In the present example, if the hypothesis of Newton is true, then all the objects should have to be subjected to earth's magnetic attraction and fall down.

Verification and Proof

After deduction of consequences, in the final step of scientific method, one has to verify whether these consequences are really present. Truth or falsity of hypothesis is verified in this step on the basis of presence or absence of consequences respectively.

In the current example, it is verified and proved that all objects fall on to earth and the hypothesis is considered to be true. Keeping this process of scientific method in mind, let us. Now, peep in into the context where experimental research is necessary in education.

EXPERIMENTAL RESEARCH

Experiments in education may be carried out in both action research and fundamental research. Action research experiments are generally preferred for classroom problems and experiments in fundamental research are preferred for theoretical problems. Let us confine our discussion only to action research.

In day-to-day classroom teaching, teachers may face several problems in bringing out desired changes among learners. In such situations they think about the problem and also about possible solutions. They face difficulty in giving shape to their ideas in terms of well-defined problem.

Even if they define the problem correctly, they may not be able to decide the strategy of research, statistical treatment of data and drawing conclusions. On this premise it may not be apt to train them in research methodology, but it is necessary to make them understand the need to systematically practice an idea and test it in a manner that can be appreciated.

We cannot expect teachers to undertake a systematic and sophisticated research to solve their classroom problems. Hence teachers are to be acquainted with the process by which they can study their problems scientifically in order to correct their actions and evaluate their decisions.

Most of the teachers face problems of various types and complexity relating to their teaching and many of them attempt to do something about these problems. They think of number of ways to overcome such problems and tries out the efficacy of their actions within normal classroom situation. Most of these efforts may involve experimentation at least to some extent. Hence it is necessary to acquaint teachers with the nature of experimental research. Experimental research involves finding out the functional relationship among phenomena under controlled conditions. The aim of experimental research is to study the cause and effect relationships between two variables.

In the process of experimental research, an experimenter manipulates or introduces some changes in one variable and observes the consequent changes in the other variable. In fact scientific method is the basis for experimental research. This can be best be understood when both the processes are compared.

Scientific Method	Experimental Research
1. Observation: Scientific observation gives raise to some doubts	1. A question for which the experimenter seeks an answer.
2. Formulation of hypothesis	2. Hypothesis that describes nature of relationship between two variables.
3. Deduction of consequences	3. Measurement and implementation of experiment.
4. Verification and proof	4. Data analysis to verify whether there is any relationship between the variables.

Characteristics of Experimental Research:

The essential characteristics of experimental research are:

- Control
- Manipulation
- Observation

CONTROL

Researcher has to control all relevant variables except the

independent variable. In experimental research control plays a very important role. It is not possible to infer the effects of independent variable without control. In order to understand the concept of control in experimentation, it is necessary to know about two basic laws, on which the experimental research is based.

Law of the Single Variable

This law states that if two situations are equal in all respects except for an independent variable, any change between two situations can be attributed to the independent variable.

Law of the only Significant Variable

This law states that if significant variables are made equal in two situations, any change between the two situations after manipulation of independent variable to one of the situation can be attributed to the independent variable.

Manipulation

In the process of manipulation, a predetermined set of varied conditions is imposed on the subjects selected for the experiment. The set of varied conditions is referred to as independent variable, the experimental variable or the treatment variable.

Observation

The experimenter is supposed to observe the changes that take place in a dependent variable as a result of manipulation of an independent variable.

Steps in Experimental Research

The steps in experimental research are similar to that of scientific method. The important steps in experimental research are:

- Selection of the problem
- Stating the hypotheses
- Preparing experimental plan

- Execution of the experimental plan
- Data analysis

SELECTION OF THE PROBLEM

The first step of experimental research is selection of problem. Scientific observation leads to certain doubts and these doubts would be formulated into research problems. In classroom researches, teachers' introspection into their own practices is one of the potential sources of locating the classroom problems.

After selection of the problem it is to be defined. The variables to be studied should be defined in operational terms. For example, in a problem that intends to study the effect of source materials on the achievement of in history, the variables, namely, source materials and achievement in history, are to be defined operationally. The experimenter has to explain what exactly the meaning of these terms in his/her experiment. Here, source materials are epigraphs, archaeological findings and minutes of various rulers and achievement in history is the achievement test score.

Stating the Hypotheses:

The second step of experimental research is stating the hypothesis in terms of the causal link between two variables under study. In the present example, the hypothesis cab be stated as, 'use of source material will improve the achievement in history.'

Preparing the Experimental Plan:

The third step of experimental research is to plan the procedure of experimentation. Following points are to be kept in mind while planning the experiment.

- Identify non-experimental variables and decide the procedure of control
- Select the procedures of collecting evidences
- Select the procedure of experimental treatment
- Prepare time schedule
- Decide the statistical procedures

In the present example, intelligence and interest may be considered as non-experimental variables and one group pretest post-test design may help to control inter-subject differences.

Execution of Experimental Plan:

After preparing the plan, it is to be meticulously executed. In this fourth step of experimental research, an experimenter is expected to introduce his/her experimental treatment and administer the tools as per the experimental plan to collect necessary evidences to test the hypothesis.

Data Analysis:

The final step of experimental research is analysis of data/ evidences. The data obtained should be subjected to statistical treatment using the statistical techniques decided in the experimental plan.

LIMITATIONS OF EXPERIMENTAL RESEARCH

While conducting experimental research, teachers should keep in view the following precautions.

- The experiment should be based on classroom problems or the concerns that are bothering teachers in their practices.
- The results of an experiment conducted on a group under certain conditions cannot be applied to other groups unless the experimental group is representative of a large population.
- The results should not be over generalized.
- The results should be interpreted with utmost caution because it is difficult to control so many variables.
- The teacher should not reflect her/his personal bias for a particular method or factor during experimentation.
- The experiment should be conducted under normal conditions of the schools.

HELPING TEACHERS TO EXPERIMENT

The general atmosphere of the school is very important to motivate teachers to undertake action research. Teachers also require help in each aspect of action research/experimental research process.

School Conditions:

The general conditions of school that help a teacher to conduct experimentation are:

- Encouragement
- Freedom to conduct experiments
- Providing staff cooperation
- Staff meetings or academic discussions
- Providing material facilities

Teachers are allowed to express their views on their success and also failures. This kind of self-examination and self-criticism would help teachers to undertake classroom researches.

Freedom should be given to teachers for conducting experiments to solve their classroom problems. For conducting experiments, cooperation from other teachers is necessary.

All teachers are encouraged to experiment together collectively and cooperatively as action research is collaborative.

During staff meetings, the progress of experimental projects may be reviewed and necessary feedback is provided to classroom researchers.

Time and material that is needed to a teacher who conducts experiment should be provided.

Helping in each aspect of the Action Research Process: besides school conditions, it is necessary to help teachers in each aspect of the action research or experimental research process. Teachers are helped to –

- Become constructively and constantly dissatisfied with their own teaching.
- Develop hope that his/her problem can be solved.
- Define the classroom problem.
- Diagnose the difficulty.
- Search for promising solutions.
- Formulation of hypothesis.
- Plan their experiment.
- Execute the experiment.
- Analyse data.
- Write report.

TYPES OF SAMPLING PROCEDURE

Sampling in educational research is generally conducted in order to permit the detailed study of part, rather than the whole, of a population.

The information derived from the resulting sample is customarily employed to develop useful generalizations about the population.

These generalizations may be in the form of estimates of one or more characteristics associated with the population, or they may be concerned with estimates of the strength of relationships between characteristics within the population.

Provided that scientific sampling procedures are used, the selection of a sample often provides many advantages compared with a complete coverage of the population. For example, reduced costs associated with gathering and analyzing the data, reduced requirements for trained personnel to conduct the fieldwork, improved speed in most aspects of data summarization and reporting, and greater accuracy due to the possibility of more intense supervision of fieldwork and data preparation operations.

The social science research situations in which sampling is used may be divided into the following three broad categories: experiments – in which the introduction of treatment variables occurs according to a pre-arranged experimental design and all extraneous variables are either controlled or randomized; surveys – in which all members of a defined target population have a known non-zero probability of selection into the sample; and investigations – in which data are collected without either the randomization of experiments or the probability sampling of surveys.

Experiments are strong with respect to internal validity because they are concerned with the question of whether a true measure of the effect of a treatment variable has been obtained for the subjects in the experiment.

Surveys, on the other hand, are strong with respect to external validity because they are concerned with the question of whether the findings obtained for the subjects in the survey may be generalized to a wider population. Investigations are weak with respect to both internal and external validity and their use is due mainly to convenience or low cost.

POPULATIONS: DESIRED, DEFINED, AND EXCLUDED

In any educational research study it is important to have a precise description of the population of elements (persons, organizations, objects, etc.) that is to form the focus of the study.

In most studies this population will be a finite one that consists of elements which conform to some designated set of specifications. These specifications provide clear guidance as to which elements are to be included in the population and which are to be excluded.

In order to prepare a suitable description of a population it is essential to distinguish between the population for which the results are ideally required, the desired target population, and the population which is actually studied, the defined target population. An ideal situation, in which the researcher had complete control over the research environment, would lead to both of these populations containing the same elements. However, in most studies, some differences arise due, for example, to

- Noncoverage: the population description may accidently omit some elements because the researcher has no knowledge of their existence,
- Lack of resources: the researcher may intentionally exclude some elements from the population description because the costs of their inclusion in data gathering operations would be prohibitive, or
- An ageing population description: the population description may have been prepared at an earlier date and therefore it includes some elements which have ceased to exist.

The defined target population provides an operational definition which may be used to guide the construction of a list of population elements, or sampling frame, from which the sample may be drawn. The elements that are excluded from the desired target population in order to form the defined target population are referred to as the excluded population.

SAMPLING FRAMES

The selection of a sample from a defined target population requires the construction of a sampling frame. The sampling frame is commonly prepared in the form of a physical list of population elements – although it may also consist of rather unusual listings, such as directories or maps, which display less obvious linkages between individual list entries and population elements. A well-constructed sampling frame allows the researcher to 'take hold' of the defined target population without the need to worry about contamination of the listing with incorrect entries or entries which represent elements associated with the excluded population. Generally the sampling frame incorporates a great deal more structure than one would expect to find in a simple list of elements.

For example, in a series of large-scale studies of Reading Literacy carried out in 30 countries during 1991, sampling frames were constructed which listed schools according to a number of stratification variables: size (number of students), programme (for example, comprehensive or selective), region (for example, urban or rural), and sex composition (single sex or coeducational). The use of these stratification variables in the construction of sampling frames was due, in part, to the need to present research results for sample data that had been drawn from particular strata within the sampling frame.

REPRESENTATIVENESS

The notion of 'representativeness' is a frequently used, and often misunderstood, notion in social science research. A sample is often described as being representative if certain percentage frequency distributions of element characteristics within the sample data are similar to corresponding distributions within the whole population. The population characteristics selected for these comparisons are referred to as 'marker variables'. These variables are usually selected from among those demographic variables that are readily available for both population and sample. Unfortunately, there are no objective rules for deciding which variables should be nominated as marker variables. Further, there are no agreed benchmarks for assessing the degree of similarity required between percentage frequency distributions for a sample to be judged as 'representative of the population'.

It is important to note that a high degree of representativeness in a set of sample data refers specifically to the marker variables selected for analysis. It does not refer to other variables assessed by the sample data and therefore does not necessarily guarantee that the sample data will provide accurate estimates for all element characteristics. The assessment of the accuracy of sample data can only be discussed meaningfully with reference to the value of the mean square error, calculated separately, for particular sample estimates.

The most popular marker variables in the field of education have commonly been demographic factors associated with students (sex, age, socio-economic status, etc.) and schools (type of school, school location, school size, etc.). For example, in a series of educational research studies carried out in the United States during the early 1970's, Wolf (1977) selected the following marker variables: sex of student, father's occupation, father's education, and mother's education. These variables were selected because their percentage frequency distributions could be obtained for the population from tabulations prepared by the Bureau of the Census.

PROBABILITY SAMPLES AND NON-PROBABILITY SAMPLES

The use of samples in educational research is usually followed by the calculation of sample estimates with the aim of either (a) estimating the values of population parameters from sample statistics, or (b) testing statistical hypotheses about population parameters. These two aims require that the researcher has some knowledge of the accuracy of the values of sample statistics as estimates of the relevant population parameters. The accuracy of these estimates may generally be derived from statistical theory – provided that probability sampling has been employed. Probability sampling requires that each member of the defined target population has a known, and non-zero, chance of being selected into the sample.

In contrast, the stability of sample estimates based on non-probability sampling cannot be discovered from the internal evidence of a single sample. That is, it is not possible to determine whether a non-probability sample is likely to provide very accurate or very inaccurate estimates of population parameters. Consequently, these types of samples are not appropriate for dealing objectively with issues concerning either the estimation of population parameters or the testing of hypotheses. The use of non-probability samples is sometimes carried out with the (usually implied) justification that estimates derived from the sample may be linked to some hypothetical universe of elements rather than to a real population.

This justification may lead to research results which are not meaningful if the gap between the hypothetical universe and any relevant real population is too large. In some circumstances, a well-planned probability sample design can be turned accidentally into a non-probability sample design if subjective judgement is exercised at any stage during the execution of the sample design. Some researchers fall into this trap through a lack of control of field operations at the final stage of a multi-stage sample design.

The most common example of this in educational settings occurs when the researcher goes to great lengths in drawing a probability sample of schools, and then leaves it to the initiative of teaching staff in the sampled schools to select a 'random sample' of students or classes.

TYPES OF NON-PROBABILITY SAMPLES

There are three main types of non-probability samples: judgement, convenience, and quota samples. These approaches to sampling result in the elements in the target population having an unknown chance of being selected into the sample. It is always wise to treat research results arising from these types of sample design as suggesting statistical characteristics about the population – rather than as providing population estimates with specifiable confidence limits.

Judgement Sampling

The process of judgement, or purposive, sampling is based on the assumption that the researcher is able to select elements which represent a 'typical sample' from the appropriate target population. The quality of samples selected by using this approach depends on the accuracy of subjective interpretations of what constitutes a typical sample.

It is extremely difficult to obtain meaningful results from a judgement sample because no two experts will agree upon the exact composition of a typical sample. Therefore, in the absence of an external criterion, there is no way in which in the research results obtained from one judgement sample can be judged as being more accurate than the research results obtained from another.

Convenience Sampling

A sample of convenience is the terminology used to describe a sample in which elements have been selected from the target population on the basis of their accessibility or convenience to the researcher. Convenience samples are sometimes referred to as 'accidental samples' for the reason that elements may be drawn into the sample simply because they just happen to be situated, spatially or administratively, near to where the researcher is conducting the data collection. The main assumption associated with convenience sampling is that the members of the target population are homogeneous.

That is, that there would be no difference in the research results obtained from a random sample, a nearby sample, a co-operative sample, or a sample gathered in some inaccessible part of the population. As for judgement sampling, there is no way in which the researcher may check the precision of one sample of convenience against another. Indeed the critics of this approach argue that, for many research situations, readily accessible elements within the target population will differ significantly from less accessible elements. They therefore conclude that the use of convenience sampling is likely to introduce a substantial degree of bias into sample estimates of population parameters.

Quota Sampling

Quota sampling is a frequently used type of non-probability sampling. It is sometimes misleadingly referred to as 'representative sampling' because numbers of elements are drawn from various target population strata in proportion to the size of these strata. While quota sampling places fairly tight restrictions on the number of sample elements per stratum, there is often little or no control exercised over the procedures used to select elements within these strata. For example, either judgement or convenience sampling may be used in any or all of the strata. Therefore, the superficial appearance of accuracy associated with proportionate representation of strata should be considered in the light that there is no way of checking either the accuracy of estimates obtained for any one stratum, or the accuracy of estimates obtained by combining individual stratum estimates.

TYPES OF PROBABILITY SAMPLES

There are many ways in which a probability sample may be drawn from a population. The method that is most commonly described in textbooks is simple random sampling. This method is rarely used in practical social research situations because (a) the selection and measurement of individual population elements is often too expensive, and (b) certain complexities may be introduced intentionally into the sample design in order to address more appropriately the objectives and administrative constraints associated with the research. The complexities most often employed in educational research include the use of stratification techniques, cluster sampling, and multiple stages of selection.

Simple Random Sampling

The selection of a simple random sample is usually carried

out according to a set of mechanical instructions which guarantees the random nature of the selection procedure. For example, Kish (1965) provides the following operational definition in order to describe procedures for the selection of a simple random sample of elements without replacement from a finite population of elements: From a table of random digits select with equal probability n different selection numbers, corresponding to n of the N listing numbers of the population elements. The n listings selected from the list, on which each of the N population elements is represented separately by exactly one listing, must identify uniquely n different elements.

Simple random sampling, as described in this definition, results in an equal probability of selection for all elements in the population. This characteristic, called 'epsem sampling' (equal probability of selection method), is not restricted solely to this type of sample design. Equal probability of selection can result from either the use of equal probabilities of selection throughout the sampling process, or from the use varying probabilities that compensate for each other through several stages of multistage sampling. Epsem sampling is widely applied in educational research because it usually leads to self-weighting samples in which the simple arithmetic mean obtained from the sample data is an unbiased estimate of the population mean.

Stratified Sampling

The technique of stratification is often employed in the preparation of sample designs because it generally provides increased accuracy in sample estimates without leading to substantial increases in costs. Stratification does not imply any departure from probability sampling – it simply requires that the population be divided into subpopulations called strata and that probability sampling be conducted independently within each stratum. The sample estimates of population parameters are then obtained by combining information from each stratum. In some studies, stratification is used for reasons other than obtaining gains in sampling accuracy. For example, strata may be formed in order to employ different sample designs within strata, or because the subpopulations defined by the strata are designated as separate 'domains of study'.

Variables used to stratify populations in education generally describe demographic aspects concerning schools (for example, location, size, and programme) and students (for example, age, sex, grade level, and socio-economic status). Stratified sampling may result in either proportionate or disproportionate sample designs. In a proportionate stratified sample design the number of observations in the total sample is allocated among the strata of the population in proportion to the relative number of elements in each stratum of the population.

That is, a stratum containing a given percentage of the elements in the population would be represented by the same percentage of the total number of sample elements. In situations where the elements are selected with equal probability within strata, this type of sample design results in epsem sampling and therefore 'self-weighted' estimates of population parameters. In contrast, a disproportionate stratified sample design is associated with the use of different probabilities of selection, or sampling fractions, within the various population strata.

This can sometimes occur when the sample is designed to achieve greater overall accuracy than proportionate stratification by using 'optimum allocation'. More commonly disproportionate sampling is used in order to ensure that the accuracy of sample estimates obtained for stratum parameters is sufficiently high to be able to make meaningful comparisons between strata. The sample estimates derived from a disproportionate sample design are generally prepared with the assistance of 'weighting factors'.

These factors, represented either by the inverse of the selection probabilities or by a set of numbers proportional to them, are employed in order to prevent inequalities in selection probabilities from causing the introduction of bias into sample estimates of population parameters. The reciprocals of the selection probalities, sometimes called 'raising factors', refer to the number of elements in the population represented by a sample element. In the field of educational research, the weighting factors are often calculated so as to ensure that the sum of the weighting factors over all elements in the sample is equal to the sample size. This ensures that the readers of research reports are not confused by differences between actual and weighted sample sizes.

Cluster Sampling

A population of elements can usually be thought of as a hierarchy of different sized groups or 'clusters' of sampling elements. These groups may vary in size and nature. For example, a population of school students may be grouped into a number of classrooms, or it may be grouped into a number of schools. A sample of students may then be selected from this population by selecting clusters of students as classroom groups or school groups rather than individually as would occur when using a simple random sample design.

The use of cluster sampling in educational research is sometimes undertaken as an alternative to simple random sampling in order to reduce research costs for a given sample size. For example, a cluster sample consisting of the selection of 10 classes – each containing around 20 students – would generally lead to smaller data collection costs compared with a simple random sample of 200 students. The reduced costs occur because the simple random sample may require the researcher to collect data in as many as 200 schools. Cluster sampling does not prevent the application of probability sampling techniques.

This may be demonstrated by examining several ways in which cluster samples may be drawn from a population of students. Consider the hypothetical population of twenty-four students distributed among six classrooms (with four students per class) and three schools (with two classes per school). A simple random sample of four students drawn without replacement from this population would result in an epsem sample with each element having a probability of selection, p, equal to 1/6.

A range of cluster samples, listed below with their associated p values, may also be drawn in a manner which results in epsem samples.

- Randomly select one class, then include all students in this class in the sample.
- Randomly select two classes, then select a random sample of two students from within these classes.
- Randomly select two schools, then select a random sample of one class from within each of these schools, then select a random sample of two students from within these classes.

THE ACCURACY OF ESTIMATES OBTAINED FROM PROBABILITY SAMPLES

The degree of accuracy associated with a sample estimate derived from any one probability sample may be judged by the difference between the estimate and the value of the population parameter which is being estimated. In most situations the value of the population parameter is not known and therefore the actual accuracy of an individual sample estimate cannot be calculated in absolute terms. Instead, through a knowledge of the behaviour of estimates derived from all possible samples which can be drawn from the population by using the same sample design, it is possible to estimate the probable accuracy of the obtained sample estimate.

Mean Square Error

Consider a probability sample of n elements which is used to calculate the sample mean as an estimate of the population mean. If an infinite set of samples of size n were drawn independently from this population and the sample mean calculated for each sample, the average of the resulting sampling distribution of sample means would be referred to as the expected value. The accuracy of the sample mean as an estimator of the population parameter may be summarized in terms of the mean square error (MSE).

The MSE is defined as the average of the squares of the

deviations of all possible sample estimates from the value being estimated. A sample design is unbiased if the expected value of the sample mean is equal to the population mean. It is important to remember that 'bias' is not a property of a single sample, but of the entire sampling distribution, and that it belongs neither to the selection nor the estimation procedure alone, but to both jointly.

For most well-designed samples in educational research the sampling bias is usually very small – tending towards zero with increasing sample size. The accuracy of sample estimates is therefore generally assessed in terms of the magnitude of the variance term in the above equation.

The Accuracy of Individual Sample Estimates

In educational settings the researcher is usually dealing with a single sample of data and not with all possible samples from a population. The variance of sample estimates as a measure of sampling accuracy cannot therefore be calculated exactly.

Fortunately, for many probability sample designs, statistical theory may be used to derive formulae which provide estimates of the variance based on the internal evidence of a single sample of data. For a simple random sample of n elements drawn without replacement from a population of N elements, the variance of the sample mean may be estimated from a single sample of data by using the following formula: where s2 is the usual sample estimate of the variance of the element values in the population.

For sufficiently large values of N, the value of the finite population correction, (N - n)/N, tends toward unity. The variance of the sample mean in this situation may be estimated to be equal to s2/n. The sampling distribution of the sample mean is approximately normally distributed for many educational sampling situations. The approximation improves with increased sample size even though the distribution of elements in the parent population may be far from normal. This characteristic of sampling distributions is known as the Central Limit Theorem and it occurs not only for the sample mean but also for most estimators commonly used to describe survey research results.

From a knowledge of the properties of the normal distribution we know that we can be "68 per cent confident" that the population mean lies within the range specified by: (the sample mean ± one standard error of the sample mean) where the standard error of the sample mean is equal to the square root of the variance of the sample mean. Similarly the we can be "95 percent confident" that the population mean lies within the range specified by: (sample mean ± two standard errors of the sample mean) While the above discussion has concentrated mostly on sample means derived from simple random samples, the same approach may be used to set up confidence limits for many other population values derived from various types of sample designs.

For example, confidence limits may be calculated for complex statistics such as correlation coefficients, regression coefficients, multiple correlation coefficients, etc.

Comparison of the Accuracy of Probability Samples

The accuracy of probability samples is usually compared by considering the variances associated with a particular sample estimate for a given sample size. This comparison has, in recent years, been based on the recommendation put forward by Kish (1965) that the simple random sample design should be used as a standard for quantifying the accuracy of a variety of probability sample designs which incorporate such complexities as stratification and clustering. Kish (1965:162) introduced the term 'deff' (design effect) to describe the ratio of the variance of the sample mean for a complex sample design, denoted c, to the variance a simple random sample, denoted srs, of the same size.

The potential for arriving at false conclusions in educational research by using incorrect sampling error calculations has been demonstrated in a study carried out by Ross (1976). This study showed that it was highly misleading to assume that sample size was, in itself, an adequate indicator of the sampling accuracy associated with complex sample designs. For example, Ross (1976: 40) demonstrated that a two-stage cluster sample of 150 students (that was selected for a study conducted in Australia by randomly selecting 6 classes followed by the random selection of 25 students within these classes) had the same sampling accuracy for sample means as would a simple random sample of 20 students.

SAMPLE DESIGN FOR TWO-STAGE CLUSTER SAMPLES

The two-stage cluster sample is probably the most commonly used sample design in educational research. This design is generally employed by selecting either schools or classes at the first stage of sampling, followed by the selection of either clusters of students within schools or clusters of students within classes at the second stage. In many studies the two-stage cluster design is preferred because this design offers an opportunity for the researcher to conduct analyses at more than one level of data aggregation.

For example, the selection of students within classes at the second stage of sampling would, provided there were sufficient numbers of classes and numbers of students selected within classes, permit analyses to be carried out at (a) the between-student level (by using data describing individual students), (b) the between-class level (by using data based on class mean scores), or (c) both levels simultaneously using 'multilevel analysis' procedures. In the following discussion some properties of two-stage cluster samples have been described by using the simplifying assumption that the clusters in the population are of equal size. This assumption permits the use of 'sample design tables' which provide an excellent aid for designing two-stage cluster samples with pre-specified levels of sampling accuracy.

The Design Effect for two-stage Cluster Samples

The value of the design effect for a two-stage cluster sample design depends, for a given cluster size, on the value of the coefficient of intraclass correlation. The coefficient of intraclass correlation, often referred to as roh, provides a measure of the degree of homogeneity within clusters. In educational settings the notion of homogeneity within clusters may be observed in the tendency of student characteristics to more homogeneous within schools, or classes, than would be the case if students were assigned to schools, or classes, at random.

This homogeneity may be due to common selective factors (for example, residential zoning of schools), or to joint exposure to the same external influences (for example, teachers and school programs), or to mutual interaction (for example, peer group pressure), or to some combination of these.

The Effective Sample size for two-stage Cluster Samples

The "effective sample size" for a given two-stage cluster sample is equal to the size of the simple random sample which has a level of sampling accuracy, as measured by the variance of the sample mean, which is equal to the sampling accuracy of the given two-stage cluster sample. A little algebra may be used to demonstrate that the actual sample size, n c, and the effective sample size, n, for a two-stage cluster sample are related to the design effect associated with that sample in the following manner.

From previous discussion, we may replace deff in this formula by an expression which is a function of the cluster size and the coefficient of intraclass correlation.

For example, consider a two-stage cluster sample based on a sample of 10 schools followed by the selection of 20 students per school. In addition, consider a student characteristic (for example, a test score or attitude scale score) for which the value of the coefficient of intraclass correlation is equal to 0.1. This value of roh would be typical for clusters of students selected randomly from within secondary schools in Australia. In this situation, the above formula simplifies to the following expression.

Solving this equation for n gives a value of 69 for the value of the effective sample size. That is, given the value of 0.1 for roh, a two-stage cluster sample of size 200 that is selected by sampling 10 schools followed by sampling 20 students per school would have sampling accuracy equivalent to a simple random sample of 69 students. For a given population of students, the value of roh tends to be higher for clusters based on classes rather than clusters based on schools. Ross (1978) has obtained values of roh as high as 0.5 for mathematics test scores based on classes within Australian secondary schools.

SAMPLE DESIGN TABLES FOR TWO-STAGE CLUSTER SAMPLES

Sample design tables are often prepared for well-designed research studies in which it is intended to employ two-stage cluster sampling. These tables present a range of sample design options – each designed to have a pre-specified level of sampling accuracy. A hypothetical example has been presented in the following discussion in order to illustrate the sequence of calculations and decisions involved in the preparation of these tables. Consider an educational research study in which test items are administered to a two-stage cluster sample of students with the aim of estimating the percentage of students in the population that are able to obtain correct answers. In addition, assume that a sampling accuracy constraint has been placed on the design of the study so as to ensure that the sample estimate of the percentage of students providing the correct answer, p, will provide p + 5 per cent as 95 per cent confidence limits for the value of the percentage in the population.

For reasonably large samples it is possible to assume normality of the distribution of sample estimates and therefore confidence limits of p + 5 per cent are approximately equivalent to an error range of plus or minus two standard errors of p. Consequently, the error constraint placed on the study means that one standard error of p needs to be less than or equal to 2.5 per cent. Consider a simple random sample of n * students selected from this population in order to calculate values of p. Statistical theory may be employed to show that, for large populations, the variance of the sample estimate of p as an estimate of the population value may be calculated by using the following formula.

The maximum value of p(100 - p) occurs for p = 50. Therefore, in order to ensure that we could satisfy the error constraints described above, the following inequality would need to be valid. That is, the size of the simple random sample, n, would have to be greater than, or equal to, about 400 students in order to obtain 95 per cent confidence limits of p + 5 per cent. Now consider the size of a two-stage cluster sample design which would provide equivalent sampling accuracy to a simple random sample of 400 students. The design of this cluster sample would require knowledge of the numbers of primary sampling units (for example, schools or classes) and the numbers of secondary sampling units (students) which would be required.

From previous discussion, the relationship between the size of the cluster sample, n c, which has the same accuracy as a simple random sample of size n * = 400 may be written in the following fashion. This expression is often described as a 'planning equation' because it may be used to explore sample design options for two-stage cluster samples. The value of n c is equal to the product of the number of primary sampling units, a, and the number of secondary sampling units selected from each primary sampling unit, b. Substituting for n c in this formula, and then transposing provides the following expression for a in terms of b and roh.

As an example, consider roh = 0.1, and b = 20. Then we have the following value for a. That is, for roh = 0.1, a two-stage cluster sample of 1160 students (consisting of the selection of 58 primary sampling units followed by the selection of clusters of 20 students) would have sampling accuracy equivalent to a simple random sample of 400 students. In Table, the planning equation has been employed to list sets of values for a, b, deff, and n c which describe a group of two-stage cluster sample designs that have sampling accuracy equivalent to a simple random sample of 400 students.

Three sets of sample designs have been listed in the table – corresponding to roh values of 0.1, 0.2, and 0.4. In a study of school systems in ten developed countries, Ross (1983: 54) has shown that values of roh in this range are typical for achievement test scores obtained from clusters of students within schools. The most striking feature of Table is the rapidly diminishing effect that increasing b, the cluster size, has on a, the number of clusters that are to be selected. This is particularly noticeable when the cluster size reaches 10 to 15 students. Consider, for example, two sample designs applied in a situation where a value of roh = 0.4 may be assumed: (a) a total sample of 2640 students obtained by selecting 15 students per cluster from 176 clusters, and (b) a total sample of 8250 students obtained by selecting 50 students per cluster from 165 clusters.

These two sample designs have equivalent sampling accuracy, however there is a striking difference between the each design in terms of total sample size. Further, the magnitude of this difference is not reflected proportionately in the difference between the number of clusters selected.

This result illustrates an important point for the planning of educational research studies that seek to make stable estimates of student population characteristics. This is that the sampling accuracy levels of two-stage cluster sample designs, for cluster sizes of 10 or more, tend to be greatly influenced by small changes in the number of clusters that are selected at the first stage of sampling, and relatively less influenced by small changes in the size of the selected clusters.

The final choice between equally accurate options is usually guided by cost factors, or data analysis strategies, or a combination of both of these.

For example, the cost of collecting data by using 'group administration' of tests, questionnaires, etc. often depends more on the number of selected schools than on the number of students surveyed within each selected school. This occurs because the use of this methodology usually leads to higher marginal costs associated with travel to many schools, compared with the marginal costs of increasing the number of students surveyed within each selected school. In contrast, the cost of collecting data by using 'individual administration' of one-to-one tests, interviews, etc., normally depends more on the total sample size than on the number of selected schools. The choice of a sample design option may also depend upon the data analysis strategies that are being employed in the research.

For example, analyses may be planned at both the between-student and between-school levels of analysis. In order to conduct analyses at the between-school level, data obtained from individual students may need to be aggregated to obtain files consisting of school records based on student mean scores. This type of analysis requires that sufficient students be selected per school so as to ensure that stable estimates are able to be made for individual schools. At the same time, it requires that sufficient schools are available so as to ensure that meaningful results may be obtained for estimates of population characteristics.

The numbers of schools and students in the example have been made very small so that all calculations and tabulations can be carried out by hand. In the next section of this module a 'real' example has been presented in which the required calculations and tabulations must be carried out by computer. The desired target population for the example consists of 1100 students attending 20 schools located in two administrative regions of Country X. The sample design requires that five schools be selected across four strata with probability proportional to the number of students in the defined target population. Within the five selected schools a simple random sample of 20 students is to be selected. The 12 steps required to complete the sample design cover the following five areas.

Specification of Sample (Steps 1 to 4)

The development and listing of 'specifications' for the sample design – including target population, sample size, sampling stages, stratification, sample allocation, cluster size, and pseudoschool rules. In most research situations the specifications are prepared following a detailed investigation of the availability of information that is suitable for the construction of sampling frames, and an evaluation of the nature and scope of the data that are to be collected.

Stratification and Sample Allocation (Steps 5 to 7)

A description of the stratification variables and an analysis of the breakdown of the defined target population across strata. The breakdown is used with the sample design specifications to guide the allocation of the sample across strata.

Marker Variables (Step 8)

This is an 'optional' area. It provides information that can be used to make comparisons between the population and sample. However, it has no real impact on the scientific quality of the final sample.

Construction of Sampling Frame (Steps 9 and 10)

The construction of a separate list of schools for each stratum. Each school is listed in association with the number of students in the defined target population. Schools that are smaller than a specified size are linked to a similar (and nearby) school to form a 'pseudoschool'.

Sample Selection (Steps 11 and 12)

The selection of the sample of schools within strata (by using a 'lottery tickets' approach), and the selection of a sample of students within schools (by using a table of random numbers).

CRITERIA FOR SELECTION OF SAMPLE

SAMPLE SELECTION CRITERIA

The selection of quality educational resources that support, extend and enrich the education of students, while providing good value for money, is the fundamental criteria for the selection of resources at the Library and Information Centre.

Resources range from traditional fiction and nonfiction

print to videocassettes, audiocassettes, CD-ROM, computer software, Internet sites and online curriculum resources.

Overarching Outcomes

The Library and Information Centre aims to select resources that will:

- Foster growth in factual knowledge, literary, aesthetic and cultural appreciation; moral and ethical values and will aid in daily and future decision-making.
- Ensure there are adequate resources at appropriate levels for resource-based and student-centred learning and to meet personal and recreational needs
- Include new curriculum and interest areas.
- Ensure that resources provide optimum value in terms of curriculum relevance, accuracy, authority, reliability and accessibility.
- Reflect the principles of intellectual freedom and provide students with access to information that represents diverse points of view.
- Encompass a variety of media and information formats to suit varied learning purposes and styles, including:
- Print resources eg. books (reference, fiction, non-fiction), periodicals, newspapers, pamphlets, ephemera.
- Graphic resources eg. charts, posters, pictures, maps, models, realia, kits.
- Audiovisual resources eg. videocassettes, audiocassettes, slides, film.
- Electronic resources eg. computer software, multimedia, CD-ROM, videodiscs.
- Online resources eg. Internet sites, databases, indexes.
- Consider students with particular needs, taking into account race, ethnic group, culture, gender, socioeconomic group, physical and intellectual capacity.
- Assist staff in their teaching roles by providing resources and materials for professional development. For example resources which:

- Model best practice.
- Provide a variety of teaching strategies and teaching aids.
- Reflect current trends in curriculum development and assist in further professional development.

GENERAL SELECTION CRITERIA

For all resources regardless of content or form.

Authority:

- Qualified and/or experienced author.
- Reputable sources of information.
- Recognised publisher/producer.

Physical Format & Technical Quality:

- Quality materials.
- Sturdy construction.
- Attractive presentation & clear reproduction.

Arrangement of Material:

- Content is easily accessible.
- Instructions and support materials are adequate, clear, comprehensive and effective.

Appropriateness:

- Content, language, symbols and concepts are at a suitable level for the intended user.

Cost:

- Value for money.
- May be used across a number of curriculum areas and levels.

Availability:

- Currently available to schools.
- Readily available to schools.

Format:

- The most suitable medium to present the subject matter.
- Includes paperback, hardback, big book, audiocassette, videocassette, kits, realia, games, charts, posters, slides, film, computer software, CD-ROM and online resources.

Controversial Material:

- Consider any controversial content and/or issues.

SPECIFIC SELECTION CRITERIA FOR NON-FICTION BOOKS

Non-Fiction books include encyclopedias, yearbooks, almanacs, dictionaries, thesauruses, anthologies, atlases, handbooks, pamphlets, periodicals, journals and information books.

Purpose:

- Fulfil the purpose of the item (quick reference, browsing or extensive research).
- Support and enrich the curriculum.

Readability:

- Text and print size appropriate to the intended reader.
- Style of writing appropriate to the purpose or intention of the author.
- Text is smooth to read, clear and concise, interesting and non-repetitive.
- Language used reflects the intended use of the item.
- Reading level of the item matches the user's experience and capability.

Interest Level:

- Matches the readability of the text and the interest levels of students.

Accuracy:

- Information is accurate and up-to-date.
- Vital facts are not omitted or over-simplified.

Scope:

- Topic covered adequately: in-depth, detailed account or a general overview, as appropriate.
- Approach/development of concepts suited to intended users.

Curriculum Relevance:

- Supports the West Australian/Australian curriculum.

Organisation of Information:

- Clear and functional.

- Contains index, table of contents, glossary, bibliography, as appropriate.
- Clearly defined chapters/sections.

Page Layout:

- Headings/sub-headings clearly defined.
- Text well spaced and organised into paragraphs.
- Background colour/borders/illustrations do not interfere with the readability of the text.
- Adequate use of white space.

Bias:

- Avoid stereotypes in text or illustrations.
- Avoid biased opinions/value judgements.
- Reflect gender equity principles of social justice (includes race, sex, physical and intellectual disability, cultural grouping).
- Relevant to Australian conditions, as appropriate.

Illustrations:

- Support or extend the information base of the text.
- May include diagrams, maps, graphs, photographs, drawings, paintings, tables.
- Positioned relevant to the text.
- Clear, attractive and/or interesting.
- Labelled/captioned effectively/accurately.

SPECIFIC SELECTION CRITERIA FOR FICTION BOOKS

Fiction includes picture books, beginning readers, early chapter books, graphic novels and novels.

Purpose:

- Provide enjoyment and entertainment.
- Stimulate the imagination.
- Develop language.
- Extend the student's experience vicariously.
- Develop discriminatory and independent readers.
- Support the curriculum.
- Develop life-long readers.

Readability:

- Reading level of the item matches the user's experience and capability.

Language:

- Appropriate to the plot, theme and characters.
- Imaginative and interesting with natural dialogue and vivid descriptions.
- Concepts developed by the language are appropriate for the age/maturity of the intended reader.
- Style of writing is appropriate to the genre.
- Provides the opportunity for students to practise/ develop/extend literacy skills.

Content Plot:

- Stimulates the reader's imagination.
- Encourages awareness of issues.
- Story is interesting and entertaining.
- Sequence of events is logical and (within the genre) believable.
- Factual elements are correct.

Theme:

- Easily identified.
- Resolution of conflict within acceptable moral codes and behavioural modes.
- Avoids moralising and didacticism.

Characterisation:

- Resolution of conflict within acceptable moral codes and behavioural modes.
- Convincing and credible.
- Uses natural and suitable dialogue.
- Characters develop and grow.
- Avoids stereotyping by gender, race, disability or culture.

Other Considerations:

- Comparative merit with other items by the same author, in the same genre or by other authors.

Curriculum Relevance:

- May be used to support Non-Fiction curriculum Learning Areas. ie. links can be made across all Learning Areas.

Page Layout:

- Content well spaced and logically organised.

- Background colour/borders/illustrations do not interfere with readability of the text.

Illustrations: include here cover, end papers, within text, textless.

Purpose:

- Enhance/extend elements of the story.
- Enhance readability of the text.
- appropriate to the reading/interest/maturity level of the reader.

Bias:

- Avoid stereotypes in text or illustrations.
- Avoid biased opinions/value judgements.
- Reflects gender equity principles of social justice (includes race, sex, physical and intellectual disability, cultural grouping).
- Relevant to Australian conditions, as appropriate.

Sensitive Issues:

- Elements of language appropriate in the context of the plot and characterisation.
- Treatment of issues eg. sex, violence, drugs, AIDS, death, religion, the supernatural appropriate for the to the intended reader.

SPECIFIC SELECTION CRITERIA FOR COMPUTER SOFTWARE AND CD-ROMS

Purpose:

- Using the computer/CD-ROM format is the best/most appropriate way to access this information.
- This type of resource adds value to the overall resource collection and enhances the learning process.
- Useful for more than one learning/topic area.

Authority:

- Experience of intellectual content providers, qualifications and expertise (of design and content).
- Other titles published.

Appropriateness:

- Supports the content and enhances the understanding of the user.

- Appropriate to the level of the intended user/s.
- Long term value of information.
- Encourages students to use more than once to gain new experiences.

Accuracy & Recency of Information:

- Bibliographies of further reading included, plus affiliated titles and support services.
- Accuracy of information especially Australian content.

Scope:

- Depth of coverage (as appropriate).
- Uses a variety of forms so students of different levels have access to appropriate information.
- Offers students an overview plus a more detailed analysis of subject material.

Ease of Use:

- Easy to load.
- Variable search options eg. keyword, topic, picture, alphabetical listing, freetext search, multimedia items.

Navigation:

- Oflexibility of access to information.
- Easy cross referencing with hotlinks to more specific information.
- Menus clear, of a suitable number and easy to use.
- Interpretation of icons appropriate to the intended users.

Presentation:

- Level of interaction: multimedia includes text, graphics, animated graphics, sound, video clips, facility to enable student participation. ie. offers alternative media to those found in other resources.
- Provides ancillary applications eg. records student participation, print facility, notes/word processing facility.
- High quality of production.

Include here:

- Sound.
- Video and animation.

- Diagrams, illustrations, maps and legends.
- Colour quality.
- Clarity and size of illustrations/videos/animations.
- Depth of images.
- Number of frames per second.
- Depth/pace/clarity of sound recording.

Accompanying Material

Printed instructions easy to interpret:

- contain enough detail to facilitate easy access to content. • enable easy loading of software.

Printed course material/teacher'snotes/synopsis:

- Appropriate to intended users.
- Clearly set out.
- Relevant to the curriculum (not just busy work Blackline Masters).
- Enhance the learning process.

Packaging:

- Durable and facilitates easy storage.

Cost is not prohibitive.

Alternative Formats

Specific selection criteria for Non-Fiction and Fiction books also apply to each format.

Audiocassettes:

- Sound clarity.
- Clear pronunciation and enunciation.
- Reading is well paced.
- Background music/sound effects appropriate and don't interfere with main reading.
- Abridged or full-text version as appropriate.
- Story reading or dramatised version.
- Length appropriate for intended user.
- Accompanying teachers' notes - appropriate, useful and relevant.

Charts: Includes maps, diagrams, pictures, posters, friezes, study prints:

- Clear and logical layout.

- Information and graphics uncluttered.
- Overall size and print size appropriate for intended use.
- Attractively presented to generate interest.
- Simplify information and summarise key concepts.
- Support a specific educational purpose.

Games:

- Support an educational purpose.
- Packaging/storage to facilitate long-term use.
- Durability of game pieces.
- Accompanying instructions clear and appropriate for the intended user.

Realia/Models:

- Support an educational purpose.
- Durable construction.
- Size/weight appropriate for intended use.
- Attractive and interesting.
- Easy to use.

Videocassettes:

- Clarity of sound and images.
- Visually appealing.
- Voice production clear and suited for intended purpose and user.
- Accuracy and currency of visual information.
- Content appropriate for intended user.
- Variety in presentation.
- Production well paced.
- Length appropriate for the intended user.

Slides:

- Interesting and appropriate for intended purpose.
- Clear graphics/images.
- Accompanying notes clear, appropriate, useful and relevant.
- Durable packaging/storage to facilitate long-term use.

Internet Sites

Specific selection criteria for Non-Fiction and Fiction

books also apply to each format. Include Internet sites, online indexes and online databases.

Authority:

- Consider qualifications, expertise and background experience of intellectual providers.
- Authority information must be easy to locate and verify.

Ease of Access:

- Online site must be readily accessible to users at a variety of times.

Accuracy & Recency of Information:

- Site updated regularly.
- Be aware of long/short term value of sites.

Security

- Sites are free from viruses/worms/data corruption.
- Secure from tampering/alteration by visitors.

Scope:

- Provides information not readily available through other media.

Appropriateness:

- Appropriate to level/maturity of users.
- Consider here links to other sites, content, controversial material and subject matter.

Presentation:

- Text is clear and easy to read.
- Graphics relevant, clear and attractive.
- Background colour/design does not interfere with text.
- Hotlinks easy to identify.

Navigation:

- Easy to use.
- Enhances students' information retrieval and hands-on computer skills.
- Allows user to keep track of movements.
- Keeps time wasting to a minimum.

Cost is not prohibitive

RESEARCH PROPOSAL: THE NEED AND FORMAT

REASONS FOR WRITING A RESEARCH PROPOSAL

Your research proposal: gives you an opportunity to think through your project carefully, and clarify and define what you want to research provides you with an outline and to guide you through the research process lets your supervisor and department or faculty know what you would like to research and how you plan to go about it helps the department choose an appropriate supervisor gives you an opportunity to receive feedback from your supervisor and others in the academic community as well as possible funders serves as a contract between you and your supervisor and university can be submitted to an ethics committee to gain ethical approval can be submitted to a scholarship committee or other funding agency.

DEVELOPING YOUR PROPOSAL

The process includes: choosing a topic narrowing and focussing your topic formulating research objectives or questions and ideas for analysis outlining the key literature in the topic area deciding on research methodology, research design and methods proposing an approach to data analysis proposing a format e.g. how many chapters and suggested chapter headings developing a timeline developing a budget and resources you will need developing a bibliography Writing a research proposal can be a demanding, frustrating, challenging and time-consuming process - but it can also be exciting!

Your proposal does not permanently set what you will do. It is a starting point and throughout your research you will probably adjust and change your position. You will be able to trace the development of your ideas and measure the progress you have made by referring back to your proposal.

SUGGESTED FORMAT OF YOUR RESEARCH PROPOSAL

Title page: This includes your name, department and

supervisor/s, title: Proposal for Thesis, and thesis title.

Table of Contents Abstract: This includes an outline of your proposal, what your research will involve, research questions or hypothesis, research methods and how you will analyse the data.

Background: This sets out why you chose your topic - what prompted your interest in the topic; the links with previous research; ways your thesis is different or unique; and states the research objectives, questions or hypothesis.

Theoretical framework: A review of the relevant literature you have read so far sets your research in context. It identifies the direction you will take from among the possible theoretical directions. Include a bibliography at the end of your proposal.

Research methodology: In this section identify the methodology that underpins your research and give a rationale for your approach. You may need to identify the research paradigm and epistemologies that underpin your research. Show how you have used your review of the literature to construct your own research methodology.

Research design and methods: This section outlines how you are going to get your data. By reading widely you will be familiar with methodologies followed by previous researchers and have explored possible research methods. You will be aware of problems others have encountered and be able to design your research and adapt methods for your research. Outline the methods you will use and problems you anticipate. Outline whether your research is qualitative or quantitative, whether you are using triangulation, statistics, interviewing, questionnaires, experiments, observations etc. If humans or animals are to be used, outline the ethical considerations and your application to the university ethics committee.

Analysis and discussion: This section suggests what you are going to do with the data. Outline the aims of your research again and ideas you have on how you are going to analyse the data. Include any tools for analysis you intend using or trying out.

Format: Outline the format of your thesis. Suggest how

many chapters you will have, chapter headings and the order of presentation.

Timeline: Include a timeline to guide you and keep you on track. For example estimate the time needed for tasks and assign tasks for each month.

Budget and resources: Outline the resources you need and propose a budget

COLLECTION OF DATA: ORGANISING AND ANALYSING THE DATA

It is important to keep your evaluation information organized. Depending on your needs and available resources, you may want to create a database or spreadsheet to organize your data. Readily available computer programs, such as Excel and Access, may be useful. Software is also available for quantitative and qualitative analysis (such as SPSS or Atlas-TI). Some of this software is expensive, however, and you may be able to analyse your findings without it. Before investing in software, consider seeking consultation to determine if it is needed. If you create an electronic database with your evaluation results, be thoughtful about its organization. Decisions made as you design and begin to enter information will influence how easy or difficult it will be for you to analyse your results. Tips for designing your database include: Assign a unique identifier to each individual in your dataset.

Organizing your data and designing your analysis plan frequency of specific behaviors. Qualitative data is non-numerical information, such as responses gathered through unstructured interviews, observations, focus groups, or open-ended survey questions. Include all information about an individual in one row of your database, rather than having the same person appear in multiple places. Limit responses so that incorrect information cannot be entered (such as not allowing numbers that fall outside of your response choices). Code text responses into numerical form so that they are easier to analyse (e.g., 1=yes, 2 =no).

Enter data in a consistent format, such as always using a "1" to reflect female gender, rather than using various labels (e.g., "F," "female," "girl," etc.). The best time to start thinking about your analysis plan is when you are first identifying your key evaluation questions and determining how you will collect the needed information.

It's important to match the analysis strategy to the type of information that you have and the kinds of evaluation questions that you are trying to answer While statistical analysis of quantitative information can be quite complex, some relatively simple techniques can provide useful information. Descriptive analysis is used to reduce your raw data down to an understandable level.

Common methods include: Frequency distributions – tables or charts that show how many of your participants fall into various categories. Central tendency – the number that best represents the "typical score," such as the mode (number or category that appears most frequently), median (number in the exact middle of the data set), and mean (arithmetic average of your numbers).

Variability – amount of variation or disagreement in your results, including the range (difference between the highest and lowest scores) and the standard deviation (a more complicated calculation based on a comparison of each score to the average). Inferential analysis is used to help you draw conclusions about your results.

The goal is to determine whether results are meaningful. For example, did participants change in important ways over time? Were participants different from people who did not receive services? The meaningfulness of findings is typically described in terms of "significance."

There are two common forms of significance. Using probability theory, statistical significance indicates whether a result is stronger than what would have occurred due to random error.

To be considered significant, there must be high probability that the results were not due to chance. When this occurs, we can infer that a relationship between two variables is strong and reliable. Several factors influence the likelihood of significance, including the strength of the relationship, the amount of variability in the data, and the number of people in the sample. Statistical significance can be difficult to obtain, especially when data are available for a small number of people. As a result, some evaluations focus instead on clinical significance.

Clinical significance compares results to a pre-established standard that has been determined to be meaningful (such as, average functioning of a non-problematic peer group, cultural norms, or goals set by staff or participants). Clinical significance is sometimes seen as having more practical value, but only when there is a clear and rationale for establishing the underlying standards.

Many statistical tests can be used to explore the relationships found in your data. Common statistical tests include chi-squares, correlations, t-tests, and analyses of variance. If these statistics are not familiar to you, seek consultation to ensure that you select the right type of analysis for your data and interpret the findings appropriately. On its own, or in combination with quantitative information, qualitative data can provide rich information about how programs work.

The first step in analyzing qualitative information is to reduce or simplify it. Because of its verbal nature, simplification may be difficult. Important information may be interspersed throughout interviews or focus group proceedings.

During this stage, you must make important choices about which information should be emphasized, minimized, or even left out of the analysis. It is important to remain focused on the questions that you are trying to answer and the relevance of the information to these questions. When analyzing qualitative data, look for trends or themes.

Depending on the amount and type of data that you have, you might want to code the responses to help you group the comments into categories. You can begin to develop a set of codes before you collect your information, based on the theories or assumptions you have about the anticipated responses. However, it is important to review and modify your codes as you proceed to ensure that they reflect the actual findings. When you report the findings, the codes will help you identify the most prevalent themes. You might also want to identify quotes that best illustrate the themes, for use in reports.

INTERPRETING YOUR RESULTS AND DRAWING CONCLUSIONS

While analysis can help you identify key findings, you still need to interpret the results. Drawing conclusions involves stepping back to consider what the results mean and to assess their implications. Consider the following types of questions: What patterns and themes emerged? Are there any deviations from these patterns? If yes, are there factors that might explain these deviations? Do the results make sense? Are there findings that are surprising?

If so, how do you explain these results? Are the results significant from a clinical or statistical standpoint? Are they meaningful in a practical way? Do any interesting stories emerge from the responses? Do the results suggest any recommendations for improving the programme? Do the results lead to additional questions about the programme? Do they suggest that additional data may be needed?

Involve Stakeholders

While findings must be reported objectively, interpreting the results and reaching conclusions can be challenging. Consider including key stakeholders in this process by reviewing findings and preliminary conclusions with them prior to writing a formal report.

Consider Practical value, not just Statistical Significance

Do not be discouraged if you do not obtain statistically significant results. While a lack of significance may suggest that a programme was not effective, other factors should also be considered. You may have chosen an outcome measure that was too ambitious, such as a behavioral change that takes longer to emerge. In interpreting your results, consider alternate explanations. It is also important to consider the practical significance of the findings. Some statistically significant results are not helpful in guiding programme enhancements, while some "insignificant" findings end up being useful.

Watch for, and Resolve, Inconsistencies

In some cases, you may obtain contradictory information. For example, stakeholders may describe important benefits of the services, but these improvements do not appear in pre-post test comparisons. Various stakeholders may also disagree, such as staff reporting improvements in participants that are not reported by the participants themselves.

Consider the validity of each source, and remember that stakeholders can have valid viewpoints that vary based on their unique perspectives and experiences. Try to resolve discrepancies and reflect them in your findings to the extent possible. Review and correct data before beginning your analysis. Leave enough time and money for analysis. Identify the appropriate statistics for each key question – get consultation if needed.

TIPS FOR ANALYSIS

Do not use the word "significant" to describe your findings unless it has been tested and found to be true either statistically or clinically. Keep the analysis simple.

Unit III

Research Methods

HISTORICAL

The process of learning and understanding the background and growth of a chosen field of study or profession can offer insight into organizational culture, current trends, and future possibilities. The historical method of research applies to all fields of study because it encompasses their: origins, growth, theories, personalities, crisis, etc. Both quantitative and qualitative variables can be used in the collection of historical information. Once the decision is made to conduct historical research, there are steps that should be followed to achieve a reliable result. Charles Busha and Stephen Harter detail six steps for conducting historical research:

- The recognition of a historical problem or the identification of a need for certain historical knowledge.
- The gathering of as much relevant information about the problem or topic as possible.
- If appropriate, the forming of hypothesis that tentatively explain relationships between historical factors.
- The rigorous collection and organization of evidence, and the verification of the authenticity and veracity of information and its sources.
- The selection, organization, and analysis of the most pertinent collected evidence, and the drawing of conclusions.

- The recording of conclusions in a meaningful narrative.

In the field of library and information science, there are a vast array of topics that may be considered for conducting historical research. For example, a researcher may chose to answer questions about the development of school, academic or public libraries, the rise of technology and the benefits/problems it brings, the development of preservation methods, famous personalities in the field, library statistics, or geographical demographics and how they effect library distribution.

Harter and Busha define library history as "the systematic recounting of past events pertaining to the establishment, maintenance, and utilization of systematically arranged collections of recorded information or knowledge....A biography of a person who has in some way affected the development of libraries, library science, or librarianship is also considered to be library history."

There are a variety of places to obtain historical information. Primary Sources are the most sought after in historical research. Primary resources are first hand accounts of information. "Finding and assessing primary historical data is an exercise in detective work. It involves logic, intuition, persistence, and common sense... (Tuchman, Gaye in Strategies of Qualitative Inquiry, 252). Some examples of primary documents are: personal diaries, eyewitness accounts of events, and oral histories. "Secondary sources of information are records or accounts prepared by someone other than the person, or persons, who participated in or observed an event." Secondary resources can be very useful in giving a researcher a grasp on a subject and may provided extensive bibliographic information for delving further into a research topic.

In any type of historical research, there are issues to consider. Harter and Busha list three principles to consider when conducting historical research:

- Consider the slant or biases of the information you are working with and the ones possessed by the historians themselves.

This is particularly true of qualitative research. Consider an example provided by Gaye Tuchman:

Let us assume that women's letters and diaries are pertinent to ones research question and that one can locate pertinent examples. One cannot simply read them....one must read enough examples to infer the norms of what could be written and how it could be expressed. For instance, in the early nineteenth century, some (primarily female) schoolteachers instructed girls in journal writing and read their journals to do so. How would such instruction have influenced the journals kept by these girls as adults?...it is useful to view the nineteenth-century journal writer as an informant. Just as one tries to understand how a contemporary informant speaks from specific social location, so too one would want to establish the social location of the historical figure. One might ask of these and other diaries: What is the characteristic of middle-class female diary writers? What is the characteristic of this informant? How should one view what this informant writes?

Quantitative facts may also be biased in the types of statistical data collected or in how that information was interpreted by the researcher.

- There are many factors that can contribute to "historical episodes".
- Evidence should not be examined from a singular point of view.

The resources that follow this brief introduction to the historical method in research provide resources for further in-depth explanations about this research method in various fields of study, and abstracts of studies conducted using this method.

THE CASE STUDY AS A RESEARCH METHOD

Case study research excels at bringing us to an understanding of a complex issue or object and can extend experience or add strength to what is already known through previous research. Case studies emphasize detailed contextual analysis of a limited number of events or conditions and their relationships. Researchers have used the case study research method for many years across a variety of disciplines. Social scientists, in particular, have made wide use of this qualitative research method to examine contemporary real-life situations and provide the basis for the application of ideas and extension of methods. Researcher Robert K. Yin defines the case study research method as an empirical inquiry that investigates a contemporary phenomenon within its real-life context; when the boundaries between phenomenon and context are not clearly evident; and in which multiple sources of evidence are used.

Critics of the case study method believe that the study of a small number of cases can offer no grounds for establishing reliability or generality of findings. Others feel that the intense exposure to study of the case biases the findings. Some dismiss case study research as useful only as an exploratory tool. Yet researchers continue to use the case study research method with success in carefully planned and crafted studies of real-life situations, issues, and problems. Reports on case studies from many disciplines are widely available in the literature.

This paper explains how to use the case study method and then applies the method to an example case study project designed to examine how one set of users, non-profit organizations, make use of an electronic community network. The study examines the issue of whether or not the electronic community network is beneficial in some way to non-profit organizations and what those benefits might be. Many well-known case study researchers such as Robert E. Stake, Helen Simons, and Robert K. Yin have written about case study research and suggested techniques for organizing and conducting the research successfully.

This introduction to case study research draws upon their work and proposes six steps that should be used:

- Determine and define the research questions
- Select the cases and determine data gathering and analysis techniques
- Prepare to collect the data
- Collect data in the field

- Evaluate and analyse the data
- Prepare the report

Step 1. Determine and Define the Research Questions

The first step in case study research is to establish a firm research focus to which the researcher can refer over the course of study of a complex phenomenon or object. The researcher establishes the focus of the study by forming questions about the situation or problem to be studied and determining a purpose for the study. The research object in a case study is often a programme, an entity, a person, or a group of people. Each object is likely to be intricately connected to political, social, historical, and personal issues, providing wide ranging possibilities for questions and adding complexity to the case study. The researcher investigates the object of the case study in depth using a variety of data gathering methods to produce evidence that leads to understanding of the case and answers the research questions.

Case study research generally answers one or more questions which begin with "how" or "why." The questions are targeted to a limited number of events or conditions and their inter-relationships. To assist in targeting and formulating the questions, researchers conduct a literature review. This review establishes what research has been previously conducted and leads to refined, insightful questions about the problem. Careful definition of the questions at the start pinpoints where to look for evidence and helps determine the methods of analysis to be used in the study. The literature review, definition of the purpose of the case study, and early determination of the potential audience for the final report guide how the study will be designed, conducted, and publicly reported.

Step 2. Select the Cases and Determine Data Gathering and Analysis Techniques

During the design phase of case study research, the researcher determines what approaches to use in selecting single or multiple real-life cases to examine in depth and which instruments and data gathering approaches to use. When using multiple cases, each case is treated as a single case. Each cases conclusions can then be used as information contributing to the whole study, but each case remains a single case. Exemplary case studies carefully select cases and carefully examine the choices available from among many research tools available in order to increase the validity of the study. Careful discrimination at the point of selection also helps erect boundaries around the case.

The researcher must determine whether to study cases which are unique in some way or cases which are considered typical and may also select cases to represent a variety of geographic regions, a variety of size parameters, or other parameters. A useful step in the selection process is to repeatedly refer back to the purpose of the study in order to focus attention on where to look for cases and evidence that will satisfy the purpose of the study and answer the research questions posed. Selecting multiple or single cases is a key element, but a case study can include more than one unit of embedded analysis. For example, a case study may involve study of a single industry and a firm participating in that industry. This type of case study involves two levels of analysis and increases the complexity and amount of data to be gathered and analyzed.

A key strength of the case study method involves using multiple sources and techniques in the data gathering process. The researcher determines in advance what evidence to gather and what analysis techniques to use with the data to answer the research questions. Data gathered is normally largely qualitative, but it may also be quantitative. Tools to collect data can include surveys, interviews, documentation review, observation, and even the collection of physical artifacts.

The researcher must use the designated data gathering tools systematically and properly in collecting the evidence. Throughout the design phase, researchers must ensure that the study is well constructed to ensure construct validity, internal validity, external validity, and reliability. Construct validity requires the researcher to use the correct measures for the concepts being studied. Internal validity (especially important with explanatory or causal studies) demonstrates that certain conditions lead to other conditions and requires the use of multiple pieces of evidence from multiple sources to uncover convergent lines of inquiry.

The researcher strives to establish a chain of evidence forward and backward. External validity reflects whether or not findings are generalizable beyond the immediate case or cases; the more variations in places, people, and procedures a case study can withstand and still yield the same findings, the more external validity.

Techniques such as cross-case examination and within-case examination along with literature review help ensure external validity. Reliability refers to the stability, accuracy, and precision of measurement. Exemplary case study design ensures that the procedures used are well documented and can be repeated with the same results over and over again.

Step 3. Prepare to Collect the Data

Because case study research generates a large amount of data from multiple sources, systematic organization of the data is important to prevent the researcher from becoming overwhelmed by the amount of data and to prevent the researcher from losing sight of the original research purpose and questions.

Advance preparation assists in handling large amounts of data in a documented and systematic fashion. Researchers prepare databases to assist with categorizing, sorting, storing, and retrieving data for analysis.

Exemplary case studies prepare good training programs for investigators, establish clear protocols and procedures in advance of investigator field work, and conduct a pilot study in advance of moving into the field in order to remove obvious barriers and problems.

The investigator training programme covers the basic concepts of the study, terminology, processes, and methods, and teaches investigators how to properly apply the techniques being used in the study. The programme also trains investigators to understand how the gathering of data using multiple techniques strengthens the study by providing opportunities for triangulation during the analysis phase of the study.

The programme covers protocols for case study research, including time deadlines, formats for narrative reporting and field notes, guidelines for collection of documents, and guidelines for field procedures to be used. Investigators need to be good listeners who can hear exactly the words being used by those interviewed.

Qualifications for investigators also include being able to ask good questions and interpret answers. Good investigators review documents looking for facts, but also read between the lines and pursue collaborative evidence elsewhere when that seems appropriate.

Investigators need to be flexible in real-life situations and not feel threatened by unexpected change, missed appointments, or lack of office space. Investigators need to understand the purpose of the study and grasp the issues and must be open to contrary findings. Investigators must also be aware that they are going into the world of real human beings who may be threatened or unsure of what the case study will bring.

After investigators are trained, the final advance preparation step is to select a pilot site and conduct a pilot test using each data gathering method so that problematic areas can be uncovered and corrected. Researchers need to anticipate key problems and events, identify key people, prepare letters of introduction, establish rules for confidentiality, and actively seek opportunities to revisit and revise the research design in order to address and add to the original set of research questions.

Collect Data in the Field

The researcher must collect and store multiple sources of evidence comprehensively and systematically, in formats that can be referenced and sorted so that converging lines of inquiry and patterns can be uncovered. Researchers carefully observe the object of the case study and identify causal factors associated with the observed phenomenon. Renegotiation of arrangements with the objects of the study or addition of questions to interviews may be necessary as the study progresses. Case study research is flexible, but when changes are made, they are documented systematically.

Exemplary case studies use field notes and databases to categorize and reference data so that it is readily available for subsequent reinterpretation. Field notes record feelings and intuitive hunches, pose questions, and document the work in progress.

They record testimonies, stories, and illustrations which can be used in later reports. They may warn of impending bias because of the detailed exposure of the client to special attention, or give an early signal that a pattern is emerging. They assist in determining whether or not the inquiry needs to be reformulated or redefined based on what is being observed. Field notes should be kept separate from the data being collected and stored for analysis.

Maintaining the relationship between the issue and the evidence is mandatory. The researcher may enter some data into a database and physically store other data, but the researcher documents, classifies, and cross-references all evidence so that it can be efficiently recalled for sorting and examination over the course of the study.

Step 5. Evaluate and Analyse the Data

The researcher examines raw data using many interpretations in order to find linkages between the research object and the outcomes with reference to the original research questions. Throughout the evaluation and analysis process, the researcher remains open to new opportunities and insights. The case study method, with its use of multiple data collection methods and analysis techniques, provides researchers with opportunities to triangulate data in order to strengthen the research findings and conclusions.

The tactics used in analysis force researchers to move beyond initial impressions to improve the likelihood of accurate and reliable findings. Exemplary case studies will deliberately sort the data in many different ways to expose or create new insights and will deliberately look for conflicting data to disconfirm the analysis. Researchers categorize, tabulate, and recombine data to address the initial propositions or purpose of the study, and conduct cross-checks of facts and discrepancies in accounts. Focused, short, repeat interviews may be necessary to gather additional data to verify key observations or check a fact.

Specific techniques include placing information into arrays, creating matrices of categories, creating flow charts or other displays, and tabulating frequency of events. Researchers use the quantitative data that has been collected to corroborate and support the qualitative data which is most useful for understanding the rationale, or theory underlying relationships.

Another technique is to use multiple investigators to gain the advantage provided when a variety of perspectives and insights examine the data and the patterns. When the multiple observations converge, confidence in the findings increases. Conflicting perceptions, on the other hand, cause the researchers to pry more deeply.

Another technique, the cross-case search for patterns, keeps investigators from reaching premature conclusions by requiring that investigators look at the data in many different ways. Cross-case analysis divides the data by type across all cases investigated. One researcher then examines the data of that type thoroughly. When a pattern from one data type is corroborated by the evidence from another, the finding is stronger. When evidence conflicts, deeper probing of the differences is necessary to identify the cause or source of conflict. In all cases, the researcher treats the evidence fairly to produce analytic conclusions answering the original "how" and "why" research questions.

Step 6. Prepare the Report

Exemplary case studies report the data in a way that transforms a complex issue into one that can be understood, allowing the reader to question and examine the study and reach an understanding independent of the researcher.

The goal of the written report is to portray a complex problem in a way that conveys a vicarious experience to the reader. Case studies present data in very publicly accessible ways and may lead the reader to apply the experience in his or her own real-life situation. Researchers pay particular attention to displaying sufficient evidence to gain the readers confidence that all avenues have been explored, clearly communicating the boundaries of the case, and giving special attention to conflicting propositions.

Techniques for composing the report can include handling each case as a separate chapter or treating the case as a chronological recounting. Some researchers report the case study as a story. During the report preparation process, researchers critically examine the document looking for ways the report is incomplete. The researcher uses representative audience groups to review and comment on the draft document. Based on the comments, the researcher rewrites and makes revisions. Some case study researchers suggest that the document review audience include a journalist and some suggest that the documents should be reviewed by the participants in the study.

APPLYING THE CASE STUDY METHOD TO AN ELECTRONIC COMMUNITY NETWORK

By way of example, we apply these six steps to an example study of multiple participants in an electronic community network. All participants are non-profit organizations which have chosen an electronic community network on the World Wide Web as a method of delivering information to the public. The case study method is applicable to this set of users because it can be used to examine the issue of whether or not the electronic community network is beneficial in some way to the organization and what those benefits might be.

Step 1. Determine and Define the Research Questions

In general, electronic community networks have three

distinct types of users, each one a good candidate for case study research. The three groups of users include people around the world who use the electronic community network, the non-profit organizations using the electronic community network to provide information to potential users of their services, and the "community" that forms as the result of interacting with other participants on the electronic community network.

In this case, the researcher is primarily interested in determining whether or not the electronic community network is beneficial in some way to non-profit organization participants. The researcher begins with a review of the literature to determine what prior studies have determined about this issue and uses the literature to define the following questions for the study of the non-profit organizations providing information to the electronic community network:

- Why do non-profit organization participants use the network?
- How do non-profit organization participants determine what to place on the electronic community network?
- Do the non-profit organization participants believe the community network serves a useful purpose in furthering their mission? How?

Step 2. Select the Cases and Determine Data Gathering and Analysis Techniques

Many communities have constructed electronic community networks on the World Wide Web. At the outset of the design phase, the researcher determines that only one of these networks will be studied and further sets the study boundaries to include only some of the non-profit organizations represented on that one network. The researcher contacts the Board of Directors of the community network, who are open to the idea of the case study.

The researcher also gathers computer generated log data from the network and, using this data, determines that an in-depth study of representative organizations from four categories — health care, environmental, education, and religious — is feasible. The investigator applies additional selection criteria so that an urban-based and a rural-based non-profit are represented in the study in order to examine whether urban non-profits perceive more benefits from community networks than rural organizations.

The researcher considers multiple sources of data for this study and selects document examination, the gathering and study of organizational documents such as administrative reports, agendas, letters, minutes, and news clippings for each of the organizations.

In this case, the investigator decides to also conduct open-ended interviews with key members of each organization using a check-list to guide interviewers during the interview process so that uniformity and consistency can be assured in the data, which could include facts, opinions, and unexpected insights.

In this case study, the researcher cannot employ direct observation as a tool because some of the organizations involved have no office and meet infrequently to conduct business directly related to the electronic community network. The researcher instead decides to survey all Board members of the selected organizations using a questionnaire as a third data gathering tool. Within-case and cross-case analysis of data are selected as analysis techniques.

Step 3. Prepare to Collect the Data

The researcher prepares to collect data by first contacting each organization to be studied to gain their cooperation, explain the purpose of the study, and assemble key contact information. Since data to be collected and examined includes organizational documents, the researcher states his intent to request copies of these documents, and plans for storage, classification, and retrieval of these items, as well as the interview and survey data. The researcher develops a formal investigator training programme to include seminar topics on non-profit organizations and their structures in each of the four categories selected for this study.

The training programme also includes practice sessions in conducting open-ended interviews and documenting sources, suggested field notes formats, and a detailed explanation of the purpose of the case study.

The researcher selects a fifth case as a pilot case, and the investigators apply the data gathering tools to the pilot case to determine whether the planned timeline is feasible and whether or not the interview and survey questions are appropriate and effective.

Based on the results of the pilot, the researcher makes adjustments and assigns investigators particular cases which become their area of expertise in the evaluation and analysis of the data.

Step 4. Collect Data in the Field

Investigators first arrange to visit with the Board of Directors of each non-profit organization as a group and ask for copies of the organizations mission, news clippings, brochures, and any other written material describing the organization and its purpose. The investigator reviews the purpose of the study with the entire Board, schedules individual interview times with as many Board members as can cooperate, confirms key contact data, and requests that all Board members respond to the written survey which will be mailed later.

Investigators take written notes during the interview and record field notes after the interview is completed. The interviews, although open-ended, are structured around the research questions defined at the start of the case study.

Research Question: Why do non-profit organization participants use the network?

Interview Questions: How did the organization make the decision to place data on the World Wide Web community network? What need was the organization hoping to fulfill?

Research Question: How do non-profit organization participants determine what to place on the electronic community network?

Interview Questions: What process was used to select the

information that would be used on the network? How the information is kept up to date?

Research Question: Do the non-profit organization participants believe the community network serves a useful purpose in furthering their mission? How?

Interview Questions: How does the organization know if the electronic community network is beneficial to the organization? How does the electronic community network further the mission of the organization? What systematic tracking mechanisms exist to determine how many or what types of users are accessing the organization information?

The investigators field notes record impressions and questions that might assist with the interpretation of the interview data. The investigator makes note of stories told during open-ended interviews and flags them for potential use in the final report. Data is entered into the database.

The researcher mails written surveys to all Board members with a requested return date and a stamped return envelope. Once the surveys are returned, the researcher codes and enters the data into the database so that it can be used independently as well as integrated when the case study progresses to the point of cross-case examination of data for all four cases.

Step 5. Evaluate and Analyse the Data

Within-case analysis is the first analysis technique used with each non-profit organization under study. The assigned investigator studies each organizations written documentation and survey response data as a separate case to identify unique patterns within the data for that single organization. Individual investigators prepare detailed case study write-ups for each organization, categorizing interview questions and answers and examining the data for within-group similarities and differences.

Cross-case analysis follows. Investigators examine pairs of cases, categorizing the similarities and differences in each pair. Investigators then examine similar pairs for differences, and dissimilar pairs for similarities. As patterns begin to emerge, certain evidence may stand out as being in conflict with the patterns. In those cases, the investigator conducts follow-up focused interviews to confirm or correct the initial data in order to tie the evidence to the findings and to state relationships in answer to the research questions.

Step 6. Prepare the Report

The outline of the report includes thanking all of the participants, stating the problem, listing the research questions, describing the methods used to conduct the research and any potential flaws in the method used, explaining the data gathering and analysis techniques used, and concluding with the answers to the questions and suggestions for further research.

Key features of the report include a retelling of specific stories related to the successes or disappointments experienced by the organizations that were conveyed during data collection, and answers or comments illuminating issues directly related to the research questions.

The researcher develops each issue using quotations or other details from the data collected, and points out the triangulation of data where applicable. The report also includes confirming and conflicting findings from literature reviews. The report conclusion makes assertions and suggestions for further research activity, so that another researcher may apply these techniques to another electronic community network and its participants to determine whether similar findings are identifiable in other communities. Final report distribution includes all participants.

APPLICABILITY TO LIBRARY AND INFORMATION SCIENCE

Case study research, with its applicability across many disciplines, is an appropriate methodology to use in library studies. In Library and Information Science, case study research has been used to study reasons why library school programs close, to examine reference service practices in university library settings, and to examine how questions are negotiated between customers and librarians.

Much of the research is focused exclusively on the librarian as the object or the customer as the object. Researchers could use the case study method to further study the role of the librarian in implementing specific models of service.

For example, case study research could examine how information-seeking behaviour in public libraries compares with information-seeking behaviour in places other than libraries, to conduct in-depth studies of non-library community based information services to compare with library based community information services, and to study community networks based in libraries.

Case studies are complex because they generally involve multiple sources of data, may include multiple cases within a study, and produce large amounts of data for analysis. Researchers from many disciplines use the case study method to build upon theory, to produce new theory, to dispute or challenge theory, to explain a situation, to provide a basis to apply solutions to situations, to explore, or to describe an object or phenomenon.

The advantages of the case study method are its applicability to real-life, contemporary, human situations and its public accessibility through written reports. Case study results relate directly to the common readers everyday experience and facilitate an understanding of complex real-life situations.

COMBINING QUALITATIVE AND QUANTITATIVE RESEARCH

As in other fields of education, adult education and literacy faces great pressure to conduct more scientifically based research to identify effective instructional practices to guide teaching and inform policy. Educational research, especially in adult literacy, has been criticized for employing weak methodologies that do not allow for valid and reliable conclusions.

To address this issue in the U.S., the Department of Education began an ambitious agenda to improve the quality of research, in part by establishing strict methodology guidelines for educational research that accepts only studies with experimental or quasi-experimental designs.

At the same time, adult educational researchers face increasing demands to be more responsive to the field by designing studies and presenting findings that are more accessible to teachers and other practitioners, who need to know research-based practices that will improve the literacy and language skills of adult learners.

To this end, several research to practice initiatives have arisen, including those led by the NRDC in England and NCSALL in the U.S, the major adult literacy research organizations in their respective countries.

FALSE DICHOTOMIES

Due to the nature of the research process, it has been difficult for researchers and practitioners to communicate. Researchers are expected to stay aloof from practice, to ask pre-specified questions, collect information, analyse test scores, and then write up results in formats specified by the funding source.

Typically, outside researchers do not give opinions or offer advice, since such involvement could result in a lack of objectivity. It could also pollute the data because some programs might make changes based on the researchers' input. Practitioner input into research is generally not welcome or sought only in the initial phases, most often as part of an advisory panel.

It is not surprising then that, for many literacy programs, the news that they have been selected for a national research study, while flattering, is not entirely welcome. Programs are expected to cooperate fully by providing data about their students and answering researcher questions and by offering researchers access to their classrooms and to their students.

Programs often do not hear about the results of a study that they have been part of until much later, when data collection and analysis are completed, a process that might take years. When the results are finally published, often the reports do not speak to practitioners. Methods and findings tend to be discussed in dense academic prose; statistical information is written by and for other researchers and thus is not accessible to most lay people. Implications for practice may be entirely missing or not grounded in the realities of the everyday work of literacy practitioners.

The discussion of findings in quantitative and statistical terms, is not only difficult to for non-researchers to understand, but the reduction of teaching and learning to numbers and probability tests feels too removed from reality to many practitioners.

Qualitative data, which often speaks more persuasively to teachers, is often devalued as too subjective for research. As a result, false dichotomies have arisen between research and practice, and between qualitative and quantitative research. Rigorous research is quantitative, objective, removed from practice, while qualitative research is weak and subjective.

COMBINING THE QUALITATIVE AND QUANTITATIVE

The value of, and need for, objective, methodologically sound research is undeniable. Only through sound research designs can we eliminate threats to validity and draw scientifically valid conclusions to inform practice. While we recognize the value of the more traditional research, we also believe a more interactive, reciprocal research and development model that combines evidence from previous research studies with the professional wisdom of those doing literacy work in the field has a critical role to play in conducting research.

Indeed, scientific research combined with professional wisdom is the definition of "evidence-based research" put forth by the research branch of the U.S. Department of Education.

In our view, the best research design is a mixed method design that integrates qualitative and quantitative research. This type of design begins with a strong research methodology with quantitative methods that are enhanced with qualitative measures of key processes and outcomes. Qualitative methods, such as interviews and case studies, improve the design by providing data that can give insights into how findings work and how findings can be translated to practice.

By itself, a quantitative method can identify what works, but has limited explanatory power: there is little information about how students learned and how instruction worked, for example. With qualitative designs there is rich information about learners and teaching, but the information about what worked is more subjective and cannot be generalized.

By combining the two methods, we can obtain a much richer understanding. In other words, using a rigorous design the quantitative methods can tell us what works, while the qualitative methods can tell us how it works.

IMPLEMENTING A MIXED DESIGN: THE WHAT WORKS STUDY

Over the last several years, we had the opportunity to implement a mixed method approach to research in a major study for the U.S. Department of Education, the What Works Study For Adult ESL Literacy Students. The goal of this study was to identify effective instructional practices for adult ESL literacy students.

We used a longitudinal research design where we followed two cohorts of learners for nine months from the time they entered class. We assessed them with a comprehensive assessment battery upon entry into class and three months and nine months later, regardless of how long they remained in class. We measured instruction through classroom observations to develop quantitative measures of instructional practices.

To conduct observations, we developed an observation guide that allowed us to see how teachers approached language and literacy learning and capture the learning opportunities afforded to students in each class. In designing the observation guide we combined theoretical models of how language and literacy are developed with knowledge gained from visiting classes and talking with teachers. In the end, we developed a taxonomy of instructional practices related to second language acquisition that allowed us to categorize and code teaching activities. These codes were supplemented with a running record of activities in the classroom, providing both data on what teachers did (and for long and how often) and a means for double-checking codes.

The analyses of instructional inputs and learning outcomes employed latent growth modeling, a complex statistical method for analyzing longitudinal data, to relate the instructional measures to student literacy growth measured by the student assessments.

The modeling, which included measures of student attendance and student and teacher variables, found the following instructional methods were related to increases in literacy and language development:

- "Connection to the outside" — students in classes where teachers made connections to the "outside" or real world, had more growth in reading basic skills development.
- Use of the students' native language for clarification — students in classes where teachers used students' native language for clarification during instruction (e.g., to explain concepts and provide instructions on class work) had faster growth in reading comprehension and oral communication skills.
- Varied practice and interaction strategy — use of this strategy, where the teacher taught concepts in a variety of modalities and allowed for language practice, resulted in faster growth in oral communication skills.
- Emphasis on oral communication — students in classes where the teacher explicitly emphasized oral English communication skills in instruction showed more growth in this area.

This quantitative approach met one of the major goals of the study, to identify "what works" for instructing adult ESL literacy learners. However, we wanted to obtain a richer, more complete understanding both of the classes we were studying and how the students in our study were acquiring literacy skills. To do this, we added qualitative measures of instructional content and student literacy practices and abilities.

MEASURES OF INSTRUCTION

By collecting qualitative measures of instruction, we hoped to get an understanding of it what instruction that affects literacy development looked like. We used a detailed classroom observation guide, where an observer wrote a detailed narrative and rated teaching on five dimensions as the main source of data on instructional activities. Supplementing these data were bi-weekly logs of representative lessons provided by teachers, as well as periodic formal and ad hoc discussions with teachers about their instructional approaches and goals.

These data provided us with some surprises—mainly that even though the classes were supposed to be literacy-focused, most of the instructional time was being spent on language acquisition activities, rather than literacy development. On average 60 percent of instructional time in the 38 classes we observed was spent on language acquisition activities. Of the 40 percent of instructional time spent on literacy development, about 25 percent was spent on developing basic literacy skills and 15 percent of the time was devoted to teaching reading comprehension strategies. Only 11 classes in the study spent more than 60 percent of instructional time on literacy development.

In addition, we found that the teachers in our study we not trained in teaching literacy. They were mostly using the materials and methods that they would normally use in regular ESL classes aimed at more literate students.

The qualitative data we collected also allowed us to identify and describe more fully the instructional strategies we observed. We also were able to measure how often teachers used each strategy (shown as the mean observation score in the table).

Supplementing these qualitative data with the findings

from the growth modeling allowed us to understand and describe our findings more fully than would have been possible otherwise.

These qualitative data also made it easier for us to translate these instructional findings to practice. We can tell teachers what the findings mean to them because teachers helped us interpret and understand what they were doing throughout the research process.

Student Measures

We also sought to supplement the quantitative data with qualitative data from students. We included a literacy practices interview where we discussed with students their reading and writing habits, as well as other qualitative measures of their goals and background. A second data source was an alternative reading assessment where we observed students reading common, everyday materials.

The students self-selected the materials they wanted to read from a set we offered, which ranged in difficulty from easy (soda cans and food labels), to moderately difficult (flyers, utility bills and newspaper advertisements) and more difficult items (simple stories and magazine articles).

We rated students on their ability to read the item and their comprehension of what they read. The literacy practices interview also confirmed these finding and identified other materials beginning literacy students read.

Means are the average rating of each of the strategies comprising that scale. The rating scale ranged from 0 to 3, where "0" indicated that strategy was not observed at all, and "3" indicated that the strategy was characteristic of the class to a large extent.

These qualitative data provide a greater richness to the test score data we collected, which told us that students were gaining in literacy and language skills. However, we had wanted to include an ethnographic component to the study to get a deeper understanding of students' literacy development. This information would have provided us with greater insight into student learning, since we found that

Table. Observation-Based Instructional Strategies

Strategy	Mean Observation Score	Characteristic Practices Associated with Strategy
Varied Practice and Interaction	2.09	Teachers: • engage in direct teaching • keep students involved and engaged • provide feedback on student progress • allow ample opportunities for practice Students have the opportunity to: • work together to solve problems • spend the time it takes on a`task to 'get it' • engage in different types of literacy • use multiple modes of learning • learn from each other
Open Commu-nications	1.73	Teachers: • are flexible and respond to student needs as they arise • ask open-ended questions • supports open and authentic communication Students have the opportunity to: • contribute ideas based on their experience • express themselves without immediate correction
Connect-ion to "outside" world	1.25	Teachers: • share overall lesson goals • links lesson to real life • bring 'outside' into the classroom Students have the opportunity to: • apply class lessons to challenges outside the classroom
Choices and thinking	.53	Teachers: • provide students with choices Students have the opportunity to: • make choices about the way they learn • think about tasks and decide how to approach it

relatively little time was pent in class on literacy. Students were clearly learning outside of class but due to resource limitations, we were unable to implement a component that would shed light on such learning.

Table. Percent of Students Exhibiting Comprehension of Items on the Alternative Reading Assessment

Comprehension	Time 1 (n=435)	Time 2 (n=310)	Time 3 (n=215)
Attempted to read, but could understand none of the items	25	13	8
Showed comprehension of only the easy items (Soda can, food label, or French fry bag)	24	17	18
Showed comprehension of moderately difficult items (e.g., ad, flyer, bill, both stories)	40	49	55
Showed comprehension of most difficult items (magazine or newspaper)	12	20	19

In the What Work Study, we succeeded in using a mixed research design that included qualitative and quantitative elements. The quantitative methodology allowed us to identify instructional factors that worked to promote literacy and language development among adult ESL learners.

Through the qualitative measures, we also can describe the content and frequency of instructional activities that were effective and readily translate these findings to practice. We found that literacy development was not a main focus in most classes, but that the instructional model more closely resembled a standard ESL model of oral language development, where literacy is presumed to develop naturally as a by-product of language learning.

At the same time, the study design allowed us to understand what we failed to learn. We obtained only a brief glimpse into how ESL literacy learners engage in and acquire literacy in and out of class. In other words, we need to learn more about what types of literacy interventions it takes for struggling adult ESL readers who face turbulent lives to engage in learning, literacy and language.

We plan to continue our research in adult ESL literacy by designing a new study that explicitly examines literacy interventions for adult ESL learners. Our ideal design would be based on scientific research and practitioner experience and use a rigorous methodology that includes a mix of quantitative and qualitative measures. As part of designing such a study, we first reviewed the research literature to identify promising literacy interventions for adult ESL students and then developed hypotheses to serve as the basis for a study of selected interventions that would provide insights into policy and practice.

Since adult ESL literacy is a relatively new field it has received scant research attention. Indeed, the What Works Study is the only major study ever conducted on this population of students. However, existing at the nexus of adult literacy, second language acquisition, first language literacy development, and second language reading, adult ESL literacy can benefit from studies conducted in these fields.

To identify research that would inform the development of promising literacy interventions we reviewed studies in adult basic education (ABE) and adult ESL, and research in second language acquisition (SLA) of both children and adults, English as a foreign language, ESL pedagogy and reading acquisition in both the native language and second language. We present the findings of our review below and illustrate how an intervention would work for each hypothesis using our mixed design approach.

RESEARCH IN ABE AND ADULT ESL

To conduct the review of ABE and adult ESL, we first identified the universe of research studies through a comprehensive search of all published and unpublished studies examining literacy interventions using a sample of adults that were eligible to attend adult literacy programs (aged 16 or older, who were not enrolled in a secondary or post-secondary education) and that used literacy-related outcome measures (e.g., that measured reading, writing, speaking and/or listening skills).

We included studies in the U.S. and other English speaking countries (Australia, England, Canada, New Zealand). Our intention was to cast a wide net to catch all possible studies, conducted in the years 1983-2003. Through these procedures, we identified 111 studies.

After reviewing summaries and abstracts of these studies we excluded:

- Studies with simple one-group pretest-posttest designs and simple zero-order correlations, since they resulted in findings where the connection between the intervention and outcomes was unclear or inconclusive;
- Studies employing sample size smaller than 15 for either the treatment or the comparison groups; and
- Studies with no measures of literacy (reading, writing or English fluency for ESOL students).

Following these procedures we identified 17 studies of literacy interventions to review. The 17 studies examined the literacy impacts of a very narrow range of topics in adult education: instructional models, computer assisted instruction (CAI) and general impacts of participation in adult literacy programs. However, nine of the studies examined CAI. Only *two* studies examined an adult ESL population, while five were conducted in prison settings. Nine studies employed random assignment of students to treatment and control groups (although not always successfully).

In our review we gave consideration to three studies with the strongest research designs. Rich and Shepherd (1993) and Roberts, Cheek and Mumm (1994) looked at the effect of a specific instructional method on reading in ABE learners. Rich and Shepherd showed that the reciprocal teaching strategies of summarizing and questioning could improve reading comprehension.

These findings suggest the importance of using higher

order reading strategies in low-level readers. By demonstrating that a community building process could affect reading skills, Roberts, Cheek and Mumm showed the efficacy of group interaction and cooperative learning in ABE. Gretes and Green (1994), the other study with a rigorous methodology design, found that the multi-media READY software programme was effective in improving reading skills.

This software used a content-based, sequential reading approach that allowed individualized, self-directed learning. Taken together, these three high quality studies demonstrated the effects of:

- Teaching higher order reading strategies to improve reading comprehension;
- Group, cooperative learning;
- Learner engagement through individualized, multi-media, and
- The use of content-based materials.

The information we draw from the other studies, suffering from methodological problems, is more tentative, although is supportive of these findings. For example, Cheek and Lindsay (1994) studied the diagnostic prescriptive instructional approach, which used individualized instruction with language experience approaches and real-life materials. Students taught with the approach scored higher than controls on reading measures. The other CAI studies also support the ability of the use of technology in instruction to improve reading skills.

Supporting Gretes and Green (1994), Johnston (1996) found that READY and other software improved reading test scores among students in her study, while Maclay and Askov (1988) found that software that used a whole word approach to vocabulary building improved reading scores. In a rather dated study, Meyers, Ory and Hinckley (1983) found reading improvements over controls among male prison inmates using the PLATO software.

However, five studies of CAI found no differences for their interventions over controls, and often had substantial methodological or study implementation problems. Overall, it is difficult to make conclusions from these studies. The four studies examining general effects of ABE instruction are not very helpful to us in identifying effective literacy interventions.

Since they were focused on identifying broad programmatic effects, they did not describe in detail the nature of the literacy interventions employed. In three of them – Martinson and Friedlander (1994) and both Even Start studies – the adult students were enrolled in several different instructional programs where the researchers had no control over, or monitoring of, the intervention.

In any case, the Even Start studies found no significant difference between Even Start adults and controls on the literacy measures and Friedlander and Martinson found only a site-specific effect for literacy outcomes in their study of GAIN participants. Tewksbury and Vito (1994) did find significant differences in reading and math scores for male inmates in a prison literacy programme that used a functional skills approach, although the research design was weak.

It is worth noting that *we found only two studies that used adult ESL students.* One of these studies showed no treatment-control differences for adult literacy instruction and the other had methodological flaws. Thus, the effects of literacy interventions on literacy and language development among adult ESL learners lacks a research base and we must use these ABE reading studies if we want research-based guidance from this field to identify promising literacy interventions for adult ESL literacy learners.

This approach is problematic, since not only are there differences between second language reading development and reading in the native language, but the ABE studies do not address the *language* issues inherent in ESL.

The teaching of higher order reading strategies to improve reading comprehension, such as used by Rich and Shepherd (1993), require interaction among learners and teachers – and this interaction requires a common language. Consequently, teaching these strategies is impossible in an ESL class unless the teachers and learners all speak the same language. The ABE studies also do not inform us about the role of oral language proficiency in literacy development, nor do they provide guidance on literacy interventions that might foster oral proficiency in English.

Yet another shortcoming to using the ABE studies to inform us about ESL literacy interventions is that none of the ABE studies examined literacy-level learners. Many studies used readers as low as third grade level, but even this literacy level is higher than many of the learners that would be the target of the proposed research study. Adult ESL literacy learners must learn language and literacy simultaneously, and the ABE research reviewed offers little guidance on instructional interventions that might help them meet this challenge.

The 17 studies identified reflect an unorganized approach toward studying adult literacy and were not guided by any theory, approach or school of thought about good pedagogy. They do not provide a comprehensive body of knowledge on the impacts or literacy interventions in ABE. Furthermore, seven of the studies found no significant differences between treatment and comparison groups.

Consequently, the ABE studies are very limited in the information they provide for identifying promising literacy interventions for adult ESL literacy students. To obtain further information and insights into the key elements of an effective intervention, we turned to the research in SLA, ESL pedagogy and second language reading.

RESEARCH IN ADULT SLA, ESL PEDAGOGY AND SECOND LANGUAGE READING

The literature on second language acquisition (SLA), ESL pedagogy and second language reading is extensive. We focused our review on studies that used adults or that addressed key issues in adult ESL literacy. To help organize our findings and focus the review, we started with studies conducted with ESL literacy students, including smaller studies that speak to language and literacy issues of adult immigrants and refugees.

We broadened our review to include studies in English

as a Foreign language but focused primarily on those conducted with adult learners (mostly college students learning either English or another language). We also included some of the seminal studies in second language acquisition with children and adults, focusing on those where results have been duplicated and are now generally accepted (e.g., support for the threshold hypothesis and the linguistic interdependence hypothesis).

We clustered the research around themes that were common to a several studies and highlighted those studies that involved adults learning another language. We excluded studies that only addressed sub-components of language learning, such as morphological or phonological aspects of SLA, the acquisition of tense and sentence structure and isolated vocabulary learning, since the goals of adult ESL literacy are much broader than the acquisition of structural skills.

We clustered research findings into these themes:

- The relationship between oral communication skills and literacy;
- Connecting literacy learning to real-world tasks;
- Integrating computers and multimedia into literacy instruction;
- Using the native language as support for second language development and literacy learning; and
- Improving ESL literacy through a focus on reading.

The enormous size of the literature makes it impossible for us to describe all of the significant studies cited in each area. Instead, we begin discuss the overall findings, and provide greater information on representative studies and their implications for designing a literacy intervention study.

ORAL COMMUNICATION SKILLS AND LITERACY

Several studies have examined the interrelationship between orality and reading on the one hand and oral communication and school achievement on the other. A seminal work by Alderson (1984) suggests that a greater knowledge of the target language in general facilitates L2 reading comprehension. He cites evidence that reading skills and strategies from the native language do not easily transfer to reading in the second language unless a threshold level of general language competence has been achieved, at least at the beginning levels of L2 learning. Correlational research confirms this relationship and strongly supports the view that language proficiency is a significant factor in second language reading. In other words, language ability trumps reading ability.

English learners who, for example, have good higher order reading strategies in their own language cannot call on those strategies to help them understand English texts until their understanding of English vocabulary and syntax are good enough to understand basic sentences and expressions. The interrelationship between language proficiency and literacy skills, known as the linguistic interdependence hypotheses, has now been widely accepted in the SLA field. The *What Works Study* also supports the relationship between oral proficiency and reading ability. Adult ESL literacy students whose proficiency levels of English were higher at pre-testing showed greater gains in reading than students with lower levels of oral English proficiency.

Studies of young children, particularly Snow, also provide evidence of the positive relationship between oral language and literacy, as evidenced by school achievement. She notes "although print materials may be used to support the development of English phonology, vocabulary and syntax, the postponement of formal reading instruction is appropriate until an adequate level of oral English proficiency has been achieved".

Snow has shown that children in families where parents discussed abstract ideas had greater success in school than did children from families where such oral interactions did not take place. The findings held true for both language minority students where a language other than English was spoken in the home and for native-born children. These findings suggest that adult ESL literacy students might be well served by programs that put a strong emphasis on building the overall

English competence of students, including the development of face-to-face communication skills before or while basic literacy is introduced.

CONNECTING LITERACY LEARNING TO REAL-WORLD TASKS

There is evidence from research in learning that points toward the benefits of contextualized or situated learning, compared to the learning of decontextualized skills. Studies in second language acquisition and in adult literacy also provide some evidence of the positive impact of teaching language in context, focusing on communicative interactions and task-based learning. For example, the *What Works Study* already cited found that students in classes where teachers connected instruction to real world materials and contexts showed greater gains on basic skills reading test scores that students in classes where teachers made fewer such connections.

In second language acquisition, studies in contextualized learning often appear under the rubric of "communicative competence." These studies examine the relative merits of instruction focused on oral communication, as well as reading and writing tasks that reflect real-world challenges. This approach is compared to learning through a "structural syllabus," one that focuses primarily on the syntax, vocabulary, and morphology of language.

Despite its age, a study by Savignon (1972) continues to be cited in influential research reviews such as Lightbown and Spada (2003), a key text in TESL graduate programs. This study examined the possible benefits of a communicative approach with 48 college students enrolled in French language courses at an American university. Savignon divided students into three groups, and all groups received the same number of hours per week of audio-lingual instruction where the focus was on grammar practice. The "communicative group" had an extra hour per week focused on using the target language (French) in meaningful and creative ways. The "cultural group" had an additional hour devoted to the appreciation of

French culture in workshops conducted in the native language (in this case English) to lessen the psychological distance between the home culture and the target culture.

The control group received additional work devoted to skill and drill practice in a language laboratory. All approaches included a focus on language structure. Results showed that students who spent part of their study day dealing with communicative tasks scored significantly higher on communicative tests and did as well on grammatical accuracy measures as students in classes that focused primarily on grammar and form.

A second study, conducted 10 years later with adult learners from different countries, showed similar positive results for a communication-focused model. Montgomery and Eisenstein studied 28 ESL students speaking different languages who participated either in a traditional ESL class or in a course that combined traditional grammar-focused ESL with communication activities focused around weekly field trips.

The study used a quasi-experimental design, using pre-post tests and matched pairs (matched on English proficiency, native language, length of time in the United States and SES). Progress was measured using a scale adapted from the Foreign Service Oral Interview.

Results showed that beginning learners who engaged in communicative activities around field trips in addition to their regular, required grammar course made greater improvement in accent, vocabulary, grammar, and comprehension than others who received only the standard course.

These studies (Savignon and Montgomery and Eisenstein), now widely cited, offer support for the following hypothesis: communicative approaches that include a balance between structured grammar practice on the one hand and open-ended conversation and communication tasks on the other are likely to result in greater gains in communication skills for adult learners than approaches that focus primarily on the structure and form of English.

It is important to remember that studies focused primarily

on the development of oral communication skills, rather than literacy skills, either basic or functional.

REAL-WORLD TASKS IN FUNCTIONAL CONTEXT

Another way to bring real-world activities into the classroom is through instruction that ties literacy to tasks frequently conducted in the workplace or everyday life. This type of instruction focuses on the real world literacy activities that reflect the challenges that adult learners face in their daily lives and goes beyond teaching language basics and structure. Sticht's (1997) work with literacy students in the U.S.

Army showed that learners who were taught through a functional approach where learning was tied to job tasks outperformed those who participated in a programme where learning was focused on basic skills unrelated to the work. This approach, termed the functional context approach, has received wide spread acceptance in workplace literacy training.

Sticht studied over 714 recruits in a six-week Army and Air Force reading programme to determine the effect of a functional approach to reading. The design used a quasi-experimental, pre-and posttest comparison model. The study included a treatment group, which used a contextual instructional model tied to work tasks, and two control groups, one with Army recruits and another with Navy recruits, both using a basic skills curriculum not contextualized to work tasks.

All three groups consisted of recruits with similar demographic profiles. Assessment measures included a general reading test and a test of job related reading tasks. The treatment group participating in the functional reading programme showed significantly higher gains in job related reading tasks in comparison to both control groups and similar gains on the general reading test.

Studies with ABE learners also point toward the benefits of an approach that links classroom instruction to the use of functional literacy outside of the classroom. In a study conducted for the National Centre for the Study of Adult

Learning and Literacy (NCSALL), Purcell-Gates *et al.*, (2002) examined the relationship between use of real life materials in the classroom and changes in literacy practices by learners outside of the classroom. The study involved 159 students and used descriptive and correlational methods. Teacher surveys and classroom observations were used to determine the degree of real life materials and activities in the classroom and students were interviewed to see to what degree learners increased their range of literacy practices as a result of instruction.

Students who participated in classes where authentic materials and activities were used showed greater change in their daily literacy practices in terms of both the range of texts and the amount of reading and writing being done outside of class than students who used materials and activities focused on school-based reading and writing.

Project-based learning and cooperative learning models represent a similar approach to working with authentic, real-world materials in adult learning. These approaches add another feature, namely that of working as part of a group to deal with language and literacy tasks. Reports from the field on cooperative learning show positive benefits in studies with language minority youth and with kids where students work in teams.

Slavin reviewed a total of 90 studies. Some of the studies compared multiple cooperative learning methods to control groups and he counts these as separate comparisons for a total of 99 comparisons of cooperative learning with control groups. 63 were significantly positive, 31 showed no difference and 5 were significantly negative. Results showed cooperative learning to be most effective when there are group awards and individual accountability within the group.

Not surprisingly, the opportunities to use English inside and outside of the classroom tend to accelerate language learning, particularly for adults. An early comparative study conducted in the Netherlands by Snow and Hoefnagel-Hoehle (1978) compared adults, children, and adolescents learning Dutch as a second language to see how rates of acquisition differed among the three groups. The study showed that adults and adolescents make rapid progress in proficiency in cases where they can make use of the target language on a daily basis in social, personal, professional, and academic interactions.

Given that adult immigrants and refugees come to classes to learn the skills needed in the community and at work, and given that only a few hours of classes are offered in a week, an approach that connects classroom learning with the community and encourages language and literacy use outside of school shows a great deal of promise.

INTEGRATING COMPUTERS AND MULTIMEDIA INTO LITERACY INSTRUCTION

Video, or multimedia containing video, shows particular promise for language instruction, since language and content are presented in a variety of modalities (visual, auditory, text based) that reinforce each other. As such, they offer an immediate context for language learning that is not print dependent and allows for varied inputs in terms of language variation (regional accents and foreign dialects), as well as variation in the speed of discourse, thus allowing for increases in listening comprehension and understanding of the pronunciation of American English.

In addition, skill and drill software allows students to work independently and at their individual levels of readiness. Computer-based learning of this type can provide practice in structure and vocabulary, especially at the very beginning levels of language learning where creation and construction of knowledge are still very difficult. The automatic immediate feedback offered by software can have positive results as well.

There is now some evidence of the effectiveness of the use of these approaches in literacy education in general. Some of these studies focus on the various uses of technology as part of language instruction, notably Canning (1998); Beauvois, (1998); Belz (2002) and Chapelle (2001). Various studies have shown effects in the nature and quality of communication via electronic networks and collaborative conversations. Others have pointed toward the benefits of using video as part of language teaching (e.g., Baltova, 1994). Although these studies are too numerous to review in detail here, the findings are worth considering.

A typical study by Herron, Hanley and Cole (1995) indicates that the visual support in the form of descriptive pictures significantly improved comprehension scores with language videos for English speaking students learning French. Using two classes of college students enrolled in introductory, the researchers studied the effect of using video with pictorial support on comprehension.

In one class, the teacher read aloud six sentences from cue cards that summarized the major scenes in an upcoming video segment.

In the second class, the teacher read the same six sentences aloud, but following each sentence also showed a picture related in context to the sentence, but not a direct pictorial translation of it. In this way, the picture acted as contextual support rather than a direct representation of the scene from the video.

Both classes of students then watched the video. Comprehension was tested immediately after the students watched the video when they had to answer questions about the video in English. Two judges blindly scored student's written responses. Students with the pictorial support performed significantly better than students without the visual support.

The use of multimedia in the form of video combined with text-based language learning (in print or online) is also showing some promise for ABE students. Project READY, a computer-based multimedia literacy programme for adults, showed positive results for adult literacy learners, although ESL students were not included in the study. An experimental study that looked at *Crossroads Café* reviewed above, found positive outcomes for adult ESL students, although it had methodological flaws. Anecdotal evidence from the field consistently stresses the draw that technology presents for adult literacy learners.

Cromley (2000) suggests that access to technology results in greater learner engagement and retention. Since distance learning is often problematic for non-traditional learners with low levels of skills and little experience with technology, a model that integrates multimedia with classroom teaching might have greater success than distance learning models, at least for students at the very beginning levels of English proficiency.

Such a model could also include language learning tasks designed to help students learn on their own from TV, video, and film, thereby possibly increasing both language skills and language awareness. We find this an option worth considering.

USING THE NATIVE LANGUAGE (L1) TO SUPPORT LEARNING THE SECOND LANGUAGE (L2)

There is evidence to posit a relationship between reading in the native language and the ability to process print in the target language.[5] However, this transfer of literacy skills may only come into play when higher levels of language proficiency have been achieved. Language transfer is likely to occur on the level of basic text processing and comprehension, particularly around texts that reflect the reader's background knowledge.

Various studies provide evidence that a threshold level of literacy in the native language may need to be achieved before underlying skills related to text processing will transfer to the target language. However, the question of how much literacy is enough before such transfer can occur has not been answered, and the exact nature of the threshold level has not been established. In some cases the language transfer may be negative, as when students try to apply a rule from their first language to the second language.

When threshold in the target language is sufficiently high for transfer in reading skills to occur, such transfer may not be automatic and second language learners may benefit from direct instruction on how to transfer reading strategies used in the first language to the second language. Given the possibility of such a transfer, and given that literacy in English is difficult to attain, developing the native language literacy skills of students whose languages have a fairly transparent orthographic system might be an option to study. For ESL literacy, this would mean native language literacy instruction in Spanish, Haitian Creole and Hmong.

Numerous K-12 studies in bilingual education and meta-analyses of these studies have shown that the use of the native language in the elementary grades has a positive effect on both English proficiency and academic achievement, particularly if native language use is part of a coherent programme reflecting principles of quality education.

The review by the National Research Council also supported these findings. Dual immersion programs, where language minority children learning English study side-by-side with native-born children who are learning the minority language as a foreign language (most often Spanish, but also Chinese or Korean), have also been successful. In contrast, some earlier studies show that structured ESL immersion programs where only ESL is used, is successful in terms of teaching English language and literacy skills.

Meta-analyses and reviews of these studies consistently stress that whatever approach is used, it needs to be embedded in a quality programme in order to make a difference.

While there are a great many studies exploring the role of native language instruction for children learning a second language, only two studies that attempted an experimental or quasi-experimental design exist that examine the role of first language literacy among low-literate groups trying to acquire English, Burtoff (1985) and Robson (1982). Burtoff found that Haitian Creole speakers who were taught literacy skills in their native language acquired English literacy skills faster than students who did not receive literacy instruction in Haitian Creole.

In a Thai refugee camp with Hmong learners trying to acquire English literacy, Robson showed similar results.

Teaching non-literate students to read and write in their native language has a great deal of appeal. The approach is thoroughly grounded in reading theory showing the relationship between oral language and reading and in second language acquisition, particularly the Linguistic Interdependence Theory, suggesting positive transfer between first and second language literacy skills. Studies confirming these theories strongly suggest that it is easier to become literate for the first time in a language one knows than in a language one is trying to acquire and background knowledge is more easily accessible when oral language and literacy match.

In addition, learning to decode in a home language that is orthographically regular poses fewer cognitive challenges than learning a fairly irregular system like English, which, for non-native speakers struggling with English pronunciation, poses significant challenges.

Besides teaching literacy in the native language, there may be other options for taking advantage of the students home language in adult ESL learning contexts, particularly in areas where one language group predominates (e.g., Los Angeles, El Paso, Chicago for Spanish speakers; St. Paul for the Hmong; southern Florida for Haitian Creole). The *What Works Study* provides some evidence as to the benefits of native language use with low literate ESL learners.

While the strategic use of the native language in instruction in bilingual classrooms has been explored in the K-12 literature (particularly through methods such as preview and review in the native language), this study is the only study that examined use of L1 in an adult ESL context. The study found positive gains in reading and oral English communication skills for students whose teachers used the native language for purposes such as to clarify concepts, introduce new ideas, or provide explanations.

Why students in classrooms where the native language was used showed higher gains is open to interpretation, of course, but it seems possible that use of the native language by teachers aided students in understanding directions and key concepts, thus freeing up cognitive resources for dealing with the learning tasks at hand. Given these results, investigating the difference that the judicious use of the native language within the ESL classroom might make it worth considering, particularly in bilingual communities where immigrants live and work in two languages.

IMPROVING ESL LITERACY THROUGH A FOCUS ON READING

Learning to read in a second language, particularly a language one is trying to master, is an immensely complex undertaking. Success depends on many factors including proficiency in the target language, literacy abilities in the native language, as well as factors related to disposition (motivation, interest, attitudes), personal goals, and purposes for wanting to learn the language and wanting to learn to read, both in general and in relationship to different types of texts. Cultural attitudes toward reading play a role as well, and help to determine what is to be read (types of texts) and for what purpose.

Unfortunately, the research base on what it takes to read in L2 is much smaller than the research base for reading in L1. The L2 reading studies that do exist for the most part use correlational or quasi-experimental designs and examine topics common to general reading research: how to help learners achieve fluency and automaticity, how to increase vocabulary knowledge and how to improve comprehension. Some of these studies also speak to issues particular to L2 reading, such as the relationship between L2 language proficiency and L2 reading; the possibilities of transfer between reading in the native language and reading in the second language; the role of similarities in orthography (spelling and writing systems); or the effect that knowledge of vocabulary, syntax (grammar and sentence structure) and morphology (word endings) has on comprehension.

A great many of the studies in L2 reading examine the process by which different types of learners with various backgrounds and proficiency levels manage reading tasks in a new language. A few of these reading studies have implications for instructional practice although none of them have been conducted with our target group: adults who are beginning learners of English and have low levels of literacy in the native language. Through our review of this research we have identified the following two areas as worth considering, since they provide indications of positive effects found in both L1 and L2 reading research.

Extensive exposure to print increases both vocabulary knowledge and comprehension skills (Stanovich. 2000; Cipielewski and Stanovich, 1992, studying young children learning to read in L1). Similar results were found in several studies for ESL learners in K-12. Elley (1991), in a meta-analysis of 8 empirical studies with elementary level ESL students, also showed that a programme of extensive reading can have a positive impact on reading comprehension for L2 learners in elementary school.

A study with adult ESL learners is underway at the NCSALL National ESL Lab School at Portland State University. This study, using random assignment, is exploring the effects of sustained silent reading compared to more conventional reading instruction. Results are not yet available.

According to the National Reading Panel, research in reading in L1 shows positive effects for the direct teaching of reading strategies, including those related to vocabulary acquisition and to reading comprehension (e.g., question generating and answering, summarizing information).

Strategy instruction can be effective in increasing awareness of strategies, strategy use, and reading comprehension (Brown, Pressley, Van Meter, and Schuder, 1996 using an experimental design to show the effectiveness of Transactional Strategy Instruction - TSI). The reciprocal teaching strategy has also been shown to be effective with ABE learners as discussed earlier, using a randomized design.

This approach shows promise for L2 reading as well. An experimental study in Taiwan has shown how an instructional strategy of previewing key information and key vocabulary can positively affect comprehension of texts for L2 learners. Other, non-experimental studies with L2 university students also point toward the positive effects of strategy-based teaching. For example, in a correlational study comparing the use of strategies associated with semantic mapping, Carrell showed positive results for students who used those strategies in reading and recall. She had found positive results for the direct teaching of text structures in an earlier study using a quasi-experimental design that used treatment and control groups with pre-and post testing. The sample size was fairly small (25 students).

The results of studies that look at the relationship between strategy-based teaching and reading comprehension look promising, as do the studies that have examined the effects of extended reading on general reading skills and vocabulary acquisition in particular. This latter approach has been successful with both L1 and L2 readers. However, both approaches assume at least an intermediate level of English proficiency. For those who are still struggling with English at the beginning levels, one option might be to provide strategy instruction in the native language and then guide students in using these strategies with English texts. Similarly, if extensive reading is likely to build both concept knowledge and higher-level text processing skills, and if reading in L1 is positively related to literacy in L2, extensive reading in the native language should have beneficial effect on reading in English, particularly if the subjects explored have a familiar theme.

Identifying Effective Literacy Interventions

In our review of the literature, we had hoped to find a definitive set of studies or body of research that would provide clear direction for developing effective literacy interventions for adult ESL literacy learners. Based on our review, we now know that there are no such studies. Nonetheless, both the adult ABE/ESL studies and the SLA research reviewed here suggest several directions for an intervention that can help increase our understanding of what it takes to improve the language and literacy skills of adults who are new to English and new to literacy.

Teaching Literacy in Context: Bringing in the Outside

Offering adult learners the opportunity to engage in real

life tasks and to use language and literacy outside of the classroom is supported by both the ABE and SLA studies we reviewed. A literacy intervention based on this research could test the following hypothesis:

Providing a contextualized model of instruction that includes language and literacy tasks reflective of real life language use will promote both reading comprehension and greater language proficiency in the target language (English).

IMPLICATIONS FOR POLICY AND PRACTICE

Adult immigrants in ESL classes should benefit from an approach that links classroom work with every day life and promotes language and literacy use outside of the classroom through an instructional model that integrates language tasks outside of the classroom with the work done in school. One of the key findings of the *What Works Study* was that connecting literacy teaching to every day life made a significant difference in reading basic skills development. To implement this strategy, teachers often use materials from daily life that contain information that students want to know about or with which they have some experience.

For example, a teacher might bring in grocery flyers from different stores and ask students to compare prices. Since such flyers generally use a combination of pictures, printed language and numbers, students can use their background knowledge to gain meaning from print and use supporting visuals and numbers to solve a problem, such as figuring out who may offer the best buys in a given week. Inserts from automotive stores or catalogues from department stores or cosmetic companies offer similar opportunities. In some classes we observed, teachers used phone and electricity bills, letters from schools or immigration authorities, and other items that appear in students' mailboxes to highlight literacy for adult contexts. They asked students to focus on the information contained in a bill and where key information appeared on the page, and asked them to consider the meaning of individual phrases such as "total amount due" or "late payment charges."

Another popular way to connect to the outside is to have students use literacy in real situations that call for reading and writing, such as through field trips outside of class. For example, teachers often create opportunities for their students to study menus in class and then go to a restaurant to order in English. Sometimes teachers demonstrate how to look up children's books about their home country on the Internet using an on-line bookstore and then check with the local library to see if these books are available to borrow, thus linking reading and writing with technology. Since looking for books in the library often involves both using the computer and perusing the stacks, real life literacy is once again linked to the acquisition of basic reading and writing. As the classroom is linked to the world outside, cultural knowledge of how libraries work and the selection of books of interest can be linked to the development of sub-skills such as spelling and key boarding and using the alphabet to find a book.

Investigating contextualized approaches can help us see if adults are able to acquire language and literacy skills through natural interactions with print and through communication encounters with English speakers. This model could be compared to or combined with a basic skills model of ESL that focuses primarily on teaching the sub-skills or mechanics of reading, such as those related to phonemic awareness and word knowledge.

Examining the relative contributions of each model: (1) a highly contextual, experiential approach to teaching literacy and (2) an approach that asks learners to spend a significant amount of time focusing on sub skills in isolation can go a long way in avoiding the "reading wars" in adult ESL that have plagued K-12 reading.[8] Similar models can be used to investigate the contribution that an overt focus on grammar has on language acquisition, particularly for adults who have had little experience with formal schooling.

INTEGRATING MULTIMEDIA INTO INSTRUCTION

We found research from both ABE/ESL and SLA to indicate that the use of CAI, video and other multimedia approaches to instruction might be effective for ESL literacy learners. This research suggests the following topic could be tested:

A language learning model that includes the use of visual media through pictures and computer, allows for communication via electronic means, and encourages students to learn from video and TV on their own is likely to increase the language and literacy skills of ESL literacy students.

Implications for Policy and Practice

An intervention designed to use multimedia approaches need not be limited to CAI or video, but could also exploit the possibilities of CD-ROM or on-line technology. These approaches offer opportunities for on-going self-access learning, along with the advantages of having visual materials on hand to illustrate concepts and bring language and literacy to life.

Other possibilities include collaborative projects such as "virtual visits" or key-pal relationships (e-mail version of pen-pals) with native speakers or language learners in other locations, which would provide opportunities for authentic communication and negotiation of meaning.

Case studies of individual programs that use technology creatively and show high rates of success in terms of student outcomes can help provide explanations as to why technology might be worth considering in research and practice.

The Socorro Family Literacy Programme near El Paso on the U.S.-Mexico border, for example, has adopted a model that asks learners to work in teams and create projects with technologies such as PowerPoint or video.[9] Each year the students are part of a showcase where they present their finished projects to an English speaking audience consisting of other students, parents, school administrators and community members such as social workers and officials from the Workforce Board.

Investigations into the effect of innovative approaches to technology integration can offer insights into what it takes to engage learners and help us see the difference in learning that occurs when adult literacy is used for real world purposes beyond the classroom.

Teachers know from experience that access to high-end technology (computers, video, presentation software) can act as a tremendous draw for students. An investigation into what differences hands-on work with technology can make in language and literacy learning can help programs make informed decisions about technology purchases and technology use.

Providing learners access to computer labs where they can work on their skills beyond scheduled class times can extend the learning day and may improve learning through increased time on task. Research into distance learning models that combine video-based language learning with group discussions and literacy practice through textbooks that match students' reading level show promise as well.

Direct Teaching of Literacy and Language Strategies

Many of the reading studies reviewed here suggested the effectiveness of explicitly teaching strategies related to language and literacy learning in developing reading comprehension and communication skills. Furthermore, the few well-designed ABE studies found teaching such strategies effective.. These approaches clearly appear promising, suggesting the following hypothesis:

A rich ESL literacy programme that focuses explicitly and systematically on both lower and higher level processing skills associated with reading, while at the same time creating opportunities for the exploration of a wide variety of texts, is likely to result in higher gains in English reading skills than a conventional ESL programme focused on life skills.

The use of this approach is complicated with adult ESL literacy learners. Teaching these strategies requires a common language among teacher and students and use of the strategies assumes some minimal basic skill level in reading, which literacy learners may lack. While skills related to an understanding of how English works, vocabulary development or understanding the organization of different types of functional texts can be taught in English, meta-cognitive skills may have to be taught in the native language. These could include strategies for acquiring basic literacy, particularly those related to phonemic awareness as well. Extensive teacher training would be necessary for this type of intervention since most ESL teachers are not trained in how to teach initial literacy.

Implications for Policy and Practice

Unlike children in the K-12 context who might benefit from a sequential approach to literacy that starts with decoding and slowly moves to application of these skills, adult ESL learners must deal with multiple challenges related to literacy all at the same time.

While adults many times are able to bring background knowledge to bear on these tasks or use compensatory skills to make meaning, these strategies may not help them to develop the underlying skills needed to process print effectively. A direct literacy teaching intervention we envision would target skills and strategies found to be effective in the teaching of reading and writing, such as creating phonemic awareness, developing fluency or automaticity, modeling comprehension strategies, increasing vocabulary, and fostering writing skills.

The point of such an intervention would not be to change teaching to a phonics based approach (and make ESL teachers "phonicators") but to find ways to integrate the teaching of basic literacy skills into an ESL curriculum so that non-literate or low literate students get a chance to develop the skills that they have not had the chance to attain in their first language. An intervention study of this sort would then allow us to see whether an overt focus on underlying skills associated with reading and writing will facilitate the literacy acquisition process.

Wrigley and Guth (1992) showed that teachers who were considered "effective" used examples from students' lives as starting points for highlighting patterns and helping students see the relationship between oral language and print. They might ask students which places they would like to visit and then draw their attention to common sound patterns in words such as Africa, America, Canada, California, and Alaska. They might use simple phrases to show print and sound analogies (oh, honey, give me money) and blends can be taught through fun words reflecting onomatopoeia such as "splish-splash" or "burp/slurp"). Simple poems may be used to help non-literate students focus on rhythm and rhymes ("candy is dandy, but liquor is quicker"), irregular spelling notwithstanding.

Teaching the alphabet to non-literate students can also be accomplished in the context of words that are meaningful to adult learners. Some teachers suggest that students line up by the first or last letter of their names (using a ruler that list the alphabet as a guide) or to create a grocery list that names items in alphabetical order. Asking students to predict what a news story might be all about by just looking at headlines and a picture in the paper can promote comprehension as can drawing a story board of a process that is described in print.

Dictations and language experience stories can help make connections between oral language and print transparent. Finally, teaching simple pre-fixes and roots can help develop word attack skills (uni-verse/uni-cycle/uni-form; homi-cide/sui-cide/sperm-icide, with the latter depending on the focus of the class, of course).

Native Language Literacy

Given the strong evidence of the importance of literacy in the native language to L2 learning, an intensive programme of native language literacy (in combination with training in English communication skills) might advance the literacy skills of non-readers sufficiently to allow them to engage a wide variety of texts, thus developing the underlying skills necessary to access print in English. A research study with this type of intervention could test the following hypothesis:

An instructional programme that combines native language literacy and the teaching of oral communication skills in English will increase both the literacy and language skills of adults who are not literate in their native language. Use of the native language as part of ESL instruction is likely to aid students in the cognitive processing of new information and might result in greater gains in literacy as well.

Implications for Policy and Practice

Clearly, learning to read in a language one speaks is much easier than it is to acquire text-processing skills in a language one is trying to learn.[10] In addition, acquiring basic decoding skills in a language where sound/symbol relationships are more transparent (e.g., Spanish) is likely to be more easily accomplished than trying to decode many of the high frequency words in English (e.g., meat, early, breakfast, schedule). Given these challenges, introducing literacy in the native language might provide a solid foundation in basic reading skills (decoding, fluency, and automaticity) that can facilitate English literacy development.

In the ESL literacy field, the native language is used in a variety of ways. Bilingual teachers who share the language of their students often use the native language to clarify a concept or provide an explanation when students appear confused. They may also use a "preview/review" model to introduce a lesson or task in the first language and to summarize the points made after the lesson, particularly if the discussion involved the acquisition of content knowledge related to how things work, referring to policies such as returning things to the store, or providing information related to systems such as health care, education, or schooling.

The native language is often part of the ESL classroom even when the teacher is not bilingual, since students who speak the same language invariably use the native language to ask questions of each other or to help each other out. Increasingly, we find teachers who integrate this process in a strategic way into their ESL classes.

They may invite students to discuss a problem in the native language for example, but then ask that the gist of the discussion be reported in English to the rest of the class and to the teacher. Some ESL programs set up native language literacy classes so that non-literate, non-English speaking students can acquire basic literacy skills in a language they already speak.

Designed as a transition to English literacy, these classes are offered in Spanish and to a lesser degree in Haitian Creole, Hmong or Chinese. Spanish literacy is often taught using the teaching materials developed and used in Mexico as part of popular education efforts and distributed through the Mexican consulate as part of a bi-national agreement in adult education. The Community College in San Francisco, for example, offers two levels of native language literacy to non-literate students, many of whom are Mayan students who speak Spanish as a second language. The class combines the development of basic literacy skills with strategies for dealing with functional print (both in Spanish) before transitioning students to English literacy.

In areas along the U.S.-Mexico border, where many employers require a high school diploma or a General Education Development (GED) certificate, programs may offer the GED in Spanish to allow students to complete their academic work in the home language.

This model is particularly popular in Texas, which is officially supporting bilingualism[11] in education, including bilingual vocational training for adults transitioning to work. A study on the use of the native language in the ESL classroom or an intervention that examines the effect of teaching native language literacy on the acquisition of English literacy can shed light on dual language use in English language learning settings and point toward successful ways of increasing the skills of adults who have had few years of schooling in their home country.

In addition, research in this area can help develop more nuanced approaches to literacy development and help establish policies that go beyond the use of "English Only" in adult education.

Oral Language Skills and Literacy

The SLA research shows that higher levels of language skills in L2 facilitate literacy development in that language.

This research suggests that ongoing instruction in language through face-to-face communication (in the classroom and beyond) and through various multimedia channels is likely to improve overall proficiency in English and facilitate the comprehension of different kinds of texts as students learn to transfer language knowledge to literacy tasks. A literacy intervention designed to test this language-literacy connection is embodied in the following hypothesis.

A strong emphasis on oral language development matched with the reading of texts that are accessible to low-literate students will result in significant increases in reading comprehension for adult non-readers who have low levels of English proficiency.

Implications for Policy and Practice: The intervention would include building competence in using English, particularly face-to-face communication skills, focused on listening comprehension and oral expression, along with literacy development. The teaching of oral communication skills could either precede the introduction of reading and writing or could occur simultaneously.

The oral language first model has been used successfully by agencies such as the U.S. Peace Corps, which seeks to establish a sound foundation in face-to-face communication skills in its volunteers. In adult ESL, students often complain that they do not get enough "conversation" in their classes and spend too much time listening to the teacher or filling out worksheets.

We have seen many successful teachers reverse that trend by providing students with a heavy dose of listening and speaking and face-to-face peer exchanges before asking them to focus on print. In an effort to build language skills, these teachers may offer comprehensible input through activities that involve Total Physical Response, such as demonstrating the use of an electric coffee maker in the classroom or drawing a diagram with directions for making a paper airplane.

Others may share family photographs and talk about important events and people in their lives and ask students to do the same. They may also bring in various objects, such as fruits and vegetables, tools, and household items as a basis for teaching language functions such as making offers and requests, or they may use evocative photographs and invite students to explain what they see. In this approach, only key words are introduced in print initially in order to keep students' attention on language use.

After students have a foundation in conversational skills and a store of vocabulary that they know, they work with dialogues or language experience stories that offer print versions of what has been learned orally. While literate students often find it frustrating when lessons are not written down, non-literate students can be keen language learners who are used to negotiating face-to-face communication without relying on print. This model takes advantage of their ability to take in and process language without having to deal with the complexities of acquiring print knowledge.

Since we know very little about the different ways in which non-literate adults acquire language and literacy, a study that focuses on the role of oral language as an essential part of literacy learning can provide important insights into the interaction between the two key domains of ESL literacy.

Such a study could compare the conventional model of language teaching (where language is presented in both oral and written form from the start), with a "language first" model that focuses initially on face-to face communication skills and introduces literacy slowly along the way.

MIXED DESIGNS AS PART OF AN OVERALL RESEARCH STRATEGY

Although there are few studies in adult ESL that meet the stringent requirements for rigorous scientific research, there is, nevertheless, a rich body of research that can inform future studies and provide guidance to the field. The intervention studies discussed above can form the core of a research strategy that combines large-scale experimental research into what works in instruction with qualitative research into students' lives and community contexts.

Such a strategy might include research with learners

inside and outside of programs, research that can provide invaluable insights into how language and literacy are used to negotiate environments and systems. Practitioner knowledge can serve to both inform research and to test research findings on the local level. It can also serve to highlight successes and challenges in teaching and offer insights into learning outcomes that are not easily captured by conventional assessments.

Investigations into community needs and concerns can offer important information about the social contexts that mediate language and literacy learning and can move us toward linking social service agencies with educational institutions. In the end, multiple studies focusing on different domains can provide a rich picture of how immigrants develop their language and literacy skills and highlight the contributions that formal language education can make to that process.

LANGUAGE AND STYLE OF PRESENTATION

A style sheet language, or style language, is a computer language used to describe the presentation of structured documents. A structured document is a document whose sections are clearly defined and categorized (also called "well-formed"). A programme presenting the document can present it in different styles because the content has been categorized. One modern style sheet language with widespread use is CSS (Cascading Style Sheets), which is used to style documents written in HTML, XHTML, SVG, XUL, and other markup languages. One of the most attractive features of structured documents is that the content can be reused in many contexts and presented in various ways. Different style sheets can be attached to the logical structure to produce different presentations.

In order for content in structured documents to be presented, a set of stylistic rules – describing for example, colors, fonts and layout – must be applied. A collection of stylistic rules is called a style sheet. Style sheets in the form of written documents have a long history of use by editors and typographers to ensure consistency of presentation, spelling and punctuation. In electronic publishing, style sheet languages are mostly used in the context of visual presentation rather than spelling and punctuation.

COMPONENTS

All style sheet languages offer functionality in these areas:

Syntax

A style sheet language needs a syntax in order to be expressed in a machine-readable manner. For example, here is a simple style sheet written in the CSS syntax:

h1 {font-size: 1.5em}

Selectors

Selectors specify which elements are to be influenced by the style rule. As such, selectors are the glue between the structure of the document and the stylistic rules in the style sheets. In the example above, the "h1" selector selects all h1 elements. More complex selectors can select elements based on, e.g., their context, attributes and content.

Properties

All style sheet languages have some concept of properties that can be given values to change one aspect of rendering an element. The "font-size" property of CSS is used in the above example. Common style sheet languages typically have around 50 properties to describe the presentation of documents

Values and units

Properties change the rendering of an element by being assigned a certain value. The value can be a string, a keyword, a number, or a number with a unit identifier. Also, values can be lists or expressions involving several of the aforementioned values. A typical value in a visual style sheet is a length; for example, "1.5em" which consists of a number (1.5) and a unit (em). The "em" value in CSS refers to the font size of the surrounding text. Common style sheet languages have around ten different units.

Value propagation mechanism

To avoid having to specify explicitly all values for all properties on all elements, style sheet languages have mechanisms to propagate values automatically. The main benefit of value propagation is less-verbose style sheets. In the example above, only the font size is specified; other values will be found through value propagation mechanisms. Inheritance, initial values and cascading are examples of value propagation mechanisms.

Formatting model

All style sheet languages support some kind of formatting model. Most style sheet languages have a visual formatting model that describes, in some detail, how text and other content is laid out in the final presentation. For example, the CSS formatting model specifies that block-level elements (of which "h1" is an example) extends to fill the width of the parent element. Some style sheet languages also have an aural formatting model.

CHAPTERISATION

Research means in depth study of a given subject / given area of a subject in order to bring into light the hidden Truth within it for the benefit of others. One who accepts such project has to dive into it, to discover the aspect of Truth that the subject represents. Research under Sri Aurobindo University aims at a systematic study of the vast literature and work of Sri Aurobindo and The Mother. It may lead to a spiritual ascent of a Sadhak of integral Yoga.

Those who have opted to be the honorable learners of Sri Aurobindo University should always keep in mind that research here is carried out not for any material gain nor academic degree, but purely from spiritual point of view as a medium of yoga.

THE SUBJECT OF STUDY AND RESEARCH

The subject should be one of the topics from the list prepared by Sri Aurobindo University or a similar topic relating to the writings / work of Sri Aurobindo and The Mother. It should be chosen with care keeping in mind the subject of interest and motivation of the learner. It will be advisable to the learner if he/she could consult an expert in the field, preferably the counselor, while choosing the topic. There should be a time limit chosen by the learner to complete the work. Once the topic is chosen the learner has to design the study of the subject and a brief review of related work and prepare a synopsis of the topic.

THE SYNOPSIS

The synopsis is a systematic planning of the project and it is prepared by the learner in consultation with the counselor.

Every learner has to prepare a synopsis of the project, get it approved by the counselor and then submit it to Sri Aurobindo University. Submission of the synopsis duly approved by the counselor is a necessary condition in order to allot a registration number to the learner.

The synopsis must contain:

- An introduction on the topic
- Study design with regards to methodology to be adopted in various phases
- Preparation of a working bibliograp

The Introduction

The introduction includes a survey / review of literature. It means a summerisation of previous work done by different authors on the topic and writing the gist of those in brief in a systematic and chronological manner. While doing so the learner must give footnotes in every page which indicates the source from which the contents are collected.

In the end the learner has to clearly express the aim and objective of his work which should be the continuation of the previous work. If the work includes some observations and collections of data, then it should be indicated in the introduction and the learner has to commit that the data / observation will be properly analysed and interpreted to arrive at a conclusion.

In brief, following details should be captured in the synopsis:

- Topic/Subject/Field/Area of study
- Name of the researcher

- Name of the guide or counsellor
- Name of the Institution where proposed work to be undertaken
- Acknowledgement

Chapterisation

Chapterisation means scanning of the entire project taken up by the learner. The subject of the project is to be divided into different parts, arrange them in a systematic way and mention which aspect of the work will be studied in which chapter. It should be so planned that one chapter will seem to be a continuation of the previous one. The last chapter will contain an analysis of the data / facts collected in the previous chapters and interpretation of the same to arrive at a conclusion. The conclusion will indicate to what extent the objective of the learner has been fulfilled.

3. Preparation of Working Bibliography

It is the source of materials collected by the learner in order to supplement the study. The source may be books / journals / magazines / internet etc. In some cases it may be experimental data observations collected from field tours. If the source is a book / journal / magazine the reference should be indicated.

- Name of the book / journal
- Author
- Title of the article/chapter
- Year of publication/publishers
- Place of publication/publishers
- Reference page number (first and last)
- Internet: website and date when accessed

If it is some other source, the details of the source should be given in the reference. In no case something heard from some body should be taken as a true reference, and such references should be avoided at all cost.

The references should be numbered as 1, 2, 3 etc. in order and to avoid jumbling of the references, it should be initially given as a foot note at the end of the page.

The collection of these references at one place at the end of all chapters becomes the working bibliography.

Research work

Once the synopsis is prepared and approved by the counselor, the work of the learner becomes easier and he / she has to take up deep and systematic study of the subject to develop each chapter to complete his project. While so developing, new references may come and it should be given as foot notes and collected at the end to complete the final bibliography.

Below is in brief the reccommended sections of the final dissertation

- Introduction
- Aim/ Objectives/ Relevance of the study/ Definition of the problem/ How it will benefit others
- Description of a survey of a related literature/ Review of existing literature on the topic
- Procedures or methods to be adopted to conduct the research
- Hypothesis
- Collection of data, information or facts and it's analysis
- Conclusion or suggestions or concluding observation to be based on logical reasoning from his own study

INDEXING

A database index is a data structure that improves the speed of operations on a database table. Indexes can be created using one or more columns of a database table, providing the basis for both rapid random look ups and efficient access of ordered records. The disk space required to store the index is typically less than that required by the table (since indexes usually contain only the key-fields according to which the table is to be arranged, and excludes all the other details in the table), yielding the possibility to store indexes in memory for a table whose data is too large to store in memory.

In a relational database, an index is a copy of one part of a table. Some databases extend the power of indexing by allowing indexes to be created on functions or expressions. For example, an index could be created on upper(last_name), which would only store the upper case versions of the last_name field in the index.

Another option sometimes supported is the use of "filtered" indexes, where index entries are created only for those records that satisfy some conditional expression. A further aspect of flexibility is to permit indexing on user-defined functions, as well as expressions formed from an assortment of built-in functions.

Indexes may be defined as unique or non-unique. A unique index acts as a constraint on the table by preventing duplicate entries in the index and thus, the backing table.

UNCLUSTERED

An Unclustered index is structured in a way that doesn't correspond to the order of the actual data records. It resembles the words index at the back of a book. For this reason, it will perform worse than clustered indexes on ranged searches where the result set is large, since each result could cost an additional I/O-operation to get the actual data record. One can have any number of these kinds of indexes, since all that is required is the space to store the index itself — one does not copy the actual data to create a new index.

CLUSTERED

Clustering re-orders the data block in the same order as the index, hence it is also an operation on the data storage blocks as well as on the index. A phone book ordered by last name resembles a clustered index in its structure and purpose. Exact operation of database systems varies, but because storing the row data more than once is never done in practice (since it is usually too expensive), the row data can only be stored in one order physically. Therefore, only one clustered index can be created on a given database table. Clustered indexes can greatly increase access speed, but usually only where the data is accessed sequentially in the same or reverse order of the clustered index, or when a range of items are selected.

Since the physical records are in this sort order on disk, the next row item in the sequence is immediately before or after the last one, and so fewer data block reads are required.

The primary feature of a clustered index is therefore the ordering of the physical data rows in accordance with the index blocks that point to them.

Some databases separate the data and index blocks into separate files, while others intermix the two different types of data blocks within the same physical file(s). Databases that use the latter scheme may be said to store the actual data in the leaf node of the index, whereas, in fact there is still a distinction between the index and the data block, and the data blocks can be traversed without using the index by way of a link list that links the data blocks in order.

INDEX IMPLEMENTATIONS

Indexes can be implemented using a variety of data structures. Popular indexes include balanced trees, B+ trees and hashes.

In Microsoft SQL Server, the leaf node of the clustered index corresponds to the actual data, not simply a pointer to data that resides elsewhere, as is the case with a non-clustered index. Each relation can have a single clustered index and many unclustered indexes.

COLUMN ORDER

The order in which columns are listed in the index definition is important. It is possible to retrieve a set of row identifiers using only the first indexed column. However, it is not possible or efficient (on most databases) to retrieve the set of row identifiers using only the second or greater indexed column.

For example, imagine a phone book that is organized by city first, then by last name, and then by first name. If you are given the city, you can easily extract the list of all phone numbers for that city. However, in this phone book it would be very tedious to find all the phone numbers for a given last name. You would have to look within each city's section for the entries with that last name. Some databases can do this, others just won't use the index.

APPLICATIONS AND LIMITATIONS

Indexes are useful for many applications but come with some limitations. Consider the following SQL statement: SELECT first_name FROM people WHERE last_name = 'Smith';.

To process this statement without an index the database software must look at the last_name column on every row in the table (this is known as a full table scan). With an index the database simply follows the b-tree data structure until the Smith entry has been found; this is much less computationally expensive than a full table scan.

Consider this SQL statement: SELECT email_address FROM customers WHERE email_address LIKE '%@yahoo.com';. This query would yield an email address for every customer whose email address ends with "@yahoo.com", but even if the email_address column has been indexed the database still must perform a full table scan. This is because the index is built with the assumption that words go from left to right. With a wildcard at the beginning of the search-term, the database software is unable to use the underlying b-tree data structure. This problem can be solved through the addition of another index created on reverse(email_address) and a SQL query like this: SELECT email_address FROM customers WHERE reverse(email_address) LIKE reverse('%@yahoo.com');. This puts the wild-card at the right-most part of the query (now moc.oohay@%) which the index on reverse(email_address) can satisfy.

TYPES

Bitmap index

A bitmap index is a special kind of index that stores the bulk of its data as bit arrays (bitmaps) and answers most queries by performing bitwise logical operations on these bitmaps. The most commonly used index, such as B+trees, are most efficient if the values it indexes do not repeat or repeat a relatively smaller number of times. In contrast, the bitmap index is designed for cases where the values of a variable repeat very frequently. For example, the gender field in a customer database usually contains two distinct values: male or female. For such variables, the bitmap index can have a significant performance advantage over the commonly used trees.

Dense index

A dense index in databases is a file with pairs of keys and pointers for every record in the data file. Every key in this file is associated with a particular pointer to *a record* in the sorted data file. In clustered indices with duplicate keys, the dense index points *to the first record* with that key.

Sparse index

A sparse index in databases is a file with pairs of keys and pointers for every block in the data file. Every key in this file is associated with a particular pointer *to the block* in the sorted data file. In clustered indexes with duplicate keys, the sparse index points *to the lowest search key* in each block.

COVERING INDEX

In most cases, an index is used to quickly locate the data record(s) from which the required data is read. In other words, the index is only used to locate data records in the table and not to return data. A covering index is a special case where the index itself contains the required data field(s) and can return the data.

Consider the Following Table (Other Fields Omitted):

ID	Name	Other Fields
12	Plug	...
13	Lamp	...
14	Fuse	...

To find the Name for ID 13, an index on (ID) will be useful, but the record must still be read to get the Name. However, an index on (ID, Name) contains the required data field and eliminates the need to look up the record. A covering index can dramatically speed up data retrieval but may itself be relatively large due to the additional keys, which slows down data insertion & update. To reduce such index size, some systems allow non-key fields to be included in the index. Non-key fields are not themselves part of the index ordering but only included at the leaf level, allowing for a covering index with less overall index size.

FOOTNOTE

A footnote is a note of text placed at the bottom of a page in a book or document. The note comments on and/or may cite a reference for part of the main body of text. A footnote is normally flagged by a superscript number following that portion of the text the note is in reference to.

for the first footnote on the page, for the second footnote, and so on.

Occasionally a number between brackets or parentheses is used instead, thus: Typographical devices such as the asterisk (*) or dagger (†) may also be used to point to footnotes; the traditional order of these symbols is *, †, ‡, §,, ¶. In documents like timetables, many different symbols, as well as letters and numbers, may be used to refer the reader to particular footnotes.

Endnotes are similar to footnotes, but instead of appearing at the foot of the page they are collected together at the end of the chapter or at the end of the work. They do not affect the image of the page, but may cause inconvenience for the reader who has to move back and forth between the main text and the endnotes, especially if each chapter starts afresh with number 1.

The U.S. Government Printing Office Style Manual devotes six pages to the topic. NASA has guidance for footnote usage in its historical documents.

Academic Usage

Footnotes are most often used as an alternative to long

explanatory notes that can be distracting to readers. Most literary style guidelines (including the Modern Language Association and the American Psychological Association) recommend limited use of foot and endnotes.

However, publishers often encourage note references in lieu of parenthetical references. Aside from use as a bibliographic element, footnotes are used for additional information or explanatory notes that might be too digressive for the main text.

The MLA (Modern Language Association) requires the superscript numbers in the main text to be placed following the punctuation in the phrase or clause the note is in reference to. The exception to this rule occurs when you have a hyphen in a sentence, in which case the superscript would appear before.

Aside from their technical use, authors use footnotes for a variety of reasons:

- As signposts to direct the reader to information the author has provided or where further useful information is pertaining to the subject in the main text.
- To attribute to a quote or viewpoint.
- As an alternative to parenthetical references; it is a simpler way to acknowledge information gained from another source.
- To escape the limitations imposed on the word count of various academic and legal texts which do not take into account footnotes. Aggressive use of this strategy can lead the text to be seen as affected by what some people call "footnote disease".

Footnotes as a Literary Device

At times, footnotes and endnotes have been used for their comical effect, or as a literary device.

- In The Banjo Players Must Die, footnotes constitute a significant portion of the entire text, and often serve to distract the reader from an already complex storyline. Other uses of footnotes in this work include insulting the reader, shedding more light on the alluded-to incompetence of the characters, and using expletives (presumably because no one reads the footnotes and the risk of causing offense is therefore mitigated).

- Mark Z. Danielewski's *House of Leaves* uses what are arguably some of the most extensive and intricate footnotes in literature. Throughout the novel, footnotes are used to tell several different narratives outside of the main story. The physical orientation of the footnotes on the page also works to reflect the twisted feeling of the plot (often taking up several pages, appearing mirrored from page to page, vertical on either side of the page, or in boxes in the centre of the page, in the middle of the central narrative).
- Flann O'Brien's *The Third Policeman* utilizes extensive and lengthy footnotes for the discussion of a fictional philosopher, de Selby. These footnotes span several pages and often overtake the main plotline, and add to the absurdist tone of the book.
- David Foster Wallace's *Infinite Jest* includes over 400 endnotes, some over a dozen pages long. Several literary critics suggested that the book be read with two bookmarks. Wallace uses footnotes in much of his other writing as well.
- Manuel Puig's *Kiss of the Spider Woman* (originally published in Spanish as *El beso de la mujer araña*) also makes extensive use of footnotes.
- Mark Dunn's *Ibid: A Life* is written entirely in endnotes.
- Luis d'Antin Van Rooten's, *Mots d'Heures: Gousses, Rames* (the title is in French, but when pronounced, sounds similar to the English *"Mother Goose Rhymes"*), in which he is allegedly the editor of a manuscript by the fictional François Charles Fernand d'Antin, contains copious footnotes purporting to help explain the nonsensical French text. The point of the book is

that each written French poem *sounds* like an English nursery rhyme.

- Terry Pratchett has made numerous uses within his novels. The footnotes will often set up running jokes for the rest of the novel.
- Susanna Clarke's *Jonathan Strange & Mr Norrell* uses dozens of footnotes referencing a number of fictional books including magical scholarship and biographies.
- Jonathan Stroud's *The Bartimaeus Trilogy* uses footnotes to insert comical remarks and explanations by one of the protagonists, Bartimaeus.
- Michael Gerber's *Barry Trotter* parody series used footnotes to expand one-line jokes in the text into paragraph-long comedic monologues that would otherwise break the flow of the narrative.
- John Green's *An Abundance of Katherines* uses footnotes in which he says: "[They] can allow you to create a kind of secret second narrative, which is important if, say, you're writing a book about what a story is and whether stories are significant."
- Jasper Fforde's *Thursday Next* series exploits the use of footnotes as a communication device (the *footnoterphone*) which allows communication between the main character's universe and the fictional bookworld.
- Ernest Hemingway's *Natural History of the Dead* uses a footnote to further satirize the style of a history while making a sardonic statement about the extinction of "humanists" in modern society.
- Pierre Bayle's *Historical and Critical Dictionary* follows each brief entry with a footnote (often five or six times the length of the main text) in which saints, historical figures, and other topics are used as examples for philosophical digression. The separate footnotes are designed to contradict each other, and only when multiple footnotes are read together is Bayle's core argument for Fideistic skepticism

revealed. This technique was used in part to evade the harsh censorship of 17th century France.

- Mordecai Richler's novel *Barney's Version* uses footnotes as a character device that highlights unreliable passages in the narration. As the editor of his father's autobiography, the narrator's son must correct any of his father's misstated facts. The frequency of these corrections increases as the father falls victim to both hubris and Alzheimer's disease. While most of these changes are minor, a few are essential to plot and character development.
- In Vladimir Nabokov's *Pale Fire,* the main plot is told through the footnotes of a fictional editor.

Opponents of Footnotes

Associate Justice Stephen Breyer of the Supreme Court of the United States is famous in the American legal community for his writing style, in which he never uses footnotes. He prefers to keep all citations inline (which is permitted in American legal citation).

BIBLIOGRAPHY

Bibliography as a practice, is the academic study of books as physical, cultural objects; in this sense, it is also known as bibliology. On the whole, bibliography is not concerned with the literary content of books, but rather the "bookness" of books.

A bibliography, the product of the practice of bibliography, is a systematic list of books and other works such as journal articles. Bibliographies range from "works cited" lists at the end of books and articles to complete, independent publications.

As separate works, they may be in bound volumes such as those shown on the right, or computerised bibliographic databases. A library catalog, while not referred to as a *bibliography,* is bibliographic in nature. Bibliographical works are almost always considered to be tertiary sources.

Bibliographic works differ in the amount of detail

depending on the purpose, and can be generally divided into two categories: enumerative bibliography (also called compilative, reference or systematic), which results in an overview of publications in a particular category, and analytical, or critical, bibliography, which studies the production of books.

In earlier times, bibliography mostly focused on books. Now, both categories of bibliography cover works in other formats including recordings, motion pictures and videos, graphic objects, databases, CD-ROMs and websites.

The word *bibliographia* was used by Greek writers in the first three centuries AD to mean the copying of books by hand. In the 12th century, the word started being used for "the intellectual activity of composing books". The 17th century then saw the emergence of the modern meaning, that of description of books.

Enumerative Bibliography

A bibliography is a list of writings that share a common factor: this may be a topic, a language, a period, or some other theme. The list may be comprehensive or selective. One particular instance of this is the list of sources used or considered in preparing a work, sometimes called a *reference list*.

Citation formats vary, but an entry for a book in a bibliography usually contains the following information:

- Author(s)
- Title
- Publisher
- Date of publication

An entry for a journal or periodical article usually contains:

- Author(s)
- Article title
- Journal title
- Volume
- Pages
- Date of publication

A bibliography may be arranged by author, topic, or some other scheme. Annotated bibliographies give descriptions about how each source is useful to an author in constructing a paper or argument.

These descriptions, usually a few sentences long, provide a summary of the source and describe its relevance. Reference management software may be used to keep track of references and generate bibliographies as required.

Bibliographies differ from library catalogs by including only relevant items rather than all items present in a particular library. However, the catalogs of some national libraries effectively serve as national bibliographies, as the national libraries own almost all their countries' publications.

Analytical Bibliography

The critical study of bibliography can be subdivided into descriptive (or physical), historical, and textual bibliography. Descriptive bibliography is the close examination of a book as a physical object, recording its size, format, binding, and so on, while historical bibliography takes a broader view of the context in which a book is produced, in particular, printing, publishing and bookselling. Textual bibliography is another name for textual criticism.

Non-book Material

Systematic lists of media other than books can be referred to with terms formed analogously to *bibliography*:

- Discography – recorded music
- Filmography – films
- Webography or webliography – websites (the first use of the word *webliography* recorded in the Oxford English Dictionary dates from June 1995).

Unit IV

Tabular and Graphical Methods of Data Presentation

ORGANISATION AND TABULATION OF DATA

For learner's evaluation, we usually administer a number of tests on all students of the class and scores are given in their answer-scripts. Often these are used as such, without interpreting them. If you have to interpret the scores, you must learn to tabulate them in a meaningful way and calculate various statistics from the same. In this Unit, you will study about the meaning and nature of data; the need and importance of statistics; the tabulation of data in a meaningful way and various types of graphical representation to make the data easily comprehendible.

Various types of statistics and the methods of their computation arc being discussed in the subsequent units of this block itself.

OBJECTIVES

After going through this unit, you will be able to:

- Understand the meaning and nature of data.
- Distinguish between the four measurement scales.
- Techniques of understand the need, importance and meaning of statistics.
- Appreciate the importance of the organisation of data.
- Tabulate the data obtained by you in the classroom in a meaningful way.

- Appteciate the advantages of graphical representation of data.
- Use appropriate graphic representation, for the data obtained by you in the classroom; and interpret the data given in the form of graphical representation.

MEANING OF DATA

You might be reading a newspaper regularly. Almost every newspaper gives the minimum and the maximum temperatures recorded in the city on the previous day. It also indicates the rainfall recorded, and the time of sunrise and sunset. In your school, you regularly take attendance of children and record it in a register. For a patient, the doctor advises recording of the body temperature of the patient at regular intervals.

If you record the minimum and maximum temperature, or rainfall, or the time of sunrise and sunset, or attendance of children, or the body temperature of the patient, over a period of time, what you are recording is known as data. Here, you are recording the data of minimum and maximum temperature of the city, data of rainfall, data for the time of sunrise and sunset, and the data pertaining to the attendance of children.

NATURE OF DATA

For understanding the nature of data, it becomes necessary to study about the various forms of,$ data, as shown below:

- Qualitative and Quantitative Data.
- Continuous and Discrete Data I L.
- Primary and Secondary Data.

QUALITATIVE AND QUANTITATIVE DATA

- Tabulation and Graphical.
- Representation of Data.

So the schools have been classified into 4 categories, namely, Government Schools, Local Body Schools, Private Aided Schools and Private Unaided Schools. A given school belongs to any one of the four categories. Such data is shown as Categorical or Qualitative Data. Here the category or the quality referred to is management.

Thus categorical or qualitative data result from information which has been classified into categories. Such categories are listed alphabetically or in order of decreasing frequencies or in some other conventional way.

Each piece of data clearly belongs to one classification or category. We frequently come across categorical or qualitative data in the form of schools categorised according to Boys, Girls and Co-educational; Students' Enrolment categorised according to SC, ST, OBC and 'Others'; number of persons employed in various categories of occupations, and so on.

Schools with enrolment varying in a specified range are grouped together, e.g. there are 15 schools where the students enrolled are any number between 51 and 100. As the grouping is based on numbers, such data are called Numerical or Quantitative Data.

Thus, numerical or quantitative data result from counting or measuring. We frequently come across numerical data in newspapers, advertisements etc. related to the temperature of the cities, cricket averages, incomes, expenditures and so on.

CONTINUOUS AND DISCRETE DATA

Numerical or quantitative data may be continuous or discrete depending on the nature of the elements or objects being observed. The height varies from 4' 8" to 5' 10". The height of an individual may be anywhere from 4' 8" to 5' 10". Two students may vary by almost zero inch height. Even if we take two adjacent points, say 4' 8.00" and 4' 8.01" there may be several values between the two points.

Such data are called Continuous Data, as the height is continuous. Continuous Data arise from the measurement of continuous attributes or variables, in which individual may differ by amounts just approaching zero. Weights and heights of children; temperature of a body; intelligence and achievement level of students, etc. are the examples of continuous data.

Let us consider the enrolment of 2 schools as 60 and 61. Now in between 60 and 61, there cannot be any number, as the enrolment will always be in whole numbers. Thus there is a gap of one unit from 60 to 61. Such data, where the elements being observed have gaps are called Discrete Data. Such data are usually expressed in whole numbers. The size of a family, enrolment of children, number of books etc. are the examples of discrete data.

Generally data arising from measurement are continuous, while data arising from counting or arbitrary classification are discrete. The achievement scores of students, though presented in discrete form may be considered to constitute continuous data, since a score of 24 represents any point between 23.5 and 24.5. Actually achievement is a continuous attribute or variable. All measurements of continuous attributes are approximate in character and as such do not provide a basis for distinguishing between continuous and discrete data.

FINDING THE DATA

With the advances in information technology over the past decade, there has been a revolution in the amount and availability of statistical indicators provided by governments and nongovernmental public and private organizations.

In addition to the volumes of data provided by the U.S. Census Bureau, many federal departments now have their own statistics agency, such as the National Centre for Education Statistics, the Bureau of Justice Statistics, the National Centre for Health Statistics, the Bureau of Labour Statistics, and the Bureau of Transportation Statistics, providing convenient online access to comprehensive data collections and statistical reports.

In recent years, the greatest growth in the shear quantity of statistical indicators has been in the field of education. The mandated testing under the No Child Left Behind law and the expansion of the Department of Education's National Assessment of Educational Progress have produced massive databases of measures of the performance of the nation's schools that, for better or worse, fundamentally transformed the administration of educational institutions. There has also been significant growth in the quantity and quality of comparative international data.

The Organisation for Economic Co-operation and Development (OECD) now provides a comprehensive range of governmental, social, and economic data for developed nations. For developing nations, the World Bank's development of poverty indicators and measures of business and economic conditions and the United Nations' Millennium Development Goals database have contributed greatly to public debate and analysis of national and international policies affecting impoverished people across the world.

With the Trends in International Math and Science Study (TIMSS) and the Programme in International Student Assessment (PISA) both having completed multiyear international educational achievement testing, rich databases of educational system conditions and student performance are now easily accessible.

Similar growth has taken place in the availability of social indicator data derived from nongovernmental public opinion surveys that offer consistent times series and cross-national measures of public attitudes and social behaviors.

Time series indicators can be readily obtained online from the U.S. National Elections Study and the National Opinion Research Center's annual General Social Survey and comparative cross-national data indicators can be accessed from Comparative Study of Electoral Systems, the International Social Survey Programme, and World Values Survey.

Finding the best data relevant to the analysis of contemporary social and political issues requires a basic familiarity with the kinds of data likely to be available from these sources. Social science research methods courses often give short shrift to this crucial stage of the research process that involves skills and expertise usually acquired by years of experience in specific fields of study.

Too often, the data are a "given": the instructor gives a dataset to the students and asks them to analyse it. The concluding chapter of this book addresses the topic in some detail, but finding the best data is the subtext for all of the chapters and the examples and illustrations that follow.

PRESENTING THE DATA

Good data presentation skills are to data-based analysis what good writing is to literature, and some of the same basic principles apply to both. More important, poor graphical and tabular presentations often lead both readers and writers to draw erroneous conclusions from their data and obscure facts that better presentations would reveal. Some of these practices involve deliberate distortions of data, but more commonly they involve either unintentional distortions or simply ineffective approaches to presenting numerical evidence.

The past two decades have seen the development of a substantial literature on the art and science of data presentation, much of it following Edward R. Tufte's pathbreaking work, *The Visual Display of Quantitative Information*. With his admonitions to "show the data," "minimize the ink-to-data ratio," and avoid "ChartJunk", Tufte established many of the basic rules and principles of data presentation and demonstrates over and over again how effective data presentations combined with clear thinking can reveal truths hidden in the data. Howard Wainer's work extends Tufte's standards and demonstrates the many errors that have ensued from statistical fallacies and faulty tabular and graphic design.

Few research methods and statistics texts address these standards of data presentation in more than a cursory manner and many demonstrate some of the worst data presentation practices. Although the development of spreadsheet and other software has greatly simplified the tasks of tabular and graphical data presentation, it has also greatly facilitated some very bad data presentation practices.

INTERPRETING THE DATA

Good data analysis entails little more than finding the best data relevant to a given research questions, making meaningful comparisons among the data, and drawing sound conclusions from the comparisons. To evaluate arguments based on numerical evidence, one must assess the reliability and validity of the individual measures used and validity of conclusions drawn from comparisons of the data.

Assessing the reliability and validity of social indicator measurements requires that one understand how the data are collected and how the indicators are constructed. Many research methods and statistics texts address issues of measurement merely as matters of choosing the appropriate level of measurement for variables (nominal, ordinal, or interval) and of calculating sampling error.

As a practical matter, such issues are usually irrelevant or trivial when one undertakes just plain data analysis. With just plain data analysis, almost all of the data are interval measures, in the form of ratios, percentages, and means, even if the base question for the indicator is nominal or ordinal. Measures of sampling error usually constitute the least important aspect of measurement reliability. Although assessing sampling error sometimes has a crucial role in some data analysis, in both academic research and news reporting the emphasis on sampling error often conveys a false sense of the reliability of data and distracts attention from more serious measurement problems.

WHY WE SHOULD TEACH JUST PLAIN DATA ANALYSIS

Often a fear of mathematics, combined with nonsequential curricular requirements, leads students to take a research methods and statistics course only in their last semester of study. In departments that require freshmen to take introductory methods courses, the required course is often the last time in students' academic careers that they will actually do the quantitative analysis that is taught. It may even be the last time they will have to read research employing the methods that are taught.

Just plain data analysis involves skills and expertise that students can readily apply to the analysis of evidence presented in their course literature and in conducting their own research for term papers and independent study projects. Moreover, the data analysis and data presentation skills described here have widespread application in a wide range of future careers in both government and the private sector.

It is a primary mode of communication in government and is found in the studies, annual reports, and PowerPoint presentations of almost every governmental agency and advocacy group or any career that requires writing clearly and succinctly with numbers.

It is not too late to read this text in the last semester of your senior year of college, but it is later than it should have been.

For departments that offer courses in both quantitative and qualitative methodology, just plain data analysis fills the methodological chasm that divides the social sciences. Those students who will go on to learn and apply the knowledge of the central limit theorem, multiple regression, factor analysis, and other less-plain statistical applications will discover that many of the principles of just plain data analysis will greatly improve the quality of the work.

Those who embrace qualitative analysis out of bewilderment at the often tortuous mathematical complexities of contemporary quantitative social science may find less madness in the methods presented here.

Students in almost every field of study encounter just plain data analysis all the time in the charts and tables presented in their textbooks.

In today's world the exercise of effective citizenship increasingly requires a public competent to evaluate arguments grounded in numerical evidence.

As the role of government has expanded to affect almost every aspect of people's daily lives, the role of statistics in shaping governmental policies has expanded as well. To the extent the public lacks the skills to critically evaluate the statistical analyses that shape public policy, more crucial decisions that affect our daily lives will be made by technocrats who have these statistical skills or by those who would use their mastery of these skills to serve their own partisan or special interest ends.

HISTOGRAM

In statistics, a histogram is a graphical display of tabulated frequencies, shown as bars. It shows what proportion of cases fall into each of several categories: it is a form of data binning. The categories are usually specified as non-overlapping intervals of some variable.

The categories (bars) must be adjacent. The intervals (or bands, or bins) are generally of the same size, and are most easily interpreted if they are. Histograms are used to plot density of data, and often for density estimation: estimating the probability density function of the underlying variable.

The total area of a histogram always equals 1. If the length of the intervals on the x-axis is all 1, then a histogram is identical to a relative frequency plot. An alternative to the histogram is kernel density estimation, which uses a kernel to smooth samples. This will construct a smooth probability density function, which will in general more accurately reflect the underlying variable. The histogram is one of the seven basic tools of quality control, which also include the Pareto chart, check sheet, control chart, cause-and-effect diagram, flowchart, and scatter diagram.

The word *histogram* is derived from the Greek *histos* 'anything set upright' (as the masts of a ship, the bar of a loom, or the vertical bars of a histogram); and *gramma* 'drawing, record, writing'.

EXAMPLES

As an example we consider data collected by the U.S. Census Bureau on time to travel to work (2000 census). The census found that there were 124 million people who work outside of their homes. This rounding is a common phenomenon when collecting data from people.

Histogram of travel time, US 2000 census. Area under the curve equals the total number of cases. This diagram uses Q/ width from the table.

Data by absolute numbers

Interval	*Width*	*Quantity*	*Quantity/width*
0	5	4180	836
5	5	13687	2737
10	5	18618	3723
15	5	19634	3926
20	5	17981	3596
25	5	7190	1438
30	5	16369	3273
35	5	3212	642
40	5	4122	824
45	15	9200	613
60	30	6461	215
90	60	3435	57

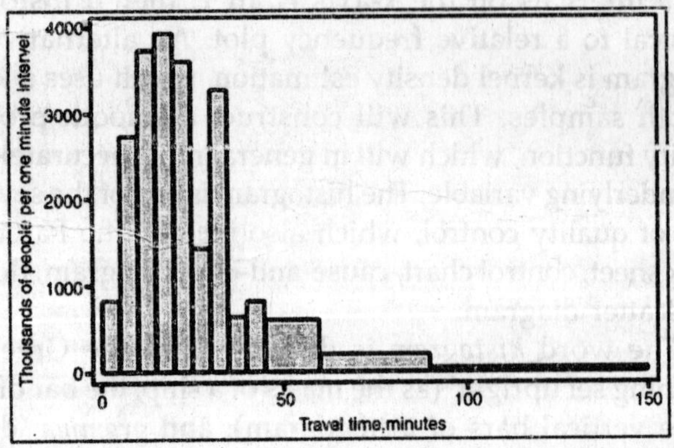

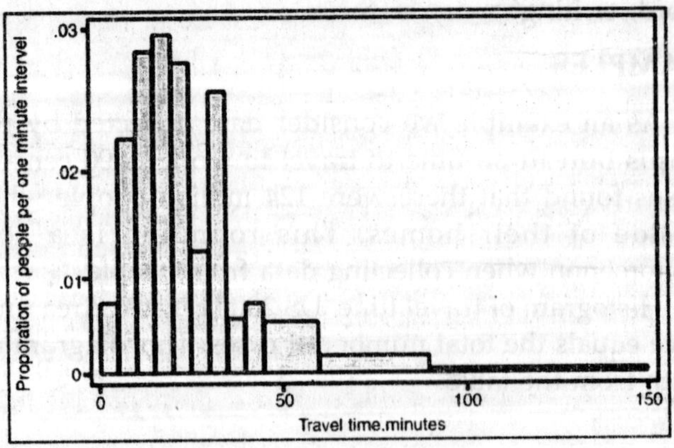

The histogram shows the number of cases per unit interval so that the height of each bar is equal to the proportion of total people in the survey who fall into that category. The area under the curve represents the total number of cases (124 million). This type of histogram shows absolute numbers.

Histogram of travel time, US 2000 census. Area under the curve equals 1. This diagram uses Q/total/width from the table.

Data by proportion

Interva	*Width*	*Quantity (Q)*	*Q/total/width*
0	5	4180	0.0067
5	5	13687	0.0221
10	5	18618	0.0300
15	5	19634	0.0316
20	5	17981	0.0290
25	5	7190	0.0116
30	5	16369	0.0264
35	5	3212	0.0052
40	5	4122	0.0066
45	15	9200	0.0049
60	30	6461	0.0017
90	60	3435	0.0005

This histogram differs from the first only in the vertical scale. The height of each bar is the decimal percentage of the total that each category represents, and the total area of all the bars is equal to 1, the decimal equivalent of 100%.

The curve displayed is a simple density estimate. This version shows proportions, and is also known as a unit area histogram.

In other words a histogram represents a frequency distribution by means of rectangles whose widths represent class intervals and whose areas are proportional to the corresponding frequencies. They only place the bars together to make it easier to compare data.

ACTIVITIES AND DEMONSTRATIONS

The SOCR resource pages contain a number of hands-on interactive activities demonstrating the concept of a histogram,

histogram construction and manipulation using Java applets and charts.

MATHEMATICAL DEFINITION

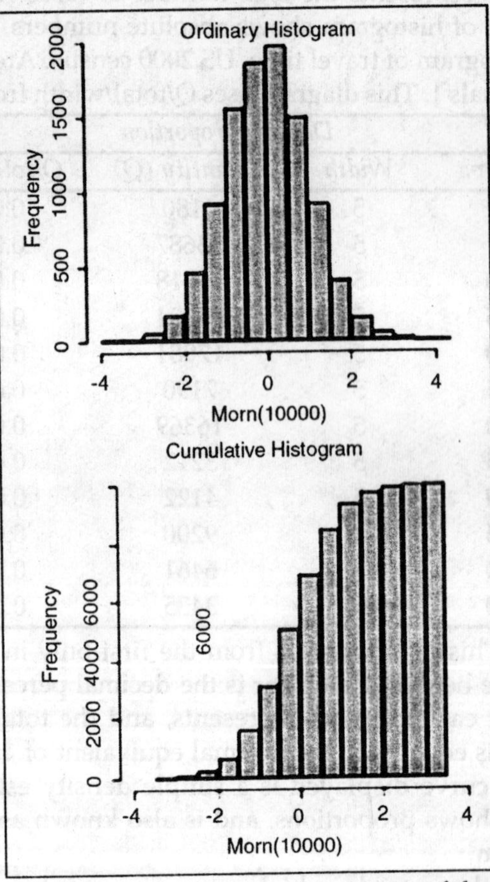

An ordinary and a cumulative histogram of the same data. The data shown is a random sample of 10,000 points from a normal distribution with a mean of 0 and a standard deviation of 1.

In a more general mathematical sense, a histogram is a mapping m_i that counts the number of observations that fall into various disjoint categories (known as *bins*), whereas the graph of a histogram is merely one way to represent a histogram. Thus, if we let n be the total number of observations and k be the total number of bins, the histogram m_i meets the following conditions:

$$N = \sum_{i=1}^{K} m_i.$$

CUMULATIVE HISTOGRAM

A cumulative histogram is a mapping that counts the cumulative number of observations in all of the bins up to the specified bin. That is, the cumulative histogram M_i of a histogram m_i is defined as:

$$M_i = \sum_{j=1}^{i} m_j.$$

NUMBER OF BINS AND WIDTH

There is no "best" number of bins, and different bin sizes can reveal different features of the data. Some theoreticians have attempted to determine an optimal number of bins, but these methods generally make strong assumptions about the shape of the distribution. You should always experiment with bin widths before choosing one (or more) that illustrate the salient features in your data.

The number of bins k can be calculated directly, or from a suggested bin width h:

$$k = \left\lceil \frac{\max x - \min x}{h} \right\rceil.$$

The braces indicate the ceiling function.

Sturges' formula

$$k = \lceil \log_2 n + 1 \rceil,$$

which implicitly bases the bin sizes on the range of the data, and can perform poorly if $n < 30$.

$$h = \frac{3.5\sigma}{n^{1/3}},$$

where σ is the sample standard deviation.

Freedman-Diaconis' choice

$$h = 2\frac{IQR(x)}{n^{1/3}},$$

which is based on the interquartile range.

CONTINUOUS DATA

The idea of a histogram can be generalized to continuous data. Let $f \in L^1(R)$, then the cumulative histogram operator H can be defined by:

$H(f)(y)$ = with only finitely many intervals of monotony this can be rewritten as

$$h(f)(y) = \sum_{\xi \in \{x : f(x) = y\}} \frac{1}{|f'(\xi)|}.$$

$h(f)(y)$ is undefined if y is the value of a stationary point.

FREQUENCY POLYGON

Frequency polygons are a graphical device for understanding the shapes of distributions. They serve the same purpose as histograms, but are especially helpful in comparing sets of data. Frequency polygons are also a good choice for displaying cumulative frequency distributions.

To create a frequency polygon, start just as for histograms, by choosing a class interval. Then draw an X-axis representing the values of the scores in your data. Mark the middle of each class interval with a tick mark, and label it with the middle value represented by the class. Draw the Y-axis to indicate the frequency of each class.

Place a point in the middle of each class interval at the height corresponding to its frequency. Finally, connect the points. You should include one class interval below the lowest value in your data and one above the highest value. The graph will then touch the X-axis on both sides. The first label on the X-axis is 35. This represents an interval extending from 29.5 to 39.5. Since the lowest test score is 46, this interval has a frequency of 0. The point labeled 45 represents the interval from 39.5 to 49.5.

There are three scores in this interval. There are 150 scores in the interval that surrounds 85. You can easily discern the shape of the distribution. Most of the scores are between 65 and 115. It is clear that the distribution is not symmetric inasmuch as good scores (to the right) trail off more gradually than poor scores (to the left).

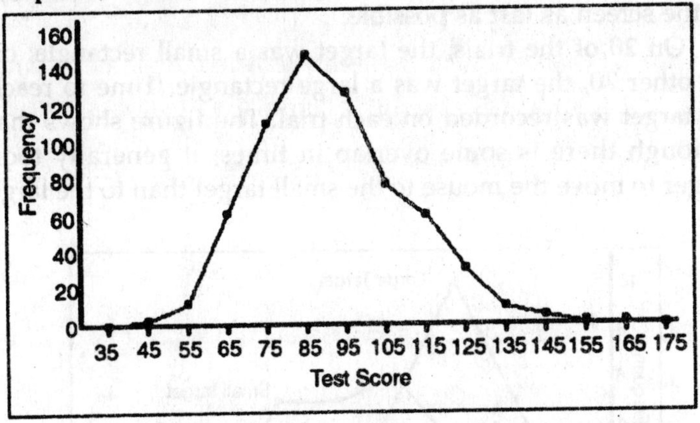

Fig. Frequency polygon for the psychology test scores.

The graph is the same as before except that the YY value for each point is the number of students in the corresponding class interval plus all numbers in lower intervals. For example, there are no scores in the interval labeled "35," three in the interval "45,"and 10 in the interval "55."Therefore the YY value corresponding to "55" is 13. Since 642 students took the test, the cumulative frequency for the last interval is 642.

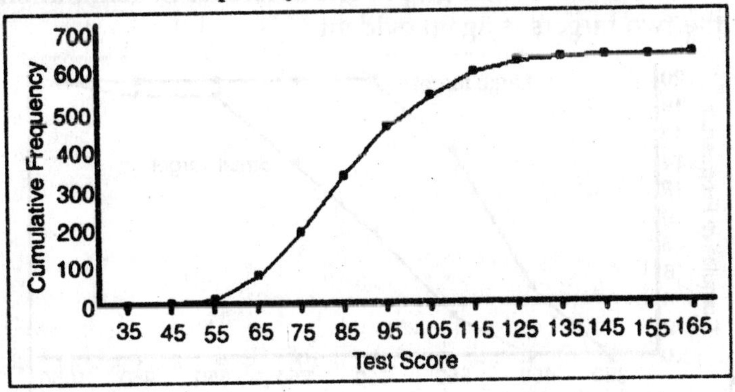

Fig. Cumulative Frequency Polygon for the Psychology Test Scores.

Frequency polygons are useful for comparing distributions. This is achieved by overlaying the frequency polygons drawn for different data sets. The data come from a task in which the goal is to move a computer mouse to a target on the screen as fast as possible.

On 20 of the trials, the target was a small rectangle; on the other 20, the target was a large rectangle. Time to reach the target was recorded on each trial. The figure shows that although there is some overlap in times, it generally took longer to move the mouse to the small target than to the large one.

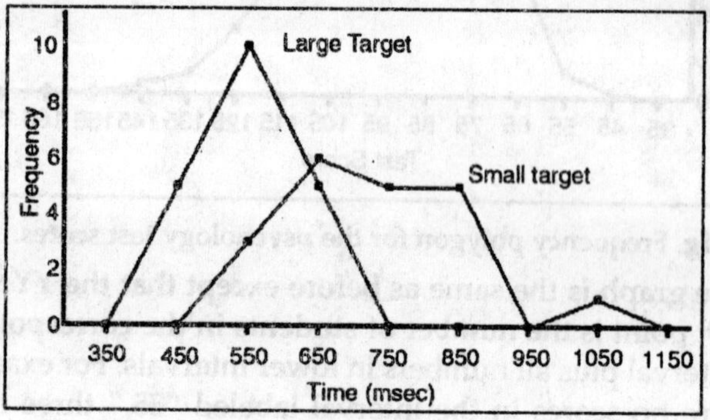

Fig. Overlaid Frequency Polygons.

It is also possible to plot two cumulative frequency distributions in the same graph. The difference in distributions for the two targets is again evident.

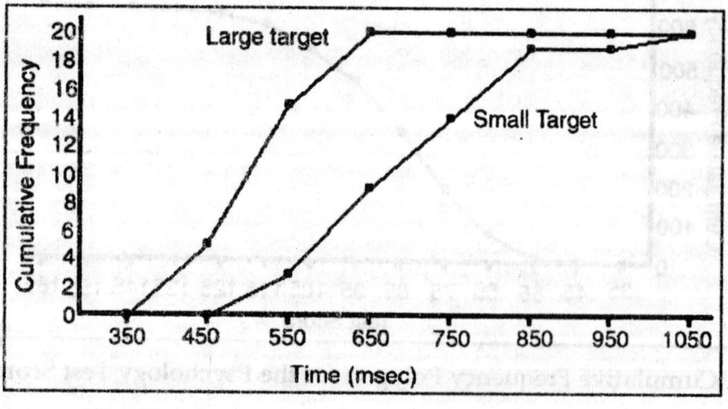

Fig. Overlaid Cumulative Frequency Polygons.

OGIVE AND OVERLAPPING DISTRIBUTION

An ogive ("Oh-jive") is a curved shape, figure, or feature. In ballistics or aerodynamics, an ogive is a pointed, curved surface mainly used to form the approximately streamlined nose of a bullet or other projectile. The traditional or secant ogive is a surface of revolution of the same curve that forms a Gothic arch; that is, a circular arc, of greater radius than the diameter of the cylindrical section ("shank"), is drawn from the edge of the shank until it intercepts the axis.

If this arc is drawn so that it meets the shank at zero angle (that is, the distance of the centre of the arc from the axis, plus the radius of the shank, equals the radius of the arc), then it is called a tangential or spitzer ogive. This is a very common ogive for high velocity (supersonic) rifle bullets. The sharpness of this ogive is expressed by the ratio of its radius to the diameter of the cylinder; a value of one half being a hemispherical dome, and larger values being progressively more pointed. Values of 4 to 10 are commonly used in rifles, with 6 being the most common.

Another common ogive for bullets is the elliptical ogive. This is a curve very similar to the spitzer ogive, except that the circular arc is replaced by an ellipse defined in such a way that it meets the axis at exactly 90°. This gives a somewhat rounded nose regardless of the sharpness ratio. An elliptical ogive is normally described in terms of the ratio of the length of the ogive to the diameter of the shank. A ratio of one half would be, once again, a hemisphere. Values close to 1 are common in practice. Elliptical ogives are mainly used in pistol bullets.

Missiles and aircraft generally have much more complex ogives, such as the von Kármán ogive. In Gothic architecture, ogives are the intersecting transverse ribs of arches that establish the surface of a Gothic vault. An ogive or ogival arch is a pointed, "Gothic" arch, drawn with compasses as outlined above, or with arcs of an ellipse as described. A very narrow, steeply pointed ogive arch (like the one in the construction above) is sometimes called a "lancet arch."

The most common form is an equilateral arch, where the

radius is the same as the width. In the later Flamboyant Gothic style, an "ogee arch," an arch delineating a void with a pointed head, like S-shaped curves, became prevalent.

Villard de Honnecourt, a 13th century itinerant master-builder of Picardy in the north of France, was the first writer to use the word *ogive.*

The French term's origin is considered obscure by *O.E.D.*; it might come from the Late Latin *obvita,* the feminine past participle of *obvire,* to resist, *i.e.* the arches resisting the downward force of the structure's mass.

Unit V

Descriptive Measures

MEASURES OF CENTRAL TENDENCY – MEAN, MEDIAN AND MODE

The term central tendency refers to the "middle" value or perhaps a typical value of the data, and is measured using the mean, median, or mode. Each of these measures is calculated differently, and the one that is best to use depends upon the situation.

MEAN

The mean is the most commonly-used measure of central tendency. When we talk about an "average", we usually are referring to the mean.

The mean is simply the sum of the values divided by the total number of items in the set. The result is referred to as the arithmetic mean. Sometimes it is useful to give more weighting to certain data points, in which case the result is called the weighted arithmetic mean.

The notation used to express the mean depends on whether we are talking about the population mean or the sample mean:

μ = population mean

$\bar{x}$ = sample mean

The mean is valid only for interval data or ratio data. Since it uses the values of all of the data points in the population or sample, the mean is influenced by outliers that may be at the extremes of the data set.

MEDIAN

The median is determined by sorting the data set from lowest to highest values and taking the data point in the middle of the sequence. There is an equal number of points above and below the median. For example, in the data set {1,2,3,4,5} the median is 3; there are two data points greater than this value and two data points less than this value.

In this case, the median is equal to the mean. But consider the data set {1,2,3,4,10}. In this dataset, the median still is three, but the mean is equal to 4. If there is an even number of data points in the set, then there is no single point at the middle and the median is calculated by taking the mean of the two middle points.

The median can be determined for ordinal data as well as interval and ratio data. Unlike the mean, the median is not influenced by outliers at the extremes of the data set. For this reason, the median often is used when there are a few extreme values that could greatly influence the mean and distort what might be considered typical.

This often is the case with home prices and with income data for a group of people, which often is very skewed. For such data, the median often is reported instead of the mean. For example, in a group of people, if the salary of one person is 10 times the mean, the mean salary of the group will be higher because of the unusually large salary. In this case, the median may better represent the typical salary level of the group.

MODE

The mode is the most frequently occurring value in the data set. For example, in the data set {1,2,3,4,4}, the mode is equal to 4. A data set can have more than a single mode, in which case it is multimodal. In the data set {1,1,2,3,3} there are two modes: 1 and 3.

The mode can be very useful for dealing with categorical data. For example, if a sandwich shop sells 10 different types of sandwiches, the mode would represent the most popular sandwich. The mode also can be used with ordinal, interval, and ratio data. However, in interval and ratio scales, the data may be spread thinly with no data points having the same value. In such cases, the mode may not exist or may not be very meaningful.

The following table summarizes the appropriate methods of determining the middle or typical value of a data set based on the measurement scale of the data.

Measurement Scale	Best Measure of the "Middle"
Nominal (Categorical)	Mode
Ordinal	Median
Interval	Symmetrical data: Mean
	Skewed data: Median
Ratio	Symmetrical data: Mean
	Skewed data: Median

CALCULATION, INTERPRETATION AND USES

Plasma osmolality is determined mainly by Sodium (NA), its counter ions, and uncharged species such as Glucose (GLU) and Urea (UN). Knowledge of the plasma concentration of these species allows calculation of the plasma osmolality to a degree that compares quite well to measured osmolality from freezing point depression. The difference between measured osmolality (MO) and calculated osmolality (CO) is known as the osmolality gap (OG).

A large positive (>14) osmolality gap can help identify the presence in plasma of substances such as ethanol, methanol, isopropanol, ethylene glycol, propylene glycol, and acetone. The formula given below for CO was developed using the specific plasma assays available at University of Iowa Hospitals and Clinics.

1. $CO = 2 \times NA + GLU/20 + UN/3 - 2$: calculated osmolality.
2. $OG = MO - CO$: osmolality gap.

To calculate the osmolality gap, plasma determination of MO, NA, GLU, and UN are necessary. Proper interpretation of the OG also requires knowledge of the anion gap (AG = NA

- HCO_3 - CL), the blood pH, and qualitative testing of the plasma ketone bodies (KETO). Determinations of MO and for CO should be performed on the same plasma sample.

The OG was calculated in 119 patients at University of Iowa Hospitals and Clinics using formulas (1) and (2). A mean OG of 0.13 was obtained with an observed range of –11 to +13; 61% of the patients were in the interval –3 to +3, and 97% of the patients were in the interval of –10 to +10. An OG value greater than 14 has traditionally been considered a critical value or cutoff.

When the OG is combined with blood pH and AG, poisonings with toxic alcohols can be quickly recognized. The presence of low blood pH, elevated AG, and greatly elevated OG (>14) is a medical emergency that requires prompt treatment.

The specific agent(s) responsible can be identified by the gas chromatographic assays for ethanol, methanol, isopropanol, acetone, and ethylene glycol. The following table summarizes results found in intoxications and other clinical situations.

SITUATION	pH	AG	KETO	GLU	OG	(mOsm/kg H20)
Ethanol only	N	N	N	N	HI	100 mg/dl = 21.7
Methanol (late)	LO	HI	N	N or HI	N or HI	50 mg/dl = 15.6
Isopropanol	N	N	POS	N	HI	100 mg/dl = 16.7 (also acetone)
Ethylene Glycol	LO	HI	N	N	HI	50 mg/dl = 8.1
Alcoholic Ketoacidosis	LO	HI	Weak POS	300	HI	(ethanol)
Diabetic Ketoacidosis	LO	HI	POS	300	N or UP (usually < 20-25)	50 mg/dl = 8.6 (acetone)

*On the left side of the equals sign are substance concentrations, and on the right side of the equals sign equivalent osmolality contributions. By dividing the OG by the right hand factor and then multiplying by the left hand concentration for this factor, an estimated pure substance concentration can be calculated.

**Osmolar gap may be increased in early methanol poisoning.

Non-toxic examples of an elevated osmolality gap include hyperlipidemia (less plasma water), chronic renal failure, and myeloma (increased plasma proteins).

Example Case:

A sixty-seven year old white male was found pulseless and resuscitated; then brought to the emergency room. He had been reported to be drinking in a bar all afternoon, and had then fallen from a ten foot balcony to snow covered ground. He arrived in the emergency room with a fractured occiput and was unresponsive.

Admission Data:

NA=141 mEq/l	UN=8 mg/dl	pH=7.30
CL=105 mEq/l	GLU=181 mg/dl	MO=353 mOsm/kg
HCO3=19 mEq/l	KETO=Neg	

AG = NA - CL- HCO3= 141 - 105- 19 = 17

CO = 2 × NA + GLU/20 + UN/3 -2

= 282+ 181/20 + 8/3 -2 = 292

0G = MO - CO= 353 - 292 = 61

If we assume OG is due to ethanol, then ethanol concentration would be 61/21.7 × 100 mg/dl = 281 mg/dl

The measured ethanol concentration on this sample was 270 mg/dl. The OG calculated in this case was consistent with the history and indicated ethanol intoxication.

MEASURES OF VARIABILITY – RANGE, QUARTILE DEVIATION, AVERAGE DEVIATION, STANDARD DEVIATION

While mean and median tell you about the centre of your observations, it says nothing about the 'spread' of the numbers.

Example: Suppose two machines produce nails which are on average 10 inches long. A sample of 11 nails is selected from each machine.

- Machine A: 6, 8, 8, 10, 10, 10, 10, 10, 12, 12, 14

- Machine B: 6, 6, 6, 8, 8, 10, 12, 12, 14, 14, 14

To verify, let's compute the mean:

- mean for machine A: 110 / 11 = 10
- mean for machine B: 110 / 11 = 10

In both cases, the mean is 10, indeed. However, the first machine seems to be the better one, since most nails are close to 10 inches. Therefore:

We must find additional numbers indicating the 'spread' of the data.

The Range

The easiest measure of the data spread is the range. It is simply the highest data value minus the lowest data value (we have seen the range before). In the above example, the range is the same for both data, namely 14 - 6 = 8. The range is, while useful, too crude a measure of variability.

The Variance

We want to find out how much the data points are spread around the mean. To do that, we could find the difference between each data point and the mean, and average these differences.

However, we want to measure the differences to the mean regardless of the sign (positive or negative difference). Therefore, we could find the absolute value of the difference between each data point and average that.

But for theoretical reasons an absolute value function is not easy to deal with, so that one chooses a square function instead (which also neutralizes signs). Finally, for yet other theoretical reasons we shall use not the sample size n to compute an average, but instead n - 1.

Hence, we will use this formula to compute the data spread, or variance:

Variance = add up the squares of (Data points - mean), then divide that sum by (n - 1)

There are two symbols for the variance, just as for the mean:

- σ^2 is the variance for a population.

- s^2 is the variance for a sample.

In other words, the variance is computed according to the formulas:

- $\sigma^2 = \frac{\sum(x-\mu)^2}{n-1}$ (for the population variance)
- $s^2 = \frac{\sum(x-\mu)^2}{n-1}$ (for the sample variance)

We had to use two formulas because one involves the population mean, the other the sample mean. Practically, however, the formula is the same. It is useful to compute the variance at least once "by hand" before we show how to use Excel to accomplish the same feat quickly and easily.

How to find the variance "by hand":

- Make a table of all x values.
- Find the mean of the data.
- Include a column with the difference to the mean.
- Include a column with the square of difference to the mean.
- Add the last column and divide the sum by (n - 1).

Here is the table that this procedure produces for the above sample of nails from machine A and B:

Machine A:

x	$(x-\bar{x})$	$(x-\bar{x})^2$
6	4	16
8	2	4
8	2	4
10	0	0
10	0	0
10	0	0
10	0	0
10	0	0
12	-2	4
12	-2	4
14	4	16

Therefore, the variance for machine A is: (16 + 4 + 4 + 0 + 0 + 0 + 0 + 0 + 4 + 4 + 16) / 10 = 48 / 10 = 4.8

Machine B:

x	$(x-\bar{x})$	$(x-\bar{x})^2$
6	4	16
6	4	16
6	4	16
8	2	4
8	2	4
10	0	0
12	-2	4
12	-2	4
14	-4	16
14	-4	16
14	-4	16

Therefore, the variance for machine B is: (16 + 16 + 16 + 4 + 4 + 0 + 4 + 4 + 16 + 16 + 16) / 10 = 112 / 10 = 11.2

In other words, the variance - or spread around the mean, for machine A is 4.8 while machine B has a variance (spread) of 11.2. That means that machine A seems to produce nails that, as a rule, produces nails that stick pretty close to the average nail length. Machine B, on the other hand, produces nails with more variability that machine A. Therefore, Machine A would be much preferred over machine B.

The unit of the variance is the square of the original unit; hence, it is not the best number (considering units). Therefore, one introduces an additional number, called the standard deviation:

The Standard Deviation

The standard deviation is the square root of the variance. As with the mean, there are two letters for variance and standard deviation:

- σ^2 is the variance for a population and $\sigma = \sqrt{\sigma^2}$ is the population standard deviation

- s^2 is the variance for a sample and $s = \sqrt{s^2}$ is the sample standard deviation

Example: Consider the sample data 6, 7, 5, 3, 4. Compute the standard deviation for that data.

To compute the standard deviation, we must first compute the mean, then the variance, and finally we can take the square root to obtain the standard deviation. In this case we do not need to create a table since there are so few numbers:

- Computing the mean: $\mu = (6+7+5+3+4)/5 = 5$
- Computing the variance:

$$\sigma^2 = \left[(6-5)^2 + (7-5)^2 + (5-5)^2 + (3-5)^2 + (4-5)^2\right]/4 = 2.5$$

- Standard deviation: $\sigma = \sqrt{2.5} = 1.58$

Short-Cut for Variance

There is a nice short-cut to compute the variance that can be proved as an exercise:

$$\sigma^2 = \frac{1}{n-1}\sum(x-\mu)^2 = \frac{1}{n-1}\left(\sum x^2 - \frac{\left(\sum x\right)^2}{n}\right)$$

At first the second formula looks much more complicated, but it is actually easier since it does not involve computing the mean first. In other words, using the second formula we can compute the variance (and therefore the standard deviation) without first having to compute the mean.

In our above example of machine B we would compute the variance using this shortcut as follows:

x	x^2
6	36
6	36
6	36
8	64
8	64
10	100
12	144
12	144

14	196
14	196
14	196
sum(x) = 110	sum(x^2) = 1212

Therefore the variance is:

$1/(11 - 1)^* (1212 - 110^2/11) = 0.1 * (1212 - 1100) = 11.2$

which of course is the same number as before, but a little easier to arrive at. However, Excel - as usual - provides built-in function to compute the range, the variance, and the standard deviation.

Using Excel to Compute Range, Variance, and Standard Deviation

Excel provides simple formulas to compute the range, the variance, and the standard deviation:

- The Excel formula to compute the range is "= max (RANGE) - min(RANGE)"
- The Excel formula to compute the variance is "= var (RANGE)"
- The Excel formula to compute the standard deviation is "= stdev(RANGE)"

Unit VI

Measures of Association

LINEAR CORRELATION: MEANING AND USES – CO-EFFICIENT OF CORRELATION

There is little doubt that the correlation coefficient in its many forms has become the workhorse of quantitative research and analysis. And well it should be, for our empirical knowledge is fundamentally of co-varying things. We come to discern relationships among things in terms of whether they change together or separately; we come to impute causes on the basis of phenomena co-occurring; we come to classify as a result of independent variation.

Of course, many of our concepts may be apriori, our frameworks may be projected onto phenomena and create order, and our understanding may be partly intuitive. Our knowledge is a dialectical balance between that sensory reality bearing on us, and our reaching out and imposing on this reality structure and framework. Whatever the framework within which we order phenomena, however, that reality we perceive is of dependence, concomitance, covariation, coincidence, concurrence; or of independence, disassociation, or disconnectedness.

We exist in a field of relatedness: i.e., we come to understand the world around us through the multifold, interlaced and intersecting correlations it manifests. Sometimes we call these relationships cause and effect, sometimes we generalize them into assumed laws, and sometimes we simply call them natural or social uniformities or regularities. Reflecting this interrelatedness, our theories and ideas about phenomena usually are based on assumed correlations. "Birds of a feather flock together." "Time heals all wounds." "Power kills and absolute power kills absolutely."

Or at a different level: "National cohesion increases in wartime." "Prolonged severe inflation disorders society." "Institutional power aggrandizes until checked by opposing institutional power." No wonder, then, that scientists have tried to make the concept of correlation more precise, to measure and to quantitatively compare correlations. Here I will deal with one such measure, called the product moment correlation coefficient. This is the most widely used technique for assessing correlations and is the basis for techniques determining mathematical functions (such as regression analysis) or patterns of interdependence (such as factor analysis).

Although much used, however, the correlation coefficient is not widely understood by students and teachers, and even those applying the correlation in advanced research. Therefore, the purpose of this book is to convey an understanding of the correlation coefficient to students that will be generally useful. I am especially concerned with providing the student with an intuitive understanding of correlation that will enable him to better comprehend the use of correlation coefficients in the literature, while providing material helpful for applying the correlation coefficient to his own work.

Conveying understanding and facilitating application are my aims. The organization of this book and the topics included mirror these goals, as does my emphasis on figures. A picture is worth a thousand derivations and symbols. Correlation can be beautifully illustrated, but yet many statistical books solely present the mathematical derivations and statistical formula for the correlation coefficient, to the detriment of a student's learning. Here I hope to show the very simple meaning of correlation, both in vector terms and in graphical plots. With this meaning understood, the application of the correlation coefficient is straight forward and intuitively reasonable, while the usual complex statistical formula is then simply a computational tool to that end.

To convey this understanding, the first chapters look at correlation intuitively. Given certain phenomena, what does correlation mean? What about phenomena are we perceiving? How can we approach a measure of correlation? Correlated phenomena are vector phenomena: they have direction and magnitude. To appreciate the correlation intuitively it is helpful to visualize the geometric or spatial meaning of the coefficient. However, there is an alternative spatial view of correlation as a Cartesian plot. This is the usual picture of correlation presented in the statistical books. From this view will be derived the usual formulation of the correlation coefficient. The remaining chapters move on to more advanced topics concerning the correlation. Our ability to portray partial correlation in simple geometric terms exemplifies the usefulness of the geometric approach.

1. Henceforth, unless otherwise specified, correlation coefficient will mean the product moment.

Correlation Intuitively Considered

When we perceive two things that covary, what do we see? When we see one thing vary, we perceive it changing in some regard, as the sun setting, the price of goods increasing, or the alternation of green and red lights at an intersection. Therefore, when two things covary there are two possibilities. One is that the change in a thing is concomitant with the change in another, as the change in a child's age covaries with his height. The older, the taller. When higher magnitudes on one thing occur along with higher magnitudes on another and the lower magnitudes on both also co-occur, then the things vary together positively, and we denote this situation as positive covariation or *positive correlation.*

The second possibility is that two things vary inversely or oppositely. That is, the higher magnitudes of one thing go along with the lower magnitudes of the other and vice versa. Then, we denote this situation as negative covariation or *negative correlation*. This seems clear enough, but in order to be more systematic about correlation more definition is needed.

Perceived covariation must be covariation across some cases. A case is a component of variation in a thing. For example, the change in the speed of traffic with the presence or absence of a traffic policeman (a negative correlation) is a change across time periods.

Different time periods are the cases. Different levels of GNP that go along with different amounts of energy consumption may be perceived across nations. Nations are the cases, and the correlation is positive, meaning that a nation (case) with high GNP has high energy consumption; and one with low GNP has low energy consumption. The degree to which a regime is democratic is inversely correlated with the intensity of its foreign violence. The cases here are different political regimes.

The two things we perceive varying together—the variables—are 1955 GNP per capita and trade. The cases across which these vary are the fourteen nations shown. Although it is not easy to observe because of the many different magnitudes, the correlation is positive, since for more nations than not, high GNP per capita co-occurs with high trade, and low GNP per capita with low trade.

We can summarize this covariation in terms of a four-fold table. Let us define high as above the means (averages) of $481 for GNP per capita and $4,975 millions for trade, and low at or below these means. Then we get the positive correlation. The numbers that appear in the cells of the table are the number of nations that have the indicated joint magnitudes. For example, there are nine nations which have both low GNP per capita and low trade.

Table. High and Low are Divided at the Average.

		GNP Per Capita	
		Low	High
Trade	Low	9	1
	High	0	4

From the table, we can now clearly see that the correlation

between the two variables is positive, since with only one exception (in the upper right cell) high magnitudes are observed together, as are low magnitudes.

If the correlation were negative, then most cases would be counted in the lower left and upper right cells. What if there were about an equal number of cases in all the cells of the fourfold table? Then, there would be little correlation: the two variables would not covary. In other words, sometimes high magnitudes on one variable would occur as often with low as with high magnitudes on the other.

But all this is still imprecise. The four-fold table gives us a way of looking at correlation, but just considering correlation as covarying high or low magnitudes is quite a loss of information, since we are not measuring how high or low the figures are. Moreover, if we are at all going to be precise about a correlation, we should determine some *coefficient of correlation*—some one number that in itself expresses the correlation between variables.

To be a useful coefficient, however, this must be more than a number unique to a pair of variables. It must be a number *comparable between* pairs of variables. We must be able to compare correlations, so that we can determine, for example, which variables are more or less correlated, or whether variables change correlation with change in cases. Finally, we want a correlation that indicates whether the correlation is positive or negative. In the next chapter we can intuitively and precisely define such a coefficient.

STANDARD SCORES AND CORRELATION

Although the cases across which two variables covary usually will be the same, the units in which the magnitudes are expressed for each variable may differ. One variable may be in dollars per capita, another number of infant deaths. One may be in percent, another in feet. One apples, the other oranges. Clearly, we have a classic problem. How can we measure the correlation between different things in different units? We know we perceive covariation between things that are different. But determining common units for different things such that their correlations can be measured and compared to other correlations seems beyond our ability. Yet, we must make units comparable before we can jointly measure variation. But how?

Note the differences in units between the various variables, both in their nature and average magnitudes our problem, then, is to determine some way of making the units of such variables comparable, so that we can determine the correlation between any two of them, as well as compare the correlations between various pairs of variables. Is, for example, the covariation of foreign conflict and of defence budget across the fourteen nations greater or less than that of, say, foreign conflict and the freedom of group opposition?

Let us consider this problem for a moment. We want a measure of covariation, of *how much two things change together or oppositely*. Clearly, then, we have no interest in their different magnitudes. And since magnitudes are irrelevant we can at least make the different magnitudes of the two variables comparable by making their average magnitude the same. This we can do by subtracting the average or mean of each variable from all its magnitudes.

Such data resulting from subtracting the mean is called mean-deviation data, and the mean of mean-deviation data is always zero. Now that we have made the average magnitude comparable by transforming each variable to a mean of zero, the observations now represent pure variation. It is as though we had taken different statistical profile shots of each variable and overlaid them so that we could better see their covariation. The problem is that subtracting the means did not change the magnitude of variation, and that of the defence budget is very large compared to power. We still need a transformation to make their variation comparable.

Why not compute an average variation then? This average could be calculated by adding up all the mean-deviations and dividing by the number of cases. However, the summed minus magnitudes equal the summed positive magnitudes (by virtue of the subtraction of the mean), and the average variation always will be zero, regardless of the absolute magnitude of the variation. Then why not average *the absolute* mean-deviation data? That is, eliminate the negative signs. But if we did this, we would run into some mathematical difficulties in eventually determining a correlation coefficient. Absolutes create more problems than they solve.

However, we can invoke a traditional solution. If we square all the mean-deviation data, we eliminate negative signs. Then the average of these squared magnitudes will give us a measure of variation around the mean. From this point on, I will have to be more precise and use some notation towards that end. I will adopt the following definitions.

Definitions 1:

X = anything that varies; a variable;

X_j = a specific variable j;

X_k = a specific variable k;

i = a particular case i

x_{ij} = a magnitude (datum) for case i on variable j;

n = the number of cases for a variable;

$\bar{X}$ = the average or mean of variable X;

X^*_j = mean-deviation data (the mean has been subtracted from each original magnitude) for variable j;

Σx_{ij} = the first case (i = 1 for variable j) to the last case (i = n for variable j), that is $x_{1j} + x_{2j} + x_{3j} + ... + x_{nj} = \Sigma x_{ij}$.

The last definition is especially important, for it enables us to compress a lot of summations into a concise equation. Now, using this notation, we can define the mean as,

Equation 1:

$$X_j = (\Sigma x_i) / n$$

And we can also easily define mean-deviation data. Since X^*_j stands for the mean-deviation data for variable X_j, let x^*_{ij} be the corresponding mean-deviation magnitude. Then

Equation 2:

$$x^*_{ij} = x_{ij} \; \bar{X}_j$$

With these equations I can return to our measure of variation. Remember, we are going to square the mean-deviation data, add, and divide the sum by n to get an average variation. Let σ^2 (sigma squared) stand for our measure of variation. Then

Equation 3:

$$\sigma^2 = \left(\sum X^{*2}_{ij}\right)/n = \left(\sum x_{ij} - \bar{X}_j\right)^2/n$$

where the last equality follows from Equation 3.2.

We can now introduce two important definitions.

Definition 2:

σ_j^2 = the *variance* of variable X_j.

σ_j = the *standard deviation* of variable X_j, which is the positive square root of the variance.

We now have two measures of variation around the mean and we will find that each of them is a useful tool for understanding correlation. At this point, we can use the standard deviation to help resolve our original problem of making the variation in two variables comparable, since it is expressed in the original units (to get a measure of variation, we squared the mean-deviations; the standard deviation is the square root of the *average* squared mean-deviations and thus brings us back to the original units).

Subtracting the mean out of a variable does not change its standard deviation. Now that we have a comparative measure of variation for a variable, we can resolve our original problem of making the variation in two variables comparable: we can norm each by its standard deviation. That is, we can divide each variable's mean-deviation x^*_{ij} by its standard deviation.

This will transform the data to standard deviation units, *and thus make each variable's variation comparable in the same units.* Such transformed data is called *standardized* data, the application of this transformation is called *standardization,* and the transformed magnitudes are called *standard scores.* The customary notation for this should be defined.

Definition 3:

Z_j = a standardized variable j,

z_{ij} = a standard score for case i on standardized variable Z_j.

And a standard score can now be defined in terms of the other measures we have developed.

Equation 4:

$$z_{ij} = x^{*}_{ij}/\sigma_j = (x_{ij} - \overline{X}_j)/\sigma_j$$

Note that the means and standard deviations for the standardized variables are equal. Moreover, the standard deviation of standard scores is equal to unity (1.00), and thus to the variance. For standardized data, our two measures of variation are equal. At a glance, a standard score tells us how low or high the data for a case on a variable is.

Its standard score of 1.613 on power means that its magnitude is 1.613 times the standard deviation of of the 14 nations on their power; its score of 2.685 on the defence budget means its magnitude on this variable is 2.687 times the standard deviation for the data on the defence budget. Thus a standard score of 1.0 means a nation's variation is one standard deviation from the average, a score of 2.0 means two standard deviations from the average, and so on.

Standard scores enable us to measure the variation of two variables and to compare their variation in common units (of standard scores) and magnitudes, regardless of their original units and magnitudes. Now, to measure such a correlation. Of course, we could use the same averaging approach employed to get a measure of variation.

We could add the two scores for each case, sum all these additions and divide this sum by n. However, if we did this we would always end up with zero regardless of the covariation involved.

Intuitively, a reasonable alternative is to multiply the two scores for each case, add all those products, and divide by n to get an average product. Then, joint high plus or joint high negative scores will contribute positively to the sum; if one is high positive and the other high negative, they will contribute negatively to the sum.

Thus, the sum will at least discriminate positive and negative covariation. Moreover, multiplication seems to intuitively capture the notion of covariation. For if one case does not vary from the average, its standard score will be zero, and the resulting multiplication of its score by that on another variable will yield zeros, i.e., no covariation. As it should be.

We now have something like what we are after. The column of joint products of standard scores measures covariation for each case; the sum measures the overall covariation; and the average of this gives us a measure of average covariation. In truth, *this measure of average correlation is the product moment correlation coefficient.* We have arrived at that somewhat intimidating coefficient intuitively, simply through searching for some way to systematically compare variation.

Definiton 4:

r_{jk} = the product moment correlation between X_j and X_k,

r_{jk}^2 = the coefficient of determination between X_j and X_k.

The squared correlation coefficient is called the coefficient of determination. Since the standard deviation is the square root of the variance, and the correlation is computed through data standardized by the standard deviation, we can translate the results back into variance terms by squaring the correlation. The *coefficient of determination then defines the proportion of variance* in common between two variables.

Let me recap the intuitive process of arriving at the correlation coefficient. First, we recognize the existence of covariation between things and the need to systematically define it. In doing this, the first hurdle is to delimit the cases over which our observations covary. Once this is done, we then have the problem of making our observations comparable. If we are to assess covariation, we must have some way of removing differences between observations due simply to their units.

One way of doing this is to make the averages of the variables equal. But, while helpful, this does not remove differences in variation around the mean due to differences in units.

To help with this problem, we then developed a measure of variation, called the standard deviation. Now, if we subtract a variable's mean from each observation and then divide by the standard deviation, we have transformed the variables into scores with equal means and standard deviations. Their variation is now comparable. To get at covariation, then, it seems most appropriate to find some measure of average covariation of the two sets of standardized scores.

The best route to this is to multiply the two scores for each case, add the products, and divide by the number of cases.

Beforehand, a precise definition of the product moment correlation will be helpful. It is

Equation 5:

$$r_{jk} = (\Sigma z_{ij} z_{ik}) / n$$

Then, replacing z_{ij} and z_{ik} by Equation 4,

Equation 6:

$$r_{jk} = \left(\sum \left(\left(x_{ij} - \bar{X}_j\right)/\sigma_j\right)\left(\left(x_{ik} - \bar{X}_k\right)/\sigma_k\right)\right)/n$$

$$= \left(\sum \left(x_{ik} - \bar{X}_j\right)\left(x_{ik} - \bar{X}_k\right)\right)/n\sigma_j\sigma_k$$

Finally from Equation 3 and Definition 2, we can rewrite the standard deviation in terms of the raw data, and thus define the correlation entirely as a function of the variables in their original magnitudes. That is

Equation 7:

$$r_{jk} = \left(\sum \left(x_{ij} - \bar{X}_j\right)\left(x_{ik} - \bar{X}_k\right)\right)/n\sigma_j\sigma_k$$

$$= \left(\sum \left(x_{ij} - \bar{X}_j\right)\left(x_{ik} - \bar{X}_k\right)\right) / \left(\left(\sum \left(x_{ij} - \bar{X}_j\right)^2 \left(\sum x_{ik} - \bar{X}_k\right)^2\right)\right)^{1/2}$$

The terms on the right of the second equality give the formula most often presented in statistical books. It is imposing, but as we have seen, its underlying logic is intuitively reasonable.

Notes:

- There are occasions when the cases may differ, such as in lagged correlations where the case for one variable is a time period lagged behind the time period for the other.
- I am leaving the range off the Σ, which would be written as

$$\sum_{t=1}^{n}$$

In this book the range will always be from i = 1 to n, and so is omitted.

- Note that the mean of a standardized variable is always zero. Therefore simply adding the standard scores for each case, summing the result across all the cases, and taking the average of that sum will always, regardless of the data, get you:

$(\Sigma(z_{ij} + z_{ik})) / n = (\Sigma z_{ij}) / n + \Sigma z_{ik}) / n$
$= (\text{mean of } Z_j) + (\text{mean of } Z_k)$
$= 0 + 0$

CHARACTERISTICS OF THE CORRELATION COEFFICIENT

The Range

Given that the correlation coefficient measures the degree to which two things vary together or oppositely, how do we interpret it? First, the maximum positive correlation is 1.00. Since the correlation is the average product of the standard scores for the cases on two variables, and since the standard deviation of standardized data is 1.00, then if the two standardized variables covary positively and perfectly, the average of their products across the cases will equal 1.00.

On the other hand, if two things vary oppositely and perfectly, then the correlation will equal 1.00. We therefore have a measure which tells us at a glance whether two things covary perfectly, or near perfectly, and whether positively or negatively. If the coefficient is, say,.80 or.90, we know that the corresponding variables closely vary together in the same direction; if -.80 or -.90, they vary together in opposite directions.

The Zero

What then is the meaning of zero or near zero correlation? It means simply that two things vary separately. That is, when the magnitudes of one thing are high; the other's magnitudes are sometimes high, and sometimes low. It is through such uncorrelated variation—such independence of things—that we can sharply discriminate between phenomena.

I should point out that there are two ways of viewing independent variation. One is that the more distinct and unrelated the covariation, the greater the independence. Then, a zero correlation represents complete independence and -1.00 or 1.00 indicates complete dependence. Independence viewed in this way is called *statistical independence.* Two variables are then statistically independent if their correlation is zero.

There is another view of independence, however, called *linear independence,* which sees independence or dependence as a matter of presence or absence, not more or less. In this perspective, two things varying perfectly together are linear dependent. Thus, variables with correlation of -1.00 or 1.00 are linear dependent. Variables with variation less than perfect are linear independent.

Interpreting the Correlation: Correlation Squared

Seldom, indeed, will a correlation be zero or perfect. Usually, the covariation between things will be something like.43 or -.16. How are we to interpret such correlations? Clearly .43 is positive, indicating positive covariation; -.16 is negative, indicating some negative covariation. Moreover, we can say that the positive correlation is greater than the negative. But, we require more than. If we have a correlation of .56 between two variables, for example, what precisely can we say other than the correlation is positive and .56?

From my derivation of the correlation coefficient in the last chapter, we know that the squared correlation describes the proportion of variance in common between the two variables. If we multiply this by 100 we then get the percent of variance in common between two variables. That is:

$r^2_{jk} \times 100$ = percent of variance in common between X_j and X_k.

For example, we found that the correlation between a nation's power and its defence budget was .66. This correlation squared is .45, which means that across the fourteen nations constituting the sample 45 percent of their variance on the two variables is in common (or 55 percent is not in common). In thus squaring correlations and transforming covariance to percentage terms we have an easy to understand meaning of correlation. And we are then in a position to evaluate a particular correlation.

As a matter of routine it is the squared correlations that should be interpreted. This is because the correlation coefficient is misleading in suggesting the existence of more covariation than exists, and this problem gets worse as the correlation approaches zero. Consider the following correlations and their squares.

r	r^2
1.00	1.00
.90	.81
.80	.64
.70	.49
.60	.36
.50	.25
.40	.16
.30	.09
.20	.04
.10	.01
.0	.0

Note that as the correlation r decrease by tenths, the r^2 decreases by much more. A correlation of .50 only shows that 25 percent variance is in common; a correlation of .20 shows 4 percent in common; and a correlation of .10 shows 1 percent in common (or 99 percent not in common). Thus, squaring should be a healthy corrective to the tendency to consider low correlations, such as .20 and .30, as indicating a meaningful or practical covariation.

Notes:

- There are exceptions to this, as when the correlation is computed for dichotomous variables with disparate frequencies.
- I am talking about statistical independence in its

descriptive and not inferential sense. In its inferential sense, a nonzero correlation would represent independent variation insofar as its variation from zero could be assumed due to chance, within some acceptable probability of error. If it is improbable that the deviation is due to chance, then the correlation is accepted as measuring statistically dependent variation.

THE VECTOR APPROACH

There are two more approaches, each providing a different kind of insight into the nature of the correlation coefficient. One is the vector approach, to be developed here. The other is what I will call the Cartesian approach, to be developed in the next chapter.

Consider again the problem. Two things vary and we wish to determine in some systematic fashion whether they vary together, oppositely, or separately. We have seen that one approach involves a simple averaging and common sense. But let us say that we are the kind of people that must visualize things and draw pictures of relationships before we understand them. How, then, can we *visualize* covariation? That is, how can we geometrize it?

There are many ways this could be done. For example, we could plot the magnitudes for different cases on each variable to get a profile. And we could then compare the profile curves to see if they moved oppositely or together. While intuitively appealing, however, it does not lead to a precise measure. But what about this? Variables can be portrayed as vectors in a space. We are used to treating variables this way in visualizing physical forces. A vector is an ordered set of magnitudes; a variable is such an ordered set (each magnitude is for a specific case).

A vector can be plotted; therefore a variable can be plotted as a vector. Vectors pointing in the same direction have a positive relationship and those pointing in opposite directions have a negative relationship. Could this geometric fact also be useful in picturing correlation? Let us see. The first problem is how to plot a variable as a vector. Now consider the variable as located in space spanned by dimensions constituting the cases. These two cases then define the dimensions of the space containing these variables—vectors—that are plotted. We thus have a picture of variation representing the two pairs of observations for these variables. *The variation of the variables across these nations is then indicated by the length and direction of these vectors in this space.*

To give a different example, consider again the power and defence budget variables. There are fourteen cases—nations—for each variable. To consider these variables as vectors, we would therefore treat these nations as constituting the dimensions of a fourteen dimensional space. Now, if we picture both variables as vectors in this space, their relative magnitudes and orientation towards each other would show how they vary together.

To get a better handle on this, think of the vectors as forces, which is the graphical role they have played for most of us. If the vectors are pointed in a similar direction, they are pushing together.

They are working together, which is to say that they are varying together. Vectors oppositely directed are pushing against each other: their efforts are inverse, their covariation is opposite. Then we have vectors that are at right angles, such as one pushing north, another east. These are vectors working independently: their variation is independent.

First, the vectors are not pointing oppositely, and therefore their variation is not negative. But they are not pointing exactly in the same direction either, so that they do not completely covary together. Yet, they are pointing enough in the same general direction to suggest some variation in common. But how do we measure this common covariation for vectors? Again, we have the problem of units to consider.

The length and direction of the vectors is a function of the magnitudes and units involved. Thus, the defence budget vector is much longer than the power one. Since differing lengths are a problem, why not transform the vectors to equal lengths? There is indeed such a transformation called *normalization,* which divides the magnitudes of the vector by its length.

Definition:

X_j = vector j or variable j

$|X_j|$ = length of vector j = $(\Sigma x^2_{ij})^{1/2}$

That is, the length of a vector is the square root of the squared sum of its magnitudes. Then the normalization of a vector is the division of its separate magnitudes by the vector's length. All vectors so normalized have their lengths transformed to 1.00.

The problem with normalization is that there can be considerable differences in mean magnitudes on the normalized vectors, and these mean differences would then confound the measure of correlation. After all, we want a measure of pure covariation, and differences in average magnitude confound this.

Then, in reconsidering our original vectors, what about transforming the magnitudes on the vectors by subtracting their averages? If we did this we would be translating the origin of the space to the mean for each vector: the zero point on each dimension would be the mean.

By so transforming the vectors to mean-deviation data we eliminate the affect of mean differences, but we still have the differing vector lengths. Need this bother us, now? After all, we are concerned with similarity or dissimilarity in vector *direction* as an indication of correlation. Let us therefore work for the moment with mean-deviation vectors and see what we get.

Recall that codirectionality for vectors is the essence of covariation. How do we measure codirectionality, then? *By the angle between the vectors.* But measuring this angle creates a problem. In degrees it can vary from 0° to 360° and is always positive, where perfect positive covariation would be zero, independent variation would be 90° or 270° and opposite variation 180°. As with the correlation coefficient derived, it would be desirable to have some measure which would range between something like 1.00 for perfect correlation, –1.00 for perfect negative correlation, and zero for no correlation.

And we do have such a measure given by elementary trigonometry. It is the cosine. The cosine of the angle between vectors will be +1.00 for vectors with an angle of 0°, -1.00 for an angle of 180° (completely opposite directionality), and 0 for an angle of 90° or 270°. What is more, from linear algebra we can compute the cosine directly from the vectors without measuring their angles. For vectors X^*_j and X^*_k of mean-deviation data, this is

Equation:

$$\text{Cos } \theta_{jk} = (\Sigma x^*_{ij} x^*_{ik}) / |X^*_j||X^*_k|$$

Let the magnitudes of power and defence budget be transformed to mean-deviation data. Thus, the cosine between two variables transformed to mean-deviation data—to data describing the variation around the mean—gives us a measure of correlation.

But there is a coincidence here. The .66 cosine for the angle of 49° between the two vectors is the same as the .66 product moment correlation we found for the two variables using standard scores. Is there in fact a relationship between these alternatives?

To see what this relationship might be, let us expand the formula for the cosine between two mean-deviation vectors so that it is expressed in the original magnitudes.

Equation:

$$\text{Cosine } \theta_{jk} = (\Sigma x^*_{ij} x^*_{ik}) / |X^*_j||X^*_k|$$

$$= (\Sigma(x_{ij} - \bar{X}_j)(x_{ik} - \bar{X}_k)) / (\Sigma x^*_{ij}{}^2)^{1/2} (\Sigma x^*_{ik}{}^2)^{1/2}$$

$$= (\Sigma(x_{ij} - \bar{X}_j)(x_{ik} - \bar{X}_k)) / ((\Sigma(x_{ij} - \bar{X}_j)^2)\ (\Sigma(x_{ik} - \bar{X}_k)^2))^{1/2}$$

To sum up, we have found that we can geometrically treat the variation of things as vectors, with the cases across which the variation occurs as dimensions of the space containing the vector. The covariation between two things is then shown by their angle in this space.

However, we have to again transform the variation in two things to eliminate the effects of mean-differences. The resulting mean-deviation data reflects pure variation and the covariation between the vectors is then the cosine of their angle. Moreover, this cosine turns out to be precisely the product moment correlation derived from standardized data.

Instead of two alternative measures of correlation, we thus have alternative perspectives or routes to understanding correlation: the average cross-products of standardized data, or the cosine of the angle between mean-deviation (or standardized) data vectors.

Notes:

- This is not to be confused with transforming distributions to normality, an entirely different procedure.

THE CARTESIAN APPROACH

So far we have approached correlation in intuitive-conceptual and geometric fashion. But there is another approach beloved of introductory statistical tests. This is the Cartesian approach: it relies on a Cartesian coordinate system, where each variable represents a coordinate, and the cases are points plotted in this two-dimensional space.

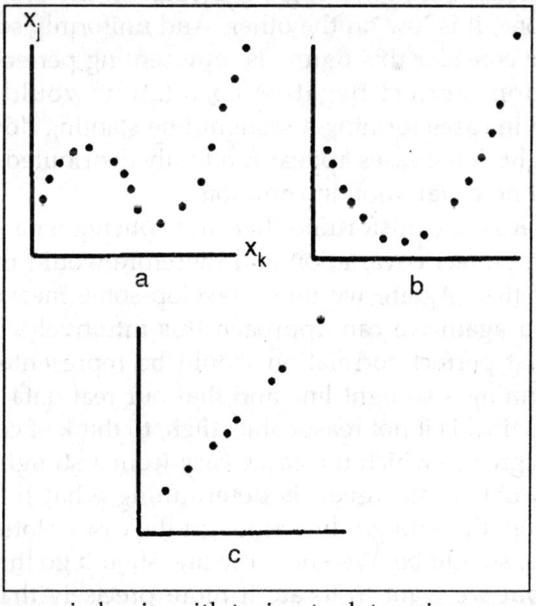

Let us again begin with trying to determine some measure

of the covariation of things. We saw that the variation of a variable could be pictured as a vector and covariation as codirectionality between vectors. We could have, however, pictured variation differently. Rather than fixing the cases as dimensions of the space, we could have treated the variables as the dimensions. Then we could plot each case on these dimensions in terms of their joint magnitudes, for variables X_j and X_k. The variation of the cases in this space then represents the covariation of the variables.

What, then, would perfect covariation look like? Here, we have a fundamental ambiguity. That is, covariation could lie along some curve, like the covariation between time and the height of a ball thrown upward which can be plotted as a parabola. Or, covariation could lie along a straight line. In intuitively assessing covariation, we were concerned with a measure of when magnitudes were both high and low or when one was high, the other low. That is, we wanted to index positive or negative correlation.

Concerning positive correlation, for as the magnitude of a case on one variable is high, it is high on the other; as it is low on one, it is low on the other. And uniformly so. We can therefore consider this figure as representing perfect positive correlation. Perfect negative correlation would then be reflected in cases forming a straight line slanting downwards to the right. If the cases appear randomly distributed, we have a case of no covariation in common.

But it is our misfortune that most phenomena will have less than perfect covariation and therefore would manifest a plot like that. Again, we must develop some measure of all this. And again we can approach this intuitively. Now, we know that perfect correlation would be represented by the cases forming a straight line and that our real data will vary from this line. Is it not reasonable, then, to think of correlation as the degree to which the cases vary from a straight line?

A problem, however, is determining what this perfect correlation, this straight line amongst the cases plotted on the variables, should be. We know the line should go through the points, but we want to locate it more precisely than this so that we can develop an exact measure of correlation. One possibility is to locate the line such that the deviations of cases from the line are minimal. Let us consider such deviations, where the deviations are computed as the difference between the case's magnitude x_{ij} on one variable (X_j), and the location x_{ij} of the case on the line if X_j and X_k were perfectly correlated. I will denote this deviation by d_i as shown. Deviations d_2 and d_3 are also shown as examples.

We could then sum these deviations for all cases and locate the line so that the sum is as small as possible. And since deviations above the line would always be positive, those below would be negative, we could always locate the line such that these deviations sum to zero. Unfortunately, however, an infinitude of lines could be fitted to the cases to yield deviations summing to zero, and we cannot define any unique line this way.

We could sum absolute deviations, but then absolutes are again difficult to deal with mathematically. Why not square deviations and sum the squares? This in fact provides a solution, for the minimization of d_i^2 leads to a unique line fitting the points. We need not go into the actual minimization. Suffice to say that the equation of the straight line is

$$X_j = \alpha + \beta X_k,$$

and the line minimizing the squared deviations is called the *least squares line* or *least squares regression.*

Now, let us say that we have such a least squares line, and the squared deviations add to the smallest possible sum. What then? This sum of squared deviations always would be zero in the case of perfect correlation, but otherwise would depend on the original data units. Therefore, different sums of squared deviations for different variables would not be easily comparable or interpretable. When this type of unit-dependent variation occurs, a solution is often to develop a ratio of some sort. For example, national government budgets in national currencies are difficult to compare between nations, but the ratio of national budget to GNP eliminates currency units and provides easily comparable measures.

But to what do we compute a ratio for our sums? Consider

that we have so far computed differences from a perfect correlation line fitted to the actual magnitudes of the variables. Could we not also introduce a hypothetical line fitted to the cases as though they had no correlation? We would then have two hypothetical lines, one measuring perfect correlation; the other measuring complete statistical independence, or noncorrelation. Would not some ratio of differences from the two lines give us what we want? Let's see.

To be consistent with the previous approach, squared deviations from the second line would also be calculated. First, the line would be horizontal, since if there is some variation in common between two variables, the line will angle upward to the right if this correlation is positive, or to the left if negative.

Okay, now where do we place the horizontal line? If there is no correlation between two variables, then from a magnitude on the one variable, we cannot predict to a magnitude in the other. Knowing one variable's variation does not reduce uncertainty about the other's. This is an opposite situation for perfectly correlated variables, where knowing a magnitude on one variable enables a precise prediction as to the magnitude of the other.

When we have complete uncertainty, as in the case of perfect statistical independence, then given the one variable, what is the best estimate of the magnitude on the other? This is the other variable's *mean*. In a situation of complete uncertainty about the magnitude of a case on a variable, the best guess as to this magnitude is the variable's mean. Since the line of perfect noncorrelation is a line of complete uncertainty about where a case would lie on the vertical axis, X_j, given its magnitude on X_kk, the most intuitively reasonable location for the line is at the average of X_j.

However, not only is this intuitively reasonable, but if in fact the two variables were perfectly uncorrelated, then the line which would minimize Σd^2_i would be this horizontal line. In other words, as the correlation approaches zero, the perfect correlation line approaches the horizontal one shown. Now, given this horizontal line for hypothetically perfect noncorrelation, we can determine the deviation of each case from it. Let me denote such a deviation as g_i, along with g_1 as an example. The sum of the squared deviations of g_i is Σg^2_i, which is a minimum if the variables are perfectly correlated.

Thus, we have two measures of deviation. One from the perfect correlation line fitting the actual data; the other from the line of hypothetical noncorrelation. Surely, there will be a relationship between Σd^2_i and Σg^2_i. Now, the less correlated the variables, the more the slanted line approaches the horizontal one. That is, the more Σd^2_i approaches Σg^2_i. If the variables were perfectly correlated, Σd^2_i would be zero, since there would be no deviation from the line of perfect correlation. And therefore the *less* the observations covary, the closer Σd^2_i approaches Σg^2_i from zero. If the observations are in fact perfectly uncorrelated, then $\Sigma d^2_i = \Sigma g^2_i$.

Thus, it appears that a ratio between Σd^2_i and Σd^2_i would measure the actual correlation between two variables. If the correlation were perfect, then the ratio would be zero; if there were no correlation, the ratio would be one. But this is the opposite of the way we measured correlation before. Therefore, reverse this measurement by subtracting the ratio from 1.00, and denote the resulting coefficient as h. Then,

Equation:

$$h = 1 - \Sigma d^2_i / \Sigma g^2_i$$

To deepen our understanding of h, and consider again the horizontal line. The deviations g_i are from the average $\overline{X}_j$. Therefore,

$$g_i = x_{ij} - \overline{X}_j,$$

$$g^2_i = (x_{ij} - \overline{X}_j)^2,$$

$$\Sigma g^2_i / n = \Sigma(x_{ij} - \overline{X}_j)^2/n = \sigma^2_j.$$

That is, what in fact Σg^2_i measures is the total variation of X_j. If we divide this by n, we would have the variance (σ^2_j) of X_j.

The other sum of squares, Σd^2_i, measures that part of the variation in X_j that does not covary with X_k—that is independent of covariation with X_k. If X_j and X_k covaried perfectly, there would be no independent variation in X_j and Σd^2_i would equal zero.

Therefore, the ratio of Σd^2_i to Σg^2_i measures the variance in X_j independent of X_k with respect to the total variance of X_j. Thus, when we subtract this ratio from 1.00 we get

$$h = 1 - \Sigma d^2_i / \Sigma g^2_i$$

$$= (\Sigma g^2_i - \Sigma d^2_i) / \Sigma g^2_i$$

= (total variance - independent variance) / total variance

= (variance in common) / total variance.

In other words, h measures the *proportion* of variance between two variables. But this is what the coefficient of determination r^2 does.

Therefore,

Equation:

$$h = r^2,$$

and our measure of correlation derived through the Cartesian approach is the product moment correlation squared. And the Cartesian approach provides an understanding of why the correlation squared measures the proportion of variance of two variables in common.

Notes:

- Through calculus we can determine the values for α and βthat define the minimizing equation. They are

$$\beta = \left(\sum(X_{ij}-\bar{X}_j)(X_{ik}-\bar{X}_k)\right)/\sum(X_{ik}-\bar{X}_k)^2$$

$$\alpha = \bar{X}_j - \beta\bar{X}_k.$$

THE PROBLEM OF EXTERNAL EFFECTS: PARTIAL CORRELATION

A problem with the correlation coefficient arises from the very way the covariation question was phrased. We wanted some systematic measure of the covariation of two things. And that is precisely what we got with the correlation coefficient: a measure confined wholly to two things and which treats them as an isolated system.

But few pairs of things are isolated. Most things are part

of larger wholes or complexes of interrelated and covarying parts, and these wholes in turn are still parts of other wholes, as a cell is a part of the leaf, which is part of the tree that is part of a forest.

Things usually covary in large clusters or patterns of interdependence and causal influences (which is the job of factor analysis to uncover). To then isolate two things, compute the correlation between them, and to interpret that correlation as measuring the relationship between the two variables alone can be misleading.

Consider two examples. First, let us assess the correlation between illiteracy and infant mortality. We may feel that a lack of education means poor infant care, resulting in higher mortality. Of course, we want to be as comparative as possible so we compute the correlation for all nations. The actual correlation for 1955 is.61, which is to say that illiteracy and infant mortality have 37 percent of their variance in common. Are we then to conclude that education helps prevent infant mortality?

If we were unwary, we might. But these two variables are not isolated. They are aspects of larger social systems and both subject to extraneous influences; and in this case, these influences flow from economic development. Many in the least developed countries have insufficient diets and inadequate health services, and live in squalid conditions.

High infant mortality follows. Also by virtue of nonexistent or poor educational systems, many people are illiterate. This is quite the opposite of the developed nations, which usually have good medical services, a varied and high protein diet, and high literacy. Thus the correlation between illiteracy and infant mortality. It has less to do with any intrinsic relationship between them then to the joint influence on illiteracy and infant mortality of national development.

A second example has to do with the covariation between economic growth rate and social conflict. Let us hypothesize that they have a negative correlation due to economic growth increasing opportunities, multiple group membership, and cross-pressures, thus draining off conflict. Let us find, however, that the actual correlation is near zero. Before rushing out into the streets to proclaim that economic growth is independent of conflict, however, we might consider whether exogenous influences are dampening the real correlation.

In this case, we could argue that the educational growth rate is the depressant. Increasing education creates new interests, broadens expectations, and generates a consciousness of deprivations. Thus, if education increases faster than opportunities, social conflict would increase. To assess the correlation between economic growth rate and conflict, therefore, we should hold constant the educational growth rate.

How do we handle these kinds of situations? There is an approach called *partial correlation*, which involves calculating the correlation between two variables holding constant the external influences of a third. Before looking at the formula for computing the partial correlation, three intuitive approaches to understanding what is involved may be helpful.

First, consider the first example of the correlation between illiteracy and infant mortality. How can we hold constant economic development of course, before we can do anything, we must have some measure of economic development, and I will use GNP (gross national product) per capita for this purpose.

Given this measure, then, a reasonable approach would be to divide the sample of nations into three groups: those with high, with moderate, and with low GNP per capita. Then the correlation between illiteracy and infant mortality rate can be calculated separately within each group.

We would then have three different correlations between illiteracy and infant mortality, at different economic levels. We could then calculate the average of these three correlations (weighting by the number of nations in each sample) to determine an overall correlation, *holding constant economic development*. The result would be the partial correlation coefficient.

As a second intuitive approach, consider the deviations d_i between the actual magnitudes and the perfect correlation line for two variables. This deviation measures the amount of variation in X_j unrelated to X_k. It is called the residual.

Now, consider two separate plots, one for the correlation between GNP per capita and illiteracy; the other for the correlation between GNP per capita and infant mortality. In each case, GNP per capita would be X_k, the horizontal axis. For each plot there will be a perfect correlation line, from which can be calculated the residuals for GNP per capita and illiteracy, and for GNP per capita and infant mortality. These two sets of residuals, di, measure the independence of illiteracy and infant mortality from GNP per capita.

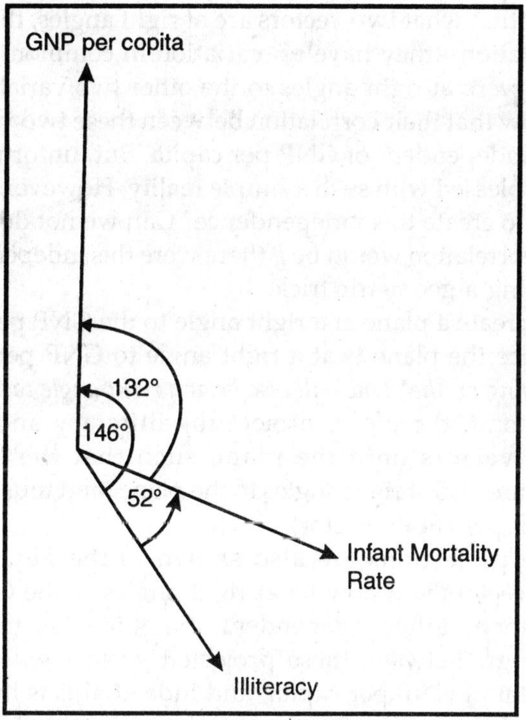

With this in mind, consider. What we are after is the correlation between the two variables with the effect of economic development, as measured by GNP per capita, removed. But are not these residuals exactly the two variables with these effects taken out? Of course. Therefore, it seems reasonable to define the partial correlation as the product moment correlation between these residuals—between the d_i for illiteracy and the d_i for infant mortality—which would be.13. And in fact, this is the partial correlation.

The third intuitive approach is geometrical. Before, I showed that the cosine of the angle between two variables, each interpreted as a vector, was identical to the correlation, when the means were subtracted from the magnitudes. It can be seen that GNP per capita has negative correlations (angles over 90°) with the other two variables, and is in fact -.67 for GNP per capita with infant mortality and -.83 with illiteracy.

Recall that what two vectors are at right angles, they have zero correlation—they have no variation in common. If GNP per capita were at right angles to the other two variables, we would know that their correlation between these two variables would be independent of GNP per capita. But, unfortunately, we are not blessed with such a simple reality. However, is there not a way to create this independence? Can we not determine what this correlation would be *if* there were this independence? Yes, by using a geometric trick.

First, create a plane at a right angle to the GNP per capita vector. Since the plane is at a right angle to GNP per capita, *anything lying on the plane will also be at a right angle to GNP per capita.* Second, therefore, project the illiteracy and infant mortality vectors onto the plane such that the lines of projection are also at right angles to the plane (and thus parallel to the GNP per capita vector).

These projections are also shown in the Figure. The projected vectors will now be at right angles to the GNP per capita vector and thus independent of it. It follows, therefore, that the angle between these projected vectors will also be independent of GNP per capita, and indeed, this is the case.

Now, since we are after the correlation between illiteracy and infant mortality, holding constant (independent of) GNP per capita, it appears intuitively reasonable to consider the cosine of between the projected vectors as this correlation. Cosine is, as we know, the product moment correlation for mean-deviation data (which we are assuming), and is the angle independent of GNP per capita. In fact, cosine (= 82.53°) is the partial correlation between illiteracy and infant mortality and equals 13.

To conclude, the three approaches—grouping, residuals, and vectors—to understanding partial correlation provide insight into what it means to assess the variation between two variables independent of a third. What remains is to present the formula for doing this, which is

Equation:

$$r_{jk.m} = (r_{jk} - r_{jm}r_{km}) / ((1 - r^2_{jm})(1 - r^2_{km}))^{1/2},$$

where:

$r_{jk.m}$ = partial correlation between X_j and X_k, holding X_m constant;

r_{jk}, r_{jm}, r_{km} = product moment correlations between X_j, X_k, and X_m.

For illiteracy and infant mortality, partialling out the influence of GNP per capita, the formula equations of GNP per capita, the formula equals

$$r_{jk.m} = (.61 - (-.67)(-.83)) / ((1 - (-.67)^2)(1 - (-.83)^2))^{1/2} = .13.$$

The partial correlation of.13 is quite a drop from the original correlation of.61 between illiteracy and infant mortality, a sharp decrease from 37 percent to 2 percent covariation. Thus, the hypothesis of an underlying economic development influencing the correlation between these two variables surely has substance.

The discussion of partial correlation has been only in terms of one external influence—a third variable. Partial correlation, however, can be generalized to any number of other variables, and formulas for their calculation are readily available in standard statistical texts. My concern here was not to present these extensions, but to provide a description of the underlying logic. Once this logic is clear for a third variable, then understanding what is involved when holding constant more than one variable is straight forward.

THE CORRELATION MATRIX

When the correlation between many variables is computed, they are often organized in matrix form for the selected sample data. Since the correlation r_{jk} between X_j and X_k is the same as r_{kj} between X_k and X_j, only the bottom triangular portion of the matrix is given.

The matrix provides a way of easily comparing correlations (this shows the virtue of having a correlation which is *comparative,* i.e., which is not dependent on the units of the original data, and which has the same upper and lower bounds of +1.00 and same interpretation regardless of the variables) and determining clusters of variables that covary.

Such is often aided visually by noting the high correlations, as dcne by parentheses in the matrix. And more systematic methods are available for defining the interrelationships among the variables as displayed in the table, such as factor analysis.

The correlation matrix is basic to many kinds of analysis. It is a bridge over which scientists can move from their data to sophisticated statistical analyses of patterns, dimensions, factors, causes, dependencies, discriminations, taxonomies, or hierarchies. In its own right, however, the correlation matrix contains much useful knowledge.

- Each coefficient measures the degree and direction (sign) of the correlation between the row and column variables.
- Each correlation squared defines the proportion of covariation between these variables.
- Each correlation is the cosine of the angle between the variables as vectors of mean-deviation data.

The correlation matrix can be directly computed from the original data matrix.

TECHNICAL APPENDIX

Let the data of given above Table be standardized by column variable and denote the standardized matrix as Z_{nxm}. Z has 14 rows (n) and 10 columns (m).

Then,

$$(1/n)Z'_{mxn}Z_{nxm} = R_{mxm}$$

where

R = the 14 × 14 variable correlation matrix (were the upper triangle of correlations filled in);

R = a symmetric, Gramian matrix.

For empirical data, R is usually (but not always) nonsingular.

SIGNIFICANCE

The correlation coefficient is descriptive. It measures the covariation in the magnitudes of two things. Often, however, this covariation is only a spring board to saying something about the population (or universe) from which the cases were taken, such as of all nations from the correlation for the variables.

But chance affects our observations in many ways, and we should have some systematic method of assessing the likelihood of our results being accidental before rushing to categorical generalizations. Then, we are concerned with one of two questions:

- What is the possibility of computing a particular correlation or greater (in absolute values) by chance?
- Considering the cases as a sample, what is the chance of getting the correlation computed or greater (in absolute values) when in fact the correlation should be zero?

The first is a question of likelihood, given a particular set of observations; the second is a question of sample significance, given a particular sample of observations from a larger universe. I will consider both questions in turn, and my approach will be intuitive and conceptual rather than statistical.

Likelihood

If we have a bowl of 50 colored balls, of which 2 are white, 5 blue, and the rest black, by chance we should blindly pull one ball out of the bowl which is white 2 times out of 50 on the average, (if each ball is returned after being selected), or with a probability (p) of $p = 2/50 = .04$. Similarly, the probability of by chance selecting a blue ball is $p = 5/50 = .10$; of a black ball is p = (50 - 2 - 5) / 50 = 43/50 = .86. Clearly, one is likely to get a black ball in a blind selection, and very unlikely to get a white ball, although such could occur, of course.

The same approach is applicable to assessing the role of chance on the correlation calculated. Consider the defence budget and trade magnitudes for the fourteen nations. Given these magnitudes, what is the likelihood of getting by chance the joint combination of trade and defence budget magnitudes that would be correlated .71 or greater?

Mathematical statisticians have developed complex formulas for determining such probabilities, from which standard tables have been computed for statistical reference books. A simplified version which divides the correlation coefficients into the five probability levels shown for differing numbers of cases N.

Using this table, we can see that a correlation of .71 or greater for 14 nations (N) has a probability of less than.005 of occurring by chance. That is, less than one out of 200 random combinations of our observations should yield a .71 correlation or greater. It follows that the .71 correlation between trade and defence budget is meaningful, in the sense of being unlikely a chance result, given all the possible paired combinations of the data for the 14 cases on the two variables.

But, of course, any result can still occur by chance. One could on a first try blindly select the one of two white balls out of 50. One could win a lottery with odds of a million to one, also. So the .71 correlation could still be a chance happening. But if on different observations for different years and nations, we continue to get such a correlation, then our confidence in discarding chance as a possibility increases—our conviction grows that there is some underlying relationship or cause, as we would suspect something other than chance if a person won the Irish sweepstakes three years in a row.

However, assume we had hypothesized that a non-zero correlation exists between trade and defence budget, that we selected nations and observation in a way not to favour our hypothesis, and then we computed the correlation of .71. The probability of getting by chances such a correlation, or higher, is less than one out of two-hundred times, if in fact the correlation should be zero. This suggests that our hypothesis is correct. Correlations among data collected to test previously stated hypothesis always have more power than correlations which are simply assessed (exploratory). Babe Ruth's famous home run slammed over the centerfield he had just pointed to, gave him stature unattainable by any unpredicted home run.

Sample Significance

A second way of looking at the magnitudes on two variables is as a sample representing a population. The data on trade and defence budget on 14 nations could have been collected such that from the correlations inferences about all nations could be made. To do this requires selecting the sample in a random or stratified manner so as to best reflect the population of nations. For example, such a sample might be collected of 100 students attending the University of Hawaii to determine the correlation between drug use and grades; of 500 Hawaiian residents to assess the correlation between ethnicity and liberalism in Hawaii; of 1,500 national television viewers to ascertain the correlation between programming and violence.

Now, assume the fourteen nations we have used to assess the correlation between trade and defence budget is a good sample, i.e., well reflects all nations. Then what inference about all nations can be made from a correlation of .71 between the two variables? A useful way of answering this is in terms of an alternative hypothesis. If in reality there were a zero or negative correlation in fact for all nations, what would be the probability of getting by chance at least the correlation found? That is, what is the chance of a plus .71 or higher being found for the sample when the correlation is zero or negative in the population?

The answer to this is given by the probability levels, where we find the probability to be less than.005, or less than one out of two hundred. This can be interpreted as follows: *The probability is less than .005 that we would be wrong in rejecting the hypothesis that the population correlation is zero or negative.* With such a low probability of error, we might confidently reject this hypothesis, and accept that there is a positive correlation between trade and defence budgets for all nations.

In other words, we can infer that our sample results reflect the nature of the population. They are statistically *significant.*

What if the alternative hypothesis were that a zero correlation exists between the two variables? Then, our concern would be with the probability of getting a plus *or* minus sample correlation of .71, or absolutely greater, were the alternative hypothesis true.

This is a "two-tailed" probability in the sense that we are after the chance of a plus or minus correlation. The probability of wrongfully rejecting the hypothesis of a population zero correlation is thus less than one out of a hundred. Therefore, most would feel confident in inferring that a non-zero correlation exists between trade and defence expenditures.

Statistical versus Practical Significance

There are, therefore, two types of statistical significance. One is the likelihood of getting by chance the particular correlation or greater between two sets of magnitudes; the second is the probability of getting a sample correlation by chance from a population. In either case, the significance of result increases—the probability of the result being by chance decreases—as the number of cases increases.

Simply consider the column in the table for the probability of .05, and notice how the correlation that meets this level decreases as N increases. For an N of 5 a correlation must be as high as.80 to be significant at .05; but for an N of 1,000, a correlation of .05 is significant.

Therefore, very small correlations can be significant at very low probabilities of their being chance results, even though the variance in common is nil.

Clearly, one can have significant results statistically, when there is very little variation in common. A high significance does not mean a strong relationship. Even though for 1,000 cases, 99.75 percent of the variation between two variables is *not in common,* the small covariation that does exist can *significantly* differ from zero.

Table. Significance Versus Covariation

N	*Significant at .05*	*Variance in common (Z)*
5	.80	64
10	.55	30
20	.38	14
100	.17	3
250	.10	1
1,000	.05	0.25

Which should one consider, then? Significance or variance in common? This depends on what one is testing or concerned about.

If one wants results from which to make forecasts or predictions, correlations of even .7 or .8 may not be sufficient, no matter how significant, since there is still much unrelated variance. If one's results are to be a base for policy decisions, only a high percent of variance in common may be acceptable. But if one is interested in uncovering relationships, no matter how small, then significance is of concern.

SAMPLE VERSUS POPULATION

Can one determine the significance of a correlation for a population? Say we had computed the correlation between trade and defence budget for all nations and found .71. Could we ask whether this is significant? Yes, when we keep in mind the two types of significance. Clearly, this is not a sample correlation and sample significance is meaningless. But, we can assess the likelihood of this being a chance correlation between the two sets of magnitudes for all nations.

Fortunately, both types of significance can be assessed using the same probability table.

Assumptions

The formulas mathematical statisticians have developed

for assessing significance require certain assumptions for this derivation. As the data depart from these assumptions, the tables of probabilities for the correlation are less applicable.

Both types of significance described here assume a normal distribution for both variables, i.e., that the magnitudes approximate a bell-shaped distribution.

When sampling significance is of concern, the observations are assumed drawn from a bivariate normal population. That is, were the frequencies of observation plotted for both variables for the population, then they would be distributed in the shape of a bell placed on the middle of a plane, with the lower flanges widening out and merging into the flat surface.

By virtue of these distributive requirements, the assessment of significance also demands that the data be interval or ratio measurements, i.e., data like that for trade, GNP per capita, defence budget, GNP for defence, or U.S. agreement. Dichotomous data, as that for stability and foreign conflict, or rank order data, as that for power, cannot have the significance of their product moment correlations assessed.

Different Coefficients Of Correlation

I have focused upon the product moment correlation coefficient throughout. It is the most widely used coefficient and for many scientists the only one. Indeed, most computer programs computing correlations employ the product moment without so informing their users in the programme write up. But useful alternatives do exist. And a good understanding of correlations requires an appreciation of these alternatives and their rationale. Here I will describe the most popular alternatives conceptually, leaving the statistical and computational details to the literature.

Alternatives

If the magnitudes on two variables are rank-order data, then two types of rank correlation coefficients offer alternatives to the product moment: the *Spearman* and the *Kendall* coefficients. Both utilize the same amount of information in the observations, although not as much as the product moment.

The statistical significance of both can be assessed, and partial correlations can be computed for the Kendall coefficient. However, the Spearman and Kendall coefficients give *different* values for the same observations and are not directly comparable. The Spearman coefficient is the product moment, revised specifically for rank order data.

Other alternative correlation coefficients are applicable to dichotomous data—observations in two variables that comprise only two magnitudes. There are the phi, phi-ove-phi-max, and tetrachoric coefficients. The *phi* is the product moment applied to dichotomous data and is also a function of the chi-square of a fourfold table, thus enabling the statistical significance of the phi to be assessed. The range of phi is between -1.00 at +1.00 if the margins of the fourfold table are equal.

For unequal marginals the range of the phi is restricted. That is, a perfect phi correlation between two dichotomous variables may be less than an absolute value of 1.00. Thus, different phi coefficients may not be comparable. The maximum possible value of phi for given marginals can be computed and used to form the *phi-over-phi-mix* correlation coefficient, which is the ratio of phi to the maximum possible phi given the marginals. Regardless of marginal values, then, phi-over-phi-max will be plus or minus 1.00 in the case of perfect correlation, and these coefficients will be comparable for different variables.

However, the phi-over-phi-max makes a strong assumption that the underlying bivariate distribution in the data is rectangular. Moreover, this coefficient has an increasingly steep approach to 1.00 as the number of cases with the two magnitudes become increasingly disproportionate. In addition to the phi-over-phi-max coefficient for dichotomous data, the *tetrachoric* coefficient could be computed.

This estimates the value of the product moment correlation, if the *dichotomous data are drawn from a normal distribution*. The basic assumption of the tetrachoric, therefore, is that the underlying distribution of the data is bivariate normal. However, in contrast to the phi coefficient, the tetrachoric does not have its range affected by unequal data marginals and its significance can be assessed using appropriate tables.

PATTERN-MAGNITUDE COEFFICIENTS

The correlation and alternative coefficients measure the *pattern* similarity of the magnitudes for two variables—their *covariation*. Sometimes, however, it may be useful to measure both pattern and *magnitude* correlation. A number of pattern-magnitude correlation coefficients have been developed. One that is particularly useful is the *intraclass* correlation coefficient, which can be applied to any number of variables.

Just restricting it to two variables, however, the intraclass divides their variance into two parts. One is the variance of each case on the two variables and is called the within-class variance. If the magnitudes for each case on the two variables are the same, this variance is zero. The second part is the variance of the variable across the cases, which is the between-class variance. The intraclass correlation is then simply the between-class minus the within-class variance as a ratio to the sum of the two kinds of variance. And the significance of this ratio can be assessed.

For two variables, the intraclass will range between -1.00 and +1.00. When it is 1.00, each case has identical magnitudes for each variable—all the variation is across cases. When it is -1.00, all the variation is due to each case having different magnitudes on each variable.

CONSIDERATIONS

Two things are correlated if they covary positively or negatively. And we have a widely used, mathematically based, coefficient called the product moment for determining this correlation. This coefficient will describe the correlation between any two variables, regardless of their type of measurement. If, however, the statistical significance of the correlation is of concern, then to assess this significance interval or ratio measurement and normal distributions are assumed. Alternative correlation coefficients are available for specific purposes and types of data. Moreover, if the data do not meet the assumptions required for assessing the significance of the product moment, then these alternative coefficients may enable significance to be determined. The product moment, and indeed, most alternative coefficients, measure pattern correlation. Alternatives, especially the intraclass, are available to also measure both pattern at magnitude correlation, however.

Whether describing the data or regarding significance, the correlation coefficient measures linear correlations, i.e., that along a straight line. Even were observations to fall exactly on a curve, the product moment or alternative coefficients would show a zero or low linear correlation. The product moment correlation is sensitive to extreme magnitudes. Extreme cases can have many times the effect of other cases on the correlation coefficient. The correlation coefficient may thus "hang" on a few cases with unusually large or small magnitudes, and data transformation or alternative correlations might be used to avoid this problem.

Errors in the data on two variables can make the correlation coefficient higher or lower than it should be. However, error that is random—uncorrelated among themselves or with the true magnitudes—only depresses the absolute correlation. Thus the correlation coefficient for data with random error understates the real correlation and is thus *a conservative measure.* The correlation between two variables may be influenced by other variables. Formulas are available, fortunately, to determine these influences and remove them from the correlation. Therefore, if outside influences are suspected, a high, low, or zero correlation between two variables should not be accepted at face value and partial correlations, holding constant these extraneous influences, can be calculated.

There is a geometry of correlation in terms of vectors that provides an intuitively and heuristically powerful picture of correlation. This is simply the cosine of the angle between two variables of mean-deviation data plotted as vectors. Correlation between magnitudes on variables for a specific time period (such as power and defence budget for 1955) do not indicate the correlations between these variables over time (such as for power and defence budget by year in the U.S., 1946-75). Similarly, over time correlations do not indicate what the correlations would be for cases at a point in time. That is, for the same variables cross-sectional and time series correlations are independent.

Finally, the correlation coefficient is a useful and potentially powerful tool. It can aid understanding reality, but it is no substitute for insight, reason, and imagination. The correlation coefficient is a flashlight of the mind.

It must be turned on and directed by our interests and knowledge; and it can help gratify and illuminate both. But like a flashlight, it can be uselessly turned on in the daytime, used unnecessarily beneath a lamp, employed to search for something in the wrong room, or become a play thing. Understanding correlations understands both the nature of the coefficient and its dependence on human intelligence, intuition, and competence.

RANK DIFFERENCE METHOD, PEARSON'S PRODUCT MOMENT METHOD – CALCULATION, INTERPRETATION AND USES

In statistics, the Pearson product-moment correlation coefficient (sometimes referred to as the MCV or PMCC, and typically denoted by *r*) is a common measure of the correlation (linear dependence) between two variables *X* and *Y*. It is very widely used in the sciences as a measure of the strength of linear dependence between two variables, giving a value somewhere between +1 and -1 inclusive. It was first introduced by Francis Galton in the 1880s, and named after Karl Pearson.

In accordance with the usual convention, when calculated for an entire population, the Pearson product-moment correlation is typically designated by the analogous Greek letter, which in this case is ñ (rho). Hence its designation by the Latin letter *r* implies that it has been computed for a sample (to provide an estimate for that of the underlying population). For these reasons, it is sometimes called "Pearson's r."

The statistic is defined as the sum of the products of the standard scores of the two measures divided by the degrees of freedom. If the data comes from a sample, then

$$r = \frac{1}{n-1}\sum_{i=1}^{n}\left(\frac{X_i - \bar{X}}{s_X}\right)\left(\frac{Y_i - \bar{Y}}{s_Y}\right)$$

where

$$\frac{X_i - \bar{X}}{s_X}, \bar{X}, \text{and } s_X$$

are the standard score, sample mean, and sample standard deviation (calculated using n " 1 in the denominator).

If the data comes from a population, then

$$\rho = \frac{1}{n}\sum_{i=1}^{n}\left(\frac{X_i - \mu_X}{\sigma_X}\right)\left(\frac{Y_i - \mu_Y}{\sigma_Y}\right)$$

where

$$\frac{X_i - \mu_X}{\sigma_X}, \mu_X, \text{and } \sigma_X$$

are the standard score, population mean, and population standard deviation (calculated using n in the denominator).

The result obtained is equivalent to dividing the covariance between the two variables by the product of their standard deviations.

INTERPRETATION

The coefficient ranges from "1 to 1. A value of 1 shows that a linear equation describes the relationship perfectly and positively, with all data points lying on the same line and with Y increasing with X. A score of "1 shows that all data points lie on a single line but that Y increases as X decreases. A value of 0 shows that a linear model is not needed – that there is no linear relationship between the variables.

The linear equation that best describes the relationship between X and Y can be found by linear regression. This equation can be used to "predict" the value of one measurement from knowledge of the other. That is, for each value of X the equation calculates a value which is the best estimate of the values of Y corresponding the specific value. We denote this predicted variable by Y'.

Any value of Y can therefore be defined as the sum of $Y2$ and the difference between Y and $Y2$:

$$Y = Y' + (Y - Y').$$

The variance of Y is equal to the sum of the variance of the two components of Y:

$$S_y^2 = S_{y'}^2 + S_{y.x}^2$$

Since the coefficient of determination implies that $s_{y.x}^2 = s_y^2(1 \text{ " } r^2)$ we can derive the identity

$$r^2 = \frac{S_{y'}^2}{S_y^2}.$$

The square of r is conventionally used as a measure of the association between X and Y. For example, if r^2 is 0.90, then 90% of the variance of Y can be "accounted for" by changes in X and the linear relationship between X and Y.

GAUSSIANITY

The use of mean and standard deviation in the calculation above may imply that the use of the coefficient requires one to assume that X and Y are normally distributed. The coefficient is fully defined without reference to such assumptions, and it has widespread practical use with the assumption being made. However, if X and Y are assumed to have a bivariate normal distribution certain theoretical results can be derived. Possibly the most useful of these are the formula for the asymptotic (large sample size) variance of the estimated correlation coefficient. Other formulae relate to the probability distribution of the sample estimate and approximations for this.

REGRESSION AND PREDICTION, CHI SQUARE TEST, ITS COMPUTATION AND USES

In statistics, linear regression is used for two things;

- To construct a simple formula that will predict a

value or values for a variable given the value of another variable.

- To test whether and how a given variable is related to another variable or variables.

Note: correlation does not imply causation. Linear regression is a form of regression analysis in which the relationship between one or more independent variables and another variable, called the dependent variable, is modelled by a least squares function, called a linear regression equation. This function is a linear combination of one or more model parameters, called regression coefficients.

A linear regression equation with one independent variable represents a straight line when the predicted value (i.e. the dependant variable from the regression equation) is plotted against the independent variable: this is called a simple linear regression. However, note that "linear" does not refer to this straight line, but rather to the way in which the regression coefficients occur in the regression equation. The results are subject to statistical analysis.

THEORETICAL MODEL

A linear regression model assumes, given a random sample, $\left(Y_i, X_{i1}, \ldots, X_{ip}\right), i = 1, \ldots, n$ a possibly imperfect relationship between Y_i, the regress, and the regressors $X_{i1}, \ldots, X_{ip}$. A disturbance term ϵ_i, which is a random variable too, is added to this assumed relationship to capture the influence of everything else on Y_i other than. Hence, the multiple linear regression model takes the following form:

$$Y_i = \beta_0 + \beta_1 X_{i1} + \beta_2 X_{i2} + \cdots + \beta_p X_{ip} + \epsilon_i, \qquad i = 1, \ldots, n$$

Note that the regressors are also called independent variables, exogenous variables, covariates, input variables or predictor variables. Similarly, regressands are also called dependent variables, response variables, measured variables, or predicted variables.

Models which do not conform to this specification may be treated by nonlinear regression. A linear regression model need not be a linear function of the independent variable: *linear* in this context means that the conditional mean of Y_i is linear in the parameters β. For example, the model

$$Y_i = \beta_1 X_i + \beta_2 X_i^2 + \epsilon_i$$

is linear in the parameters β_1 and β_2, but it is not linear in, a nonlinear function of X_i. An illustration of this model is shown in the example, below.

DATA AND ESTIMATION

It is important to distinguish the model formulated in terms of random variables and the observed values of these random variables. Typically, the observed values, or data, denoted by lower case letters, consist of n values

$$\left(y_i, x_{i1}, \ldots x_{ip}\right), i = 1, \ldots, n.$$

In general there are $p + 1$ parameters to be determined, $\beta_0, \ldots, \beta_p$. In order to estimate the parameters it is often useful to use the matrix notation

$$Y = X\beta + \epsilon$$

where Y is a column vector that includes the observed values of $Y_1, \ldots, Y_n$, ε includes the unobserved stochastic components $\varepsilon_1, \ldots, \varepsilon_n$ and the matrix X the observed values of the regressors

$$X = \begin{pmatrix} 1 & x_{11} & \cdots & x_{1p} \\ 1 & x_{21} & \cdots & x_{2p} \\ \vdots & \vdots & \ddots & \vdots \\ 1 & x_{n1} & \cdots & x_{np} \end{pmatrix}$$

X includes, typically, a constant column, that is, a column which does not vary across observations, which is used to represent the intercept term β_0.

If there is any *linear* dependence among the columns of X, then the vector of parameters β cannot be estimated by least squares unless β is constrained, as, for example, by requiring the sum of some of its components to be 0. However, some linear combinations of the components of β may still be uniquely estimable in such cases. For example, the model $Y_i = \beta_1 X_i + \beta_2 2X_i + \varepsilon_i$ cannot be solved for β_1 and β_2

independently as the matrix of observations has the reduced rank 2. In this case the model can be rewritten as

$$Y_i = (\beta_1 + 2\beta_2) X_i + \varepsilon_i$$

and can be solved to give a value for the composite entity $\beta_1 + 2\beta_2$.

Note that to only perform a least squares estimation of $\beta_0, \beta_1, \ldots, \beta_p$ it is not necessary to consider the sample as random variables. It may even be conceptually simpler to consider the sample as fixed, observed values, as we have done thus far. However in the context of hypothesis testing and confidence intervals, it will be necessary to interpret the sample as random variables

$$(Y_i, X_{i1}, \ldots, X_{ip}), i = 1, \ldots, n$$

that will produce estimators which are themselves random variables. Then it will be possible to study the distribution of the estimators and draw inferences.

CLASSICAL ASSUMPTIONS

Classical assumptions for linear regression include the assumptions that the sample is selected at random from the population of interest, that the dependent variable is continuous on the real line, and that the error terms follow identical and independent normal distributions, that is, that the errors are i.i.d. and Gaussian.

Note that these assumptions imply that the error term does not statistically depend on the values of the independent variables, that is, that is statistically independent of the predictor variables.

This article adopts these assumptions unless otherwise stated. Note that all of these assumptions may be relaxed, depending on the nature of the true probabilistic model of the problem at hand. The issue of choosing which assumptions to relax, which functional form to adopt, and other choices related to the underlying probabilistic model are known as *specification searches*.

In particular note that the assumption that the error terms are normally distributed is of no consequence unless the sample is very small because central limit theorems imply that, so long as the error terms have finite variance and are not too strongly correlated, the parameter estimates will be approximately normally distributed even when the underlying errors are not.

Under these assumptions, an equivalent formulation of simple linear regression that explicitly shows the linear regression as a model of conditional expectation can be given as

$$E(Y_i \mid X_i = x_i) = \alpha + \beta x_i$$

The conditional expected value of Y_i given X_i is an affine function of X_i. Note that this expression follows from the assumption that the mean of ε_i is zero conditional on X_i.

LEAST-SQUARES ANALYSIS

Least Squares Estimates

The first objective of regression analysis is to best-fit the data by estimating the parameters of the model. Of the different criteria that can be used to define what constitutes a best fit, the least squares criterion is a very powerful one. This estimate (or estimator, if we are in the context of a random sample), is given by

$$\hat{\beta} = \left(X^T X\right)^{-1} X^T y$$

For a full derivation see Linear least squares.

Regression inference

The estimates can be used to test various hypotheses.

Denote by σ^2 the variance of the error term ε (recall we assume that $\varepsilon_i \sim N\left(0, \sigma^2\right)$ for every $i = 1, \ldots, n$). An unbiased estimate of σ^2 is given by

$$\hat{\sigma}^2 = \frac{S}{n-p},$$

where $S := \sum_{i=1}^{n} \hat{\varepsilon}_i^2$ is the sum of square residuals. The relation between the estimate and the true value is:

$$\hat{\sigma}^2 \cdot \frac{n-p}{\sigma^2} \sim \chi_{n-p}^2$$

where χ_{n-p}^2 has Chi-square distribution with $n-p$ degrees of freedom.

The solution to the normal equations can be written as

$$\hat{\beta} = \left(X^T X\right)^{-1} X^T y.$$

This shows that the parameter estimators are linear combinations of the dependent variable. It follows that, if the observational errors are normally distributed, the parameter estimators will follow a joint normal distribution. Under the assumptions here, the estimated parameter vector is exactly distributed,

$$\hat{\beta} \sim N\left(\beta, \sigma^2 \left(X^T X\right)^{-1}\right)$$

where N denotes the multivariate normal distribution.

The standard error of a parameter estimator is given by

$$\hat{\sigma}_j = \sqrt{\frac{S}{n-p-1}\left[\left(X^T X\right)^{-1}\right]_{jj}}$$

The 100(1 " α)% confidence interval for the parameter, β_j, is computed as follows:

$$\hat{\beta}_j \pm t_{\frac{\alpha}{2}, n-p-1} \hat{\sigma}_j.$$

The residuals can be expressed as

$$\hat{r} = y - X\hat{\beta} = y - X\left(X^T X\right)^{-1} X^T y.$$

The matrix $X\left(X^T X\right)^{-1} X^T$ is known as the hat matrix and has the useful property that it is idempotent. Using this property it can be shown that, if the errors are normally distributed, the residuals will follow a normal distribution with covariance matrix $\left(I - X\left(X^T X\right) - 1X^T\right)y.$. Studentized residuals are useful in testing for outliers. The hat matrix is the matrix of the orthogonal projection onto the column space of the matrix X.

Given a value of the independent variable, x_d, the predicted response is calculated as

$$yd = \sum_{j=1}^{p} x_{dj}\hat{\beta}_j.$$

Writing the elements x_{dj}, $j = 1, p$ as, z the 100(1 – α)% mean response confidence interval for the prediction is given, using error propagation theory, by:

$$z^T\hat{\beta} \pm t_{\frac{\alpha}{2}, n-p}\, \hat{\sigma}\sqrt{z^T\left(X^TX\right)^{-1} z}.$$

The 100(1 " α)% predicted response confidence intervals for the data are given by:

$$z^T\hat{\beta} \pm t_{\frac{\alpha}{2}, n-p}\, \hat{\sigma}\sqrt{1+z^T\left(X^TX\right)^{-1} z}.$$

Univariate linear case

We consider here the case of the simplest regression model, $Y = \alpha + \beta X + \varepsilon$. In order to estimate α and β, we have a sample of observations which are, here, not seen as random variables and denoted by lower case letters. As stated in the introduction, however, we might want to interpret the sample in terms of random variables in some other contexts than least squares estimation.

The idea of least squares estimation is to minimize the following *unknown* quantity, the sum of squared errors:

$$\sum_{i=1}^{n} \epsilon_i^2 = \sum_{i=1}^{n} (y_1 - \alpha - \beta x_i)^2$$

Taking the derivative of the preceding expression with respect to α and β yields the *normal equations:*

$$n\,\alpha + \sum_{i=1}^{n} x_i\,\beta = \sum_{i=1}^{n} y_i$$

$$\sum_{i=1}^{n} x_i\ \alpha = \sum_{i=1}^{n} x_i^2\ \beta = \sum_{i=1}^{n} x_i y_i$$

This is a linear system of equations which can be solved using Cramer's rule:

$$\hat{\beta} = \frac{n\sum_{i=1}^{n} x_i y_i - \sum_{i=1}^{n} x_i \sum_{i=1}^{n} y_i}{n\sum_{i=1}^{n} x_i^2 - \left(\sum_{i=1}^{n} x_i\right)^2} = \frac{\sum_{i=1}^{n}(x_i - \bar{x})(y_i - \bar{y})}{\sum_{i=1}^{n}(x_i - \bar{x})^2}$$

$$\hat{\alpha} = \frac{\sum_{i=1}^{n} x_i^2 \sum_{i=1}^{n} y_i - \sum_{i=1}^{n} x_i \sum_{i=1}^{n} x_i y_i}{n\sum_{i=1}^{n} x_i^2 - \left(\sum_{i=1}^{n} x_i\right)^2} = \bar{y} - \bar{x}\hat{\beta}$$

$$S = \sum_{i=1}^{n}(y_i - \hat{y}_i)^2 = \sum_{i=1}^{n} y_i^2 - \frac{n\left(\sum_{i=1}^{n} x_i y_i\right)^2 + \left(\sum_{i=1}^{n} y_i\right)^2 \sum_{i=1}^{n} x_i^2 - 2\sum_{i=1}^{n} x_i \sum_{i=1}^{n} y_i \sum_{i=1}^{n} x_i y_i}{n\sum_{i=1}^{n} x_i^2 - \left(\sum_{i=1}^{n} x_i\right)^2}$$

$$\hat{\sigma}^2 = \frac{S}{n-2}.$$

The covariance matrix is

$$\frac{1}{n\sum_{i=1}^{n} x_i^2 - \left(\sum_{i=1}^{n} x_i\right)^2}\begin{pmatrix} \sum x_i^2 & -\sum x_i \\ -\sum x_i & n \end{pmatrix}$$

The mean response confidence interval is given by

$$yd = \left(\alpha + \hat{\beta}x_d\right) \pm t_{\frac{\alpha}{2},n-2}\,\hat{\sigma}\sqrt{\frac{1}{n} + \frac{(x_d - \bar{x})^2}{\Sigma(x_i - \bar{x})^2}}$$

The predicted response confidence interval is given by

$$yd = \left(\alpha + \hat{\beta}x_d\right) \pm t_{\frac{\alpha}{2},n-2}\,\hat{\sigma}\sqrt{1 + \frac{1}{n} + \frac{(x_d - \bar{x})^2}{\Sigma(x_i - \bar{x})^2}}$$

The term $t_{\frac{\alpha}{2},n-2}$ is a reference to the Student's t-distribution. $\hat{\sigma}$ is standard error.

Analysis of Variance

In analysis of variance (ANOVA), the total sum of squares is split into two or more components.

The "total (corrected) sum of squares" is

$$\text{SST} = \sum_{i=1}^{n} (y_i - \bar{y})^2,$$

where

$$\bar{y} = \frac{1}{n}\sum_i y_i$$

("corrected" means has been subtracted from each y-value). Equivalently

$$\text{SST} = \sum_{i=1}^{n} y_i^2 - \frac{1}{n}\left(\sum_i y_i\right)^2$$

The total sum of squares is partitioned as the sum of the "regression sum of squares" SSReg (or RSS, also called the "explained sum of squares") and the "error sum of squares" SSE, which is the sum of squares of residuals.

The regression sum of squares is

$$SS\text{Re}g = \sum (\hat{y}_i - \bar{y})^2 = \hat{\beta}^T \text{X}^\text{T} y - \frac{1}{n}\left(y^T u u^T y\right),$$

where u is an n-by-1 vector in which each element is 1. Note that

$$y^T u = u^\text{T} y = \sum_i y_i,$$

and

$$\frac{1}{n} y^T u u^\text{T} y = \frac{1}{n}\left(\sum_i y_i\right)^2$$

The error (or "unexplained") sum of squares SSE, which is the sum of square of residuals, is given by

$$\text{SSE} = \sum (y_i - \hat{y}_i)^2 = y^T y - \hat{\beta}^T \text{X}^T y.$$

The total sum of squares SST is

$$SSE = \sum (y_i - \bar{y}_i)^2 = y^T y - \frac{1}{n}\left(y^T uu^T y\right) = \text{SSReg+SSE.}$$

Pearson's coefficient of regression, R^2 is then given as

$$R^2 = \frac{\text{SSReg}}{\text{SST}} = 1 - \frac{\text{SSE}}{\text{SST}}.$$

If the errors are independent and normally distributed with expected value 0 and they all have the same variance, then under the null hypothesis that all of the elements in $\beta = 0$ except the constant, the statistic

$$\frac{R^2 / (n-m)}{\left(1-R^2\right)/(m-1)}$$

follows an F-distribution with (m " 1) and (n " m) degrees of freedom (m is n " p). If that statistic is too large, then one rejects the null hypothesis. How large is too large depends on the level of the test, which is the tolerated probability of type I error; see statistical significance.

Example

To illustrate the various goals of regression, we give an example. The following data set gives the average heights and weights for American women aged 30–39 (source: *The World Almanac and Book of Facts, 1975*).

Height (m)	1.47	1.5	1.52	1.55	1.57	1.60	1.63	1.65	1.68	1.7	1.73	1.75	1.78	1.8	1.83
Weight (kg)	52.21	53.12	54.48	55.84	57.2	58.57	59.93	61.29	63.11	64.47	66.28	68.1	69.92	72.19	74.46

A plot of weight against height shows that it cannot be modeled by a straight line, so a regression is performed by modeling the data by a parabola.

$$Y_i = \beta_0 + \beta_1 X_i + \beta_2 X_i^2 + \varepsilon_i$$

where the dependent variable Y_i is weight and the independent variable X_i is height.

Place the observations $x_i, x_i^2, i = 1,\ldots,n$, in the matrix X.

$$x = \begin{pmatrix} 1 & 1.47 & 2.16 \\ 1 & 1.50 & 2.25 \\ 1 & 1.52 & 2.31 \\ 1 & 1.55 & 2.40 \\ 1 & 1.57 & 2.46 \\ 1 & 1.60 & 2.56 \\ 1 & 1.63 & 2.66 \\ 1 & 1.65 & 2.72 \\ 1 & 1.68 & 2.82 \\ 1 & 1.70 & 2.89 \\ 1 & 1.73 & 2.99 \\ 1 & 1.75 & 3.06 \\ 1 & 1.78 & 3.17 \\ 1 & 1.80 & 3.24 \\ 1 & 1.83 & 3.35 \end{pmatrix}$$

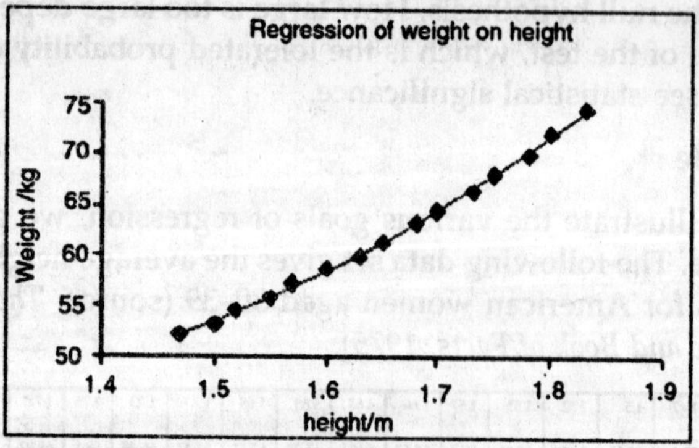

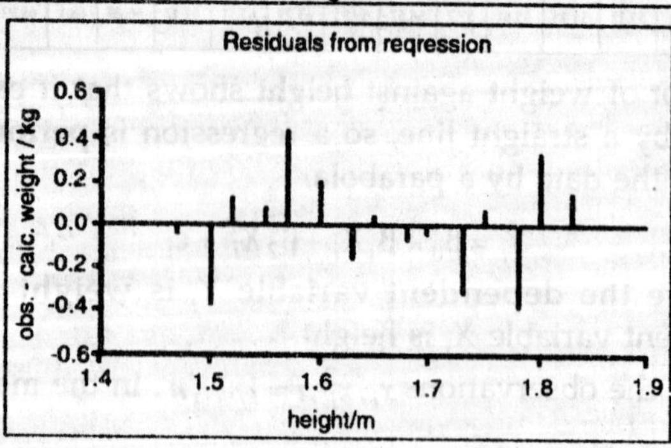

The values of the parameters are found by solving the normal equations

$$\left(X^T X\right)\hat{\beta} = X^T y$$

Element *ij* of the normal equation matrix, $X^T X$ is formed by summing the products of column *i* and column *j* of X.

$$x_{ij} = \sum_{k=1}^{15} x_{ki} x_{kj}$$

Element *i* of the right-hand side vector $X^T y$ is formed by summing the products of column *i* of X with the column of dependent variable values.

$$\left(X^T y\right)_i = \sum_{k=1}^{15} x_{ki} y_k$$

Thus, the normal equations are

$$\begin{pmatrix} 15 & 24.76 & 41.05 \\ 24.76 & 41.05 & 68.37 \\ 41.05 & 68.37 & 114.35 \end{pmatrix} \begin{pmatrix} \hat{\beta}_o \\ \hat{\beta}_1 \\ \hat{\beta}_2 \end{pmatrix} = \begin{pmatrix} 931 \\ 1548 \\ 2586 \end{pmatrix}$$

$\hat{\beta}_0 = 129 \pm 16$ (value ± standard deviation)3

$\hat{\beta}_1 = -143 \pm 20$

$$\hat{\beta}_2 = 62 \pm 6$$

The calculated values are given by

$$\hat{y}_1 = \hat{\beta}_0 + \hat{\beta}_1 x_1 + \hat{\beta}_2 x_i^2$$

The observed and calculated data are plotted together and the residuals, $y_i - \hat{y}_i$, are calculated and plotted. Standard deviations are calculated using the sum of squares, $S = 0.76$.

The confidence intervals are computed using:

$$\left[\hat{\beta}_j - \hat{\sigma}_j t_{m-n;1-\frac{\alpha}{2}};\ \hat{\beta}_j + \hat{\sigma}_j t_{m-n;1-\frac{\alpha}{2}}\right]$$

with α=5%, $t_{m-n;1-\frac{\alpha}{2}} = 2.2$. Therefore, we can say that the 95% confidence intervals are:

$$\hat{\beta}_0 \in [92.9, 164.7]$$
$$\hat{\beta}_1 \in [-186.88, -99.5]$$
$$\hat{\beta}_2 \in [-48.7, 75.2]$$

EXAMINING RESULTS OF REGRESSION MODELS

Checking model assumptions

Some of the model assumptions can be evaluated by calculating the residuals and plotting or otherwise analyzing them. The following plots can be constructed to test the validity of the assumptions:

- Residuals against the explanatory variables in the model, as illustrated above. The residuals should have no relation to these variables (look for possible non-linear relations) and the spread of the residuals should be the same over the whole range.
- Residuals against explanatory variables not in the model. Any relation of the residuals to these variables would suggest considering these variables for inclusion in the model.
- Residuals against the fitted values, $\hat{y}$.
- A time series plot of the residuals, that is, plotting the residuals as a function of time.
- Residuals against the preceding residual.
- A normal probability plot of the residuals to test normality. The points should lie along a straight line.

There should not be any noticeable pattern to the data in all but the last plot.

Assessing Goodness of fit

- The coefficient of determination gives what fraction of the observed variance of the response variable can be explained by the given variables.
- Examine the observational and prediction confidence intervals. In most contexts, the smaller they are the better.

OTHER PROCEDURES

Generalized Least Squares

Generalized least squares, which includes weighted least squares as a special case, can be used when the observational errors have unequal variance or serial correlation.

Errors-in-Variables Model

Errors-in-variables model or total least squares when the independent variables are subject to error.

Generalized Linear Model

Generalized linear model is used when the distribution function of the errors is not a Normal distribution. Examples include exponential distribution, gamma distribution, inverse Gaussian distribution, Poisson distribution, binomial distribution, multinomial distribution.

ROBUST REGRESSION

A host of alternative approaches to the computation of regression parameters are included in the category known as robust regression. One technique minimizes the mean absolute error, or some other function of the residuals, instead of mean squared error as in linear regression.

Robust regression is much more computationally intensive than linear regression and is somewhat more difficult to implement as well. While least squares estimates are not very sensitive to breaking the normality of the errors assumption, this is not true when the variance or mean of the error distribution is not bounded, or when an analyst that can identify outliers is unavailable.

Among Stata users, *Robust regression* is frequently taken to mean linear regression with Huber-White standard error estimates due to the naming conventions for regression commands. This procedure relaxes the assumption of homoscedasticity for variance estimates only; the predictors are still ordinary least squares (OLS) estimates. This occasionally leads to confusion; Stata users sometimes believe that linear regression is a robust method when this option is used, although it is actually not robust in the sense of outlier-resistance.

INSTRUMENTAL VARIABLES AND RELATED METHODS

The assumption that the error term in the linear model can be treated as uncorrelated with the independent variables will frequently be untenable, as omitted-variables bias, "reverse" causation, and errors-in-variables problems can generate such a correlation. Instrumental variable and other methods can be used in such cases.

Applications of Linear Regression

Linear regression is widely used in biological, behavioral and social sciences to describe possible relationships between variables. It ranks as one of the most important tools used in these disciplines.

TREND LINE

A trend line represents a trend, the long-term movement in time series data after other components have been accounted for. It tells whether a particular data set (say GDP, oil prices or stock prices) have increased or decreased over the period of time.

A trend line could simply be drawn by eye through a set of data points, but more properly their position and slope is calculated using statistical techniques like linear regression. Trend lines typically are straight lines, although some variations use higher degree polynomials depending on the degree of curvature desired in the line.

Trend lines are sometimes used in business analytics to show changes in data over time. This has the advantage of being simple. Trend lines are often used to argue that a particular action or event (such as training, or an advertising campaign) caused observed changes at a point in time. This is a simple technique, and does not require a control group, experimental design, or a sophisticated analysis technique.

However, it suffers from a lack of scientific validity in cases where other potential changes can affect the data.

Epidemiology

As one example, early evidence relating tobacco smoking to mortality and morbidity came from studies employing regression. Researchers usually include several variables in their regression analysis in an effort to remove factors that might produce spurious correlations. For the cigarette smoking example, researchers might include socio-economic status in addition to smoking to ensure that any observed effect of smoking on mortality is not due to some effect of education or income.

However, it is never possible to include all possible confounding variables in a study employing regression. For the smoking example, a hypothetical gene might increase mortality and also cause people to smoke more.

For this reason, randomized controlled trials are often able to generate more compelling evidence of causal relationships than correlational analysis using linear regression.

When controlled experiments are not feasible, variants of regression analysis such as instrumental variables and other methods may be used to attempt to estimate causal relationships from observational data.

Finance

The capital asset pricing model uses linear regression as well as the concept of Beta for analyzing and quantifying the systematic risk of an investment.

This comes directly from the Beta coefficient of the linear regression model that relates the return on the investment to the return on all risky assets.

Regression may not be the appropriate way to estimate beta in finance given that it is supposed to provide the volatility of an investment relative to the volatility of the market as a whole.

This would require that both these variables be treated in the same way when estimating the slope. Whereas regression treats all variability as being in the investment returns variable, i.e. it only considers residuals in the dependent variable.

Environmental Science

Linear regression finds application in a wide range of environmental science applications. For example, recent work published in the *Journal of Geophysical Research* used regression models to identify data contamination, which led to an overstatement of global warming trends over land.

Using the regression model to filter extraneous, nonclimatic effects reduced the estimated 1980–2002 global average temperature trends over land by about half.

Unit VII

Inferential Statistics

ELEMENTARY IDEAS OF PROBABILITY: THE NORMAL DISTRIBUTION - ITS PROPERTIES AND USES

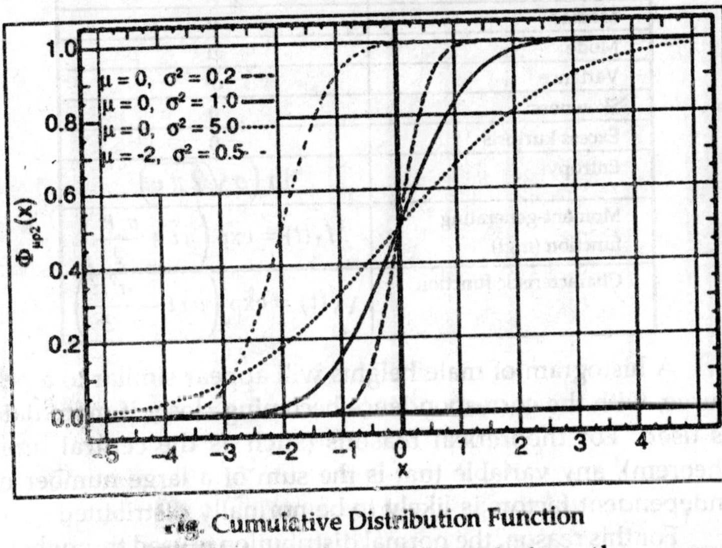

Fig. Cumulative Distribution Function

In probability theory and statistics, the normal distribution or Gaussian distribution is a continuous probability distribution that describes data that clusters around a mean or average. The graph of the associated probability density function is bell-shaped, with a peak at the mean, and is known as the Gaussian function or bell curve. The normal distribution can be used to describe, at least approximately, any variable that tends to cluster around the mean. For example, the heights of adult males in the United States are roughly normally distributed, with a mean of about 70 inches. Most men have a height close to the mean, though a small number of outliers have a height significantly above or below the mean.

Colors match the image above	
Parameters	μ location (real) $\sigma^2 > 0$ squared scale (real)
Support	$x \in \mathbb{R}$
Probability density function (pdf)	$\frac{1}{\sigma\sqrt{2\pi}} \exp\left(-\frac{(x-\mu)^2}{2\sigma^2}\right)$
Cumulative distribution function (cdf)	$\frac{1}{2}\left(1 + \text{erf}\left(\frac{x-\mu}{\sigma\sqrt{2}}\right)\right)$
Mean	μ
Median	μ
Mode	μ
Variance	σ^2
Skewness	0
Excess kurtosis	0
Entropy	$\ln\left(\sigma\sqrt{2\pi e}\right)$
Moment-generating function (mgf)	$M_X(t) = \exp\left(\mu t + \frac{\sigma^2 t^2}{2}\right)$
Characteristic function	$\chi_X(t) = \exp\left(\mu i t - \frac{\sigma^2 t^2}{2}\right)$

A histogram of male heights will appear similar to a bell curve, with the correspondence becoming closer if more data is used. For theoretical reasons (such as the central limit theorem), any variable that is the sum of a large number of independent factors is likely to be normally distributed.

For this reason, the normal distribution is used throughout statistics, natural science, and social science as a simple model for complex phenomena. For example, the observational error in an experiment is usually assumed to follow a normal distribution, and the propagation of uncertainty is computed using this assumption.

The probability density function for a normal distribution is given by the formula

$$p(x) = \frac{1}{\sigma\sqrt{2\pi}} \exp\left(-\frac{(x-\mu)^2}{2\sigma^2}\right),$$

where μ is the mean, σ is the standard deviation (a measure of the "width" of the bell), and exp denotes the exponential function. For a mean of 0 and a standard deviation of 1, this formula simplifies to

$$p(x) = \frac{1}{\sqrt{2\pi}} e^{-\frac{1}{2}x^2}$$

which is known as the standard normal distribution. When properly scaled and translated, the corresponding cumulative distribution function is known as the error function.

The Gaussian distribution is named for Carl Friedrich Gauss, who used it to analyse astronomical data, and defined the formula for its probability density function. The normal distribution was first introduced by Abraham de Moivre in an article in the year 1733, which was reprinted in the second edition of his *The Doctrine of Chances*, 1738 in the context of approximating certain binomial distributions for large *n*. His result was extended by Laplace in his book *Analytical Theory of Probabilities* (1812), and is now called the theorem of de Moivre-Laplace.

Laplace used the normal distribution in the analysis of errors of experiments. The important method of least squares was introduced by Legendre in 1805. Gauss, who claimed to have used the method since 1794, justified it rigorously in 1809 by assuming a normal distribution of the errors. The fact the distribution is sometimes called Gaussian is an example of Stigler's Law.

The name "bell curve" goes back to Esprit Jouffret who first used the term "bell surface" in 1872 for a bivariate normal with independent components. The name "normal distribution" was coined independently by Charles Sanders Peirce, Francis Galton and Wilhelm Lexis around 1875. Despite this terminology, other probability distributions may be more appropriate in some contexts.

Characterization

There are various ways to characterize a probability distribution. The most visual is the probability density function (PDF). Equivalent ways are the cumulative distribution function, the moments, the cumulants, the characteristic function, the moment-generating function, the cumulant-generating function, and Maxwell's theorem.

To indicate that a real-valued random variable X is normally distributed with mean μ and variance $\sigma^2 \geq 0$, we write

$$X \sim N(\mu, \sigma^2).$$

While it is certainly useful for certain limit theorems (e.g. asymptotic normality of estimators) and for the theory of Gaussian processes to consider the probability distribution concentrated at μ as a distribution with mean μ and variance $\sigma^2 = 0$, this degenerate case is often excluded from the considerations because no density with respect to the Lebesgue measure exists.

The normal distribution may also be parameterized using a precision parameter ô, defined as the reciprocal of σ^2. This parameterization has an advantage in numerical applications where σ^2 is very close to zero and is more convenient to work with in analysis as ô is a natural parameter of the normal distribution.

PROBABILITY DENSITY FUNCTION

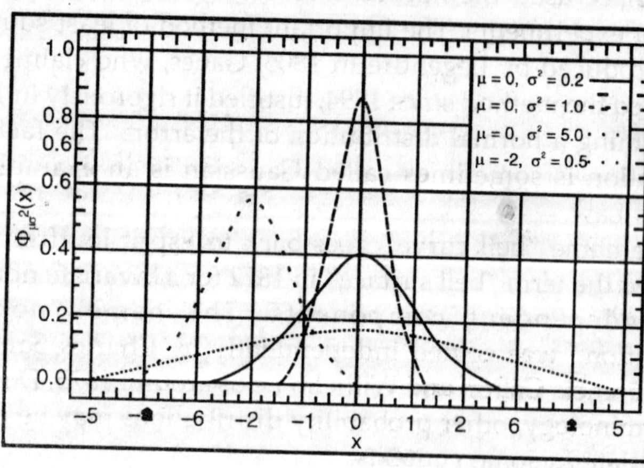

The continuous probability density function of the normal distribution is the Gaussian function

$$\varphi_{\mu,\sigma^2}(x) = \frac{1}{\sigma\sqrt{2\pi}} e^{-\frac{(x-\mu)^2}{2\sigma^2}} = \frac{1}{\sigma}\varphi\left(\frac{x-\mu}{\sigma}\right), x \in \mathbb{R},$$

where $\sigma > 0$ is the standard deviation, the real parameter μ is the expected value, and

$$\varphi(x) = \varphi_{0,1}(x) = \frac{e^{-x2/2}}{\sqrt{2\pi}} \quad x \in \mathbb{R},$$

is the density function of the "standard" normal distribution: i.e., the normal distribution with $\mu = 0$ and $\sigma = 1$. The integral of φ_{μ,σ^2} over the real line is equal to one as shown in the Gaussian integral article.

As a Gaussian function with the denominator in the exponent equal to 2, the standard normal density function φ is an eigenfunction of the Fourier transform.

The probability density function has notable properties including:

- Symmetry about its mean μ.
- The mode and median both equal the mean μ.
- The inflection points of the curve occur one standard deviation away from the mean, i.e. at $\mu - \sigma$ and $\mu + \sigma$.

Cumulative Distribution Function

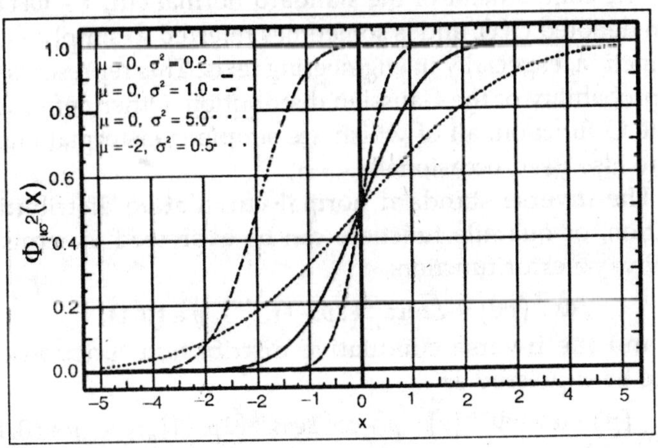

The cumulative distribution function (cdf) of a probability distribution, evaluated at a number (lower-case) x, is the probability of the event that a random variable (capital) X with that distribution is less than or equal to x. The cumulative distribution function of the normal distribution is expressed in terms of the density function as follows:

$$\Phi_{\mu,\sigma^2}(x) = \int_{-\infty}^{x} \varphi_{\mu,\sigma^2}(u)\,du$$

$$= \frac{1}{\sigma\sqrt{2\pi}} \int_{-\infty}^{x} \exp\left(-\frac{(u-\mu)^2}{2\sigma^2}\right) du, \quad x \in \mathbb{R}$$

The standard normal cdf is just the general cdf evaluated with $\mu = 0$ and $\sigma = 1$:

$$\Phi(x) = \Phi_{0,1}(x) = \frac{1}{\sqrt{2\pi}} \int_{-\infty}^{x} \exp\left(-\frac{u^2}{2}\right) du, \quad x \in \mathbb{R}.$$

The standard normal cdf can be expressed in terms of a special function called the error function, as

$$\Phi(x) = \frac{1}{2}\left[1 + \operatorname{erf}\left(\frac{x}{\sqrt{2}}\right)\right], \quad x \in \mathbb{R},$$

and the cdf itself can hence be expressed as

$$\Phi_{\mu,\sigma^2}(x) = \Phi\left(\frac{x-\mu}{\sigma}\right) = \frac{1}{2}\left[1 + \operatorname{erf}\left(\frac{x-\mu}{\sigma\sqrt{2}}\right)\right], \quad x \in \mathbb{R}.$$

The complement of the standard normal cdf, $1 - \Phi(x)$, is often denoted $Q(x)$, and is sometimes referred to simply as the Q-function, especially in engineering texts. This represents the tail probability of the Gaussian distribution. Other definitions of the Q-function, all of which are simple transformations of Φ, are also used occasionally.

The inverse standard normal cumulative distribution function, or quantile function, can be expressed in terms of the inverse error function:

$$\Phi^{-1}(p0) = \sqrt{2}\operatorname{erf}^{-1}(2p-1), \quad p \in (0,1),$$

and the inverse cumulative distribution function can hence be expressed as

$$\Phi^{-1}_{\mu,\sigma^2}(p) = \mu + \sigma\Phi^{-1}(p) = \mu + \sigma\sqrt{2}\operatorname{erf}^{-1}(2p-1), \quad p \in (0,1).$$

This quantile function is sometimes called the probit function. There is no elementary primitive for the probit function. This is not to say merely that none is known, but rather that the non-existence of such an elementary primitive has been proven. Several accurate methods exist for approximating the quantile function for the normal distribution.

The values $\Phi(x)$ may be approximated very accurately by a variety of methods, such as numerical integration, Taylor series, asymptotic series and continued fractions.

GENERATING FUNCTIONS

Moment generating function

The moment generating function is defined as the expected value of exp(tX). For a normal distribution, the moment generating function is

$$M_x(t) = E[\exp(tX)]$$

$$= \int_{-\infty}^{\infty} \frac{1}{\sigma\sqrt{2\pi}} \exp\left(-\frac{(x-\mu)^2}{2\sigma^2}\right) \exp(tx)\,dx$$

$$= \exp\left(\mu t + \frac{\sigma^2 t^2}{2}\right)$$

as can be seen by completing the square in the exponent.

CUMULANT GENERATING FUNCTION

The cumulant generating function is the logarithm of the moment generating function: $g(t) = \mu t + \sigma^2 t^2/2$. Since this is a quadratic polynomial in t, only the first two cumulants are nonzero.

CHARACTERISTIC FUNCTION

The characteristic function is defined as the expected value of exp(itX), where i is the imaginary unit. So the characteristic function is obtained by replacing t with it in the moment-generating function.

For a normal distribution, the characteristic function is

$$\chi x(t;\mu,\sigma) = M_x(it) = E[\exp(itX)]$$

$$= \int_{-\infty}^{\infty} \frac{1}{\sigma\sqrt{2\pi}} \exp\left(-\frac{(x-\mu)^2}{2\sigma^2}\right) \exp(itx)\,dx$$

$$= \exp\left(i\mu t - \frac{\sigma^2 t^2}{2}\right).$$

PROPERTIES

Some properties of the normal distribution:

- If $X \sim N(\mu,\sigma^2)$ and a and b are real numbers, then $aX + b \sim N(a\mu + b,(a\sigma)^2)$.
- The joint distribution of two independent normal random variables is a bivariante normal distribution. If $X \sim N(\mu x,\sigma_x^2)$ and $Y \sim N(\mu_Y,\sigma_Y^2)$ are independent normal random variables, then:
  - Their sum is normally distributed with $U = X + Y \sim N(\mu_X + \mu_Y,\sigma_x^2 + \sigma_Y^2)$ (proof). Thus the normal distribution is infinitely divisible. Interestingly, the converse holds: if two independent random variables have a normally-distributed sum, then they must be normal themselves — this is known as Cramér's theorem.
  - Their difference is normally distributed with $V = X - Y \sim N(\mu_X + \mu_Y,\sigma_x^2 + \sigma_Y^2)$.
  - If the variances of X and Y are equal, then U and V are independent of each other (and equal variance) – in the bivariate distribution, this corresponds to a change of coordinates in the plane from (x,y) to $(x + y, x \text{ “ } y)$, or equivalently a change of axes (rotation and dilation).
  - The Kullback-Leibler divergence is given by:

$$D_{KL}(X \,\|\, Y) = \frac{1}{2}\left(2\log\left(\frac{\sigma_Y}{\sigma_X}\right) + \frac{\sigma_X^2}{\sigma_Y^2} + \frac{(\mu_Y - \mu_X)^2}{\sigma_Y^2} - 1\right).$$

- If $X \sim N(0,\sigma_X^2)$ and $Y \sim N(0,\sigma_Y^2)$ are independent normal random variables, then:
  - Their product XY follows a distribution with density p given by $p(z)=\frac{1}{\pi\sigma_X\sigma_Y}K_0\left(\frac{|z|}{\sigma_X\sigma_Y}\right)$, where K_0 is a modified Bessel function of the second kind.
  - Their ratio follows a Cauchy distribution with $X/Y \sim \text{Cauchy}(0,\sigma_X/\sigma_Y)$. Thus the Cauchy distribution is a special kind of ratio distribution.
- If $X_1,\ldots,X_n$ are independent standard normal variables, then $X_1^2+\ldots+X_n^2$ has a chi-square distribution with n degrees of freedom.
- If $X_1,\ldots,X_n$ are independent standard normal variables, then the sample mean $\overline{X}=(X_1+\ldots+X_n)/n$

  and sample variance

  $$S^2=\left(\left(X_1-\overline{X}\right)^2+\ldots+\left(X_n-\overline{X}\right)^2\right)/(n-1)$$

  are independent. This can be proven using Basu's theorem or Cochran's theorem. This property characterizes normal distributions (and helps to explain why the F-test is non-robust with respect to non-normality!)

STANDARDIZING NORMAL RANDOM VARIABLES

As a consequence of Property 1, it is possible to relate all normal random variables to the standard normal.

If $X \sim N(\mu,\sigma^2)$, then

is a standard normal random variable: $Z \sim N(0,1)$. An important consequence is that the cdf of a general normal distribution is therefore

$$\Pr(X\le x)=\Phi\left(\frac{x-\mu}{\sigma}\right)=\frac{1}{2}\left(1+\text{erf}\left(\frac{x-\mu}{\sigma\sqrt{2}}\right)\right).$$

Conversely, if Z is a standard normal distribution, $Z \sim N(0,1)$, then

$$X = \sigma Z + \mu$$

is a normal random variable with mean μ and variance σ^2.

The standard normal distribution has been tabulated (usually in the form of value of the cumulative distribution function Φ), and the other normal distributions are the simple transformations, as described above, of the standard one. Therefore, one can use tabulated values of the cdf of the standard normal distribution to find values of the cdf of a general normal distribution.

MOMENTS

The first few moments of the normal distribution are:

Number	Raw moment	Central moment	Cumulant
0	1	1	
1	μ	0	μ
2	$\mu^2 + \sigma^2$	σ^2	σ^2
3	$\mu^3 + 3\mu\sigma^2$	0	0
4	$\mu^4 + 6\mu^2\sigma^2 + 3\sigma^4$	$3\sigma^4$	0
5	$\mu^5 + 10\mu^3\sigma^2 + 15\mu\sigma^4$	0	0
6	$\mu^6 + 15\mu^4\sigma^2 + 45\mu^2\sigma^4 + 15\sigma^6$	$15\sigma^6$	0
7	$\mu^7 + 21\mu^5\sigma^2 + 105\mu^3\sigma^4 + 105\mu\sigma^6$	0	0
8	$\mu^8 + 28\mu^6\sigma^2 + 210\mu^4\sigma^4 + 420\mu^2\sigma^6 + 105\sigma^8$	$105\sigma^8$	0

All cumulants of the normal distribution beyond the second are zero.

Higher central moments (of order $2k$) are given by the formula

$$E\left[(X-\mu)^{2k}\right] = \frac{(2k)!}{2^k k!}\sigma^{2k}.$$

The central limit theorem

Plot of the pdf of a normal distribution with $\mu = 12$ and $\sigma = 3$, approximating the pdf of a binomial distribution with $n = 48$ and $p = 1/4$

Under certain conditions (such as being independent and identically-distributed with finite variance), the sum of a large number of random variables is approximately normally distributed — this is the central limit theorem.

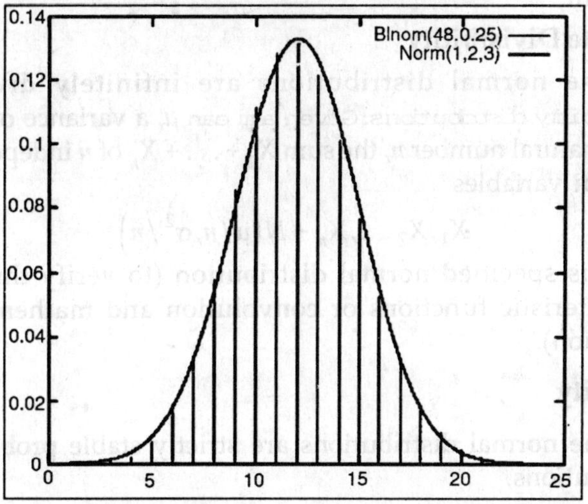

The practical importance of the central limit theorem is that the normal cumulative distribution function can be used as an approximation to some other cumulative distribution functions, for example:

- A binomial distribution with parameters n and p is approximately normal for large n and p not too close to 1 or 0 (some books recommend using this approximation only if np and $n(1 '' p)$ are both at least 5; in this case, a continuity correction should be applied). The approximating normal distribution has parameters $\mu = np$, $\sigma^2 = np(1 '' p)$.
- A Poisson distribution with parameter λ is approximately normal for large λ.

The approximating normal distribution has parameters $\mu = \sigma^2 = \lambda$.

Whether these approximations are sufficiently accurate depends on the purpose for which they are needed, and the rate of convergence to the normal distribution. It is typically the case that such approximations are less accurate in the tails of the distribution.

A general upper bound of the approximation error of the

cumulative distribution function is given by the Berry–Esséen theorem.

Infinite Divisibility

The normal distributions are infinitely divisible probability distributions: Given a mean μ, a variance σ^2 e" 0, and a natural number n, the sum $X_1 + \ldots + X_n$ of n independent random variables

$$X_1, X_2, \ldots, X_n \sim N\left(\mu/n, \sigma^2/n\right)$$

has this specified normal distribution (to verify this, use characteristic functions or convolution and mathematical induction).

Stability

The normal distributions are strictly stable probability distributions.

Standard deviation and Confidence Intervals

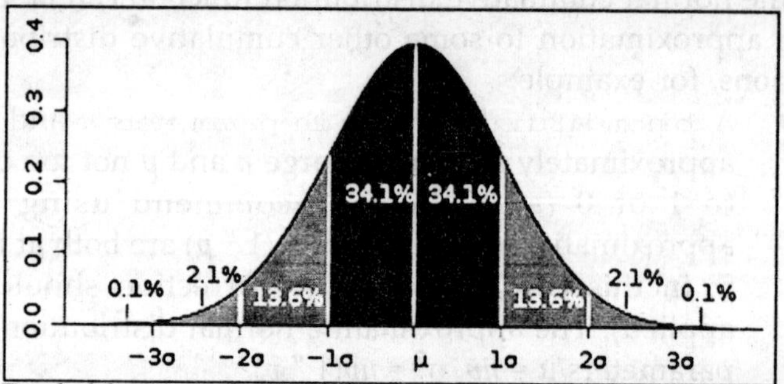

Dark blue is less than one standard deviation from the mean. For the normal distribution, this accounts for about 68% of the set (dark blue) while two standard deviations from the mean (medium and dark blue) account for about 95% and three standard deviations (light, medium, and dark blue) account for about 99.7%.

About 68% of values drawn from a normal distribution are within one standard deviation $\sigma > 0$ away from the mean μ; about 95% of the values are within two standard deviations and about 99.7% lie within three standard deviations. This is known as the "68-95-99.7 rule" or the "empirical rule."

To be more precise, the area under the bell curve between $\mu - n\sigma$ and $\mu + n\sigma$ in terms of the cumulative normal distribution function is given by:

$$\Phi_{\mu,\sigma^2}(\mu + n\sigma) - \Phi_{\mu,\sigma^2}(\mu - n\sigma)$$
$$= \Phi(n) - \Phi(-n) = 2\Phi(n) - 1 = \mathrm{erf}\left(n/\sqrt{2}\right),$$

where erf is the error function. To 12 decimal places, the values for the 1-, 2-, up to 6-sigma points are:

n	$\mathrm{erf}\left(n/\sqrt{2}\right)$
1	0.682689492137
2	0.954499736104
3	0.997300203937
4	0.999936657516
5	0.999999426697
6	0.999999998027

The next table gives the reverse relation of sigma multiples corresponding to a few often used values for the area under the bell curve. These values are useful to determine (asymptotic) confidence intervals of the specified levels based on normally distributed (or asymptotically normal) estimators:

$\mathrm{erf}\left(n/\sqrt{2}\right)$	n
0.80	1.28155
0.90	1.64485
0.95	1.95996
0.98	2.32635
0.99	2.57583
0.995	2.80703
0.998	3.09023
0.999	3.29052
0.9999	3.8906
0.99999	4.4172

where the value on the left of the table is the proportion of values that will fall within a given interval and n is a multiple of the standard deviation that specifies the width of the interval.

Exponential Family Form

The Normal distribution is a two-parameter exponential family form with natural parameters μ and $1/\sigma^2$, and natural statistics X and X^2. The canonical form has parameters $\frac{\mu}{\sigma^2}$ and $\frac{1}{\sigma^2}$ and sufficient statistics $\sum x$ and $-\frac{1}{2}\sum x^2$.

Complex normal Distribution

Consider the complex Gaussian random variable,

$$Z = X + iY$$

where X and Y are real and independent Gaussian variables with equal variances σ_r^2. The pdf of the joint variables is then

$$\frac{1}{2\pi\sigma_\tau^2} e^{-(x^2+y^2)/(2\sigma_\tau^2)}.$$

Because $\sigma_z = \sqrt{2}\sigma_\tau$, the resulting pdf for the complex Gaussian variable Z is

$$\frac{1}{\pi\sigma_Z^2} e - |Z|^2 / \sigma_Z^2.$$

Related Distributions

- R ~ Rayleigh (σ) is a Rayleigh distribution if $R = \sqrt{X^2 + Y^2}$ where $X \sim N(0, \sigma^2)$ and $Y \sim N(0, \sigma^2)$ are two independent normal distributions.
- $Y \sim \chi_\nu^2$ is a chi-square distribution with í degrees of freedom if $Y = \sum_{k=1}^{\nu} X_k^2$ where $X_k \sim N(0,1)$ for $k = 1, \ldots, \nu$ and are independent.
- $Y \sim$ Cauchy(μ= 0, θ= 1) is a Cauchy distribution if Y

= X_1 / X_2 for and are two independent normal distributions.

- $Y \sim \text{Cauchy}(\mu = 0, \theta = 1)$ is a log-normal distribution if $Y = e^X$ and $X \sim N(\mu.\sigma^2)$.
- Relation to stable distribution: if

$$X \sim \text{stable}(2, \beta, \sigma/\sqrt{2}, \mu) \text{ then } X \sim N(\mu.\sigma^2).$$

- Truncated normal distribution. If $X \sim N(\mu, \sigma^2)$, then truncating *X* below at *A* and above at *B* will lead to a random variable with mean $E(X) = \mu + \frac{\sigma(\varphi_1 - \varphi_2)}{T}$

where

$$T = \Phi\left(\frac{B-\mu}{\sigma}\right) - \Phi\left(\frac{A-\mu}{\sigma}\right), \varphi_1 = \varphi\left(\frac{A-\mu}{\sigma}\right), \varphi_2 = \varphi\left(\frac{B-\mu}{\sigma}\right)$$

and φ is the probability density function of a standard normal random variable.

- If *X* is a random variable with a normal distribution, and $Y = |X|$, then *Y* has a folded normal distribution.

DESCRIPTIVE AND INFERENTIAL STATISTICS

Scores

Many scores are derived from the normal distribution, including percentile ranks ("percentiles" or "quantiles"), normal curve equivalents, stanines, z-scores, and T-scores. Additionally, a number of behavioral statistical procedures are based on the assumption that scores are normally distributed; for example, t-tests and ANOVAs. Bell curve grading assigns relative grades based on a normal distribution of scores.

Normality tests

Normality tests check a given set of data for similarity to the normal distribution. The null hypothesis is that the data set is similar to the normal distribution, therefore a sufficiently small P-value indicates non-normal data.

- Kolmogorov–Smirnov test

- Lilliefors test
- Anderson–Darling test
- Ryan–Joiner test
- Shapiro–Wilk test
- Normal probability plot (rankit plot)
- Jarque–Bera test
- Spiegelhalter's omnibus test

ESTIMATION OF PARAMETERS

Estimators

For a normal distribution with mean μ and variance σ^2, the sample mean $\overline{X}$:

- Is the UMVU estimator for the population mean μ, by the Lehmann–Scheffé theorem (because it is an unbiased, complete, sufficient statistic),
- Is the maximum likelihood estimator for the population mean μ,
- Has sampling distribution $N(\mu,\sigma^2 / n)$, since the sum of n i.i.d. random variables has distribution $N(n\mu,n\sigma^2)$, and thus
- The standard error of the sample mean is $\sigma / \sqrt{n}$.

As the number of samples grows, the standard error of the sample mean decays as $1 / \sqrt{n}$– so if one wishes to decrease the standard error by a factor of 10, one must increase the number of samples by a factor of 100. This fact is widely used in determining sample sizes for opinion polls and number of trials in Monte Carlo simulation. The sample distribution of the mean depends on the standard deviation σ – it is not an ancillary statistic – and thus to estimate the error of the sample mean, one must estimate the standard deviation.

The sample standard deviation, defined as:

$$s = \sqrt{\frac{1}{n-1}\sum_{i=1}^{n}(x_1 - \overline{x})^2},$$

is a common estimator for the population standard deviation:

- s^2 is an unbiased estimator for the variance σ^2,
- The sampling distribution of s^2 is, up to scale, a chi-

square distribution with n–1 degrees of freedom; properly $(n-1)s_n^2/\sigma^2 \sim \chi_{n-1}^2$;,

- s is an ancillary statistic of the population mean μ – its sampling distribution does not depend on the population mean, and
- s^2 (and thus s) are independent of the sample mean X by Cochran's theorem.

Correction factor c_4 in unbiased estimation of standard deviation of a normal distribution.

Note that:

- There is a factor of n–1, not n, in the definition – this corresponds to the number of degrees of freedom (the residuals sum to 1, which removes one degree of freedom), and is known as Bessel's correction.
- The normal distribution is the *only* distribution whose sample mean and sample variance are independent.
- While s^2 is an unbiased estimator for the variance σ^2, s is a *biased* estimator for the standard deviation σ.

For the normal distribution, one can compute a correction factor, which depends on n, to arrive at an unbiased estimator of the standard deviation. This is denoted by c_4, and the corrected (unbiased) estimator is s / c_4. For n=2 $c_4 \approx 0.97$, while for n=10 so this correction is rarely used outside of high-precision estimation of small samples.

The standard error of the uncorrected (biased) sample standard deviation s is $\sigma\sqrt{1-c_4^2} \approx \sigma/\sqrt{2n}$ thus it also decays as $a/\sqrt{n}$.

Unbiased Estimation of Parameters

The maximum likelihood estimator of the population mean μ from a sample is an unbiased estimator of the mean. The maximum likelihood estimator of the variance is unbiased if we assume the population is known *a priori*, but in practice that does not happen. However, if we are faced with a sample and have no knowledge of the mean or the variance of the population from which it is drawn, as assumed in the maximum likelihood derivation above, then the maximum likelihood estimator of the variance is biased. An unbiased estimator of the variance σ^2 is:

$$S^2 = \frac{1}{n-1}\sum_{i=1}^{n}(X_i - \overline{X})^2.$$

This "sample variance" follows a Gamma distribution if all X_i are independent and identically-distributed:

$$S^2 \sim \Gamma\left(\frac{n-1}{2}, \frac{2\sigma^2}{n-1}\right),$$

with mean $E\left(S^2\right) = \sigma^2$ and variance

$$Var\left(S^2\right) = 2\sigma^4 / (n-1).$$

The maximum likelihood estimate of the standard deviation is the square root of the maximum likelihood estimate of the variance. However, neither this nor the square root of the sample variance provides an unbiased estimate for standard deviation.

Maximum Likelihood Estimation of Parameters

Suppose $X_1,\ldots, X_n$ are independent and each is normally distributed with expectation μ and variance $\sigma^2 > 0$. In the language of statisticians, the observed values of these n random variables make up a "sample of size n from a normally distributed population." It is desired to estimate the "population mean" μ and the "population standard deviation" σ, based on the observed values of this sample. The continuous joint probability density function of these n independent random variables is

$$f(x_1,\ldots,x_n;\mu,\sigma) = \prod_{i=1}^{n}\varphi_{u,\sigma^2}(x_i)$$

$$= \frac{1}{\left(\sigma\sqrt{2\pi}\right)^n}\prod_{i=1}^{n}\exp\left(-\frac{1}{2}\left(\frac{x_1-\mu}{\sigma}\right)^2\right), \quad (x_1,\ldots x_n) \in \mathbb{R}^n.$$

As a function of μ and σ, the likelihood function based on the observations $X_1,\ldots, X_n$ is

$$L(\mu,\sigma)=\frac{C}{\sigma^n}\exp\left(-\frac{\sum_{i=1}^{n}(X_i-\mu)^2}{2\sigma^2}\right),\quad \mu\in\mathbb{R},\ \sigma>0,$$

with some constant $C>0$ (which in general would be even allowed to depend on $X_1,\ldots,X_n$, but will vanish anyway when partial derivatives of the log-likelihood function with respect to the parameters are computed).

In the method of maximum likelihood, the values of μ and σ that maximize the likelihood function are taken as estimates of the population parameters μ and σ.

Usually in maximizing a function of two variables, one might consider partial derivatives. But here we will exploit the fact that the value of μ that maximizes the likelihood function with σ fixed does not depend on σ. Therefore, we can find that value of μ, then substitute it for μ in the likelihood function, and finally find the value of σ that maximizes the resulting expression.

It is evident that the likelihood function is a decreasing function of the sum

$$\sum_{i=1}^{n}(X_i-\mu)^2.$$

So we want the value of μ that *minimizes* this sum. Let

$$\bar{X}_n=(X_1+\cdots+X_n)/n$$

be the "sample mean" based on the n observations. Observe that

$$\begin{aligned}\sum_{i=1}^{n}(X_1=\mu)^2&=\sum_{i=1}^{n}\left((X_i-\bar{X}_n)+(\bar{X}_n-\mu)\right)^2\\&=\sum_{i=1}^{n}(X_i-\bar{X}_n)^2+2(\bar{X}_n-\mu)\underbrace{\sum_{i=1}^{n}(X_i-\bar{X}_n)}_{=0}\\&\qquad+\sum_{i=1}^{n}(\bar{X}_n-\mu)^2\\&=\sum_{i=1}^{n}(X_1-\bar{X}_n)^2+n(\bar{X}_n-\mu)^2.\end{aligned}$$

Only the last term depends on μ and it is minimized by

$$\hat{\mu}_n = \bar{X}_n.$$

That is the maximum-likelihood estimate of μ based on the n observations $X_1, \ldots, X_n$. When we substitute that estimate for μ into the likelihood function, we get

$$L(\bar{X}_n, \sigma) = \frac{C}{\sigma^n}\exp\left(-\frac{\sum_{i-1}^{n}(X_i - \bar{X}_n)^2}{2\sigma^2}\right), \quad \sigma > 0,$$

It is conventional to denote the "log-likelihood function", i.e., the logarithm of the likelihood function, by a lower-case – ℓ, and we have

$$\ell(\bar{X}_n, \sigma) = \log C - n\log\sigma - \frac{\sum_{i-1}^{n}(X_i - \bar{X}_n)^2}{2\sigma^2}, \quad \sigma > 0,$$

and then

$$\frac{\partial}{\partial\sigma}\ell(\bar{X}_n, \sigma) = -\frac{n}{\sigma} + \frac{\sum_{i-1}^{n}(X_i - \bar{X}_n)^2}{\sigma^3}$$

$$= -\frac{n}{\sigma^3}\left(\sigma^2 - \frac{1}{n}\sum_{i=1}^{n}(X_i - \bar{X}_n)^2\right), \quad \sigma > 0.$$

This derivative is positive, zero, or negative according as σ^2 is between 0 and

$$\hat{\sigma}_n^2 := \frac{1}{n}\sum_{i=1}^{n}(X_i - \bar{X}_n)^2,$$

or equal to that quantity, or greater than that quantity. (If there is just one observation, meaning that $n = 1$, or if $X_1 = \ldots = X_n$, which only happens with probability zero, then $\hat{\sigma}_n^2 = 0$ by this formula, reflecting the fact that in these cases the likelihood function is unbounded as σ decreases to zero.)

Consequently this average of squares of residuals is the maximum-likelihood estimate of σ^2, and its square root is the maximum-likelihood estimate of σ based on the n observations. This estimator $\hat{\sigma}_n^2$ is biased, but has a smaller mean squared error than the usual unbiased estimator, which is $n/(n-1)$ times this estimator.

Surprising Generalization

The derivation of the maximum-likelihood estimator of the covariance matrix of a multivariate normal distribution is subtle. It involves the spectral theorem and the reason it can be better to view a scalar as the trace of a 1×1 matrix than as a mere scalar.

Occurrence

Approximately normal distributions occur in many situations, as explained by the central limit theorem. When there is reason to suspect the presence of a large number of small effects *acting additively and independently*, it is reasonable to assume that observations will be normal. There are statistical methods to empirically test that assumption, for example the Kolmogorov-Smirnov test. Effects can also act as *multiplicative* (rather than additive) modifications. In that case, the assumption of normality is not justified, and it is the logarithm of the variable of interest that is normally distributed. The distribution of the directly observed variable is then called log-normal. Finally, if there is a single external influence which has a large effect on the variable under consideration, the assumption of normality is not justified either. This is true even if, when the external variable is held constant, the resulting marginal distributions are indeed normal. The full distribution will be a superposition of normal variables, which is not in general normal. This is related to the theory of errors.

To summarize, here is a list of situations where approximate normality is sometimes assumed.

- In counting problems, where the central limit theorem includes a discrete-to-continuum approximation and where infinitely divisible and decomposable distributions are involved, such as
  - Binomial random variables, associated with yes/no questions.
  - Poisson random variables, associated with rare events.
- In physiological measurements of biological specimens:

  - The *logarithm* of measures of size of living tissue (length, height, skin area, weight);
  - The *length* of *inert* appendages (hair, claws, nails, teeth) of biological specimens, *in the direction of growth*; presumably the thickness of tree bark also falls under this category;
  - Other physiological measures may be normally distributed, but there is no reason to expect that *a priori*;
- Measurement errors are often *assumed* to be normally distributed, and any deviation from normality is considered something which should be explained;
- Financial variables, in the Black–Scholes model
  - Changes in the *logarithm* of exchange rates, price indices, and stock market indices; these variables behave like compound interest, not like simple interest, and so are multiplicative;
  - While the Black–Scholes model assumes normality, in reality these variables exhibit heavy tails, as seen in stock market crashes;
  - Other financial variables may be normally distributed, but there is no reason to expect that *a priori*;
- Light intensity
  - The intensity of laser light is normally distributed;
  - Thermal light has a Bose–Einstein distribution on very short time scales, and a normal distribution on longer timescales due to the central limit theorem.

Of relevance to biology and economics is the fact that complex systems tend to display power laws rather than normality.

PHOTON COUNTING

Light intensity from a single source varies with time, as thermal fluctuations can be observed if the light is analyzed at sufficiently high time resolution. Quantum mechanics interprets measurements of light intensity as photon counting, where the natural assumption is to use the Poisson distribution. When light intensity is integrated over large times longer than the coherence time, the Poisson-to-normal approximation is appropriate.

MEASUREMENT ERRORS

Normality is the *central assumption* of the mathematical theory of errors. Similarly, in statistical model-fitting, an indicator of goodness of fit is that the residuals (as the errors are called in that setting) be independent and normally distributed. The assumption is that any deviation from normality needs to be explained. In that sense, both in model-fitting and in the theory of errors, normality is the only observation that need not be explained, being expected. However, if the original data are not normally distributed (for instance if they follow a Cauchy distribution), then the residuals will also not be normally distributed. This fact is usually ignored in practice.

Repeated measurements of the same quantity are expected to yield results which are clustered around a particular value. If all major sources of errors have been taken into account, it is *assumed* that the remaining error must be the result of a large number of very small *additive* effects, and hence normal. Deviations from normality are interpreted as indications of systematic errors which have not been taken into account. Whether this assumption is valid is debatable.

A famous and oft-quoted remark attributed to Gabriel Lippmann says: "Everyone believes in the [normal] law of errors: the mathematicians, because they think it is an experimental fact; and the experimenters, because they suppose it is a theorem of mathematics."

PHYSICAL CHARACTERISTICS OF BIOLOGICAL SPECIMENS

The sizes of full-grown animals are approximately lognormal. The evidence and an explanation based on models of growth was first published in the 1932 book *Problems of*

Relative Growth by Julian Huxley. Differences in size due to sexual dimorphism, or other polymorphisms like the worker/ soldier/queen division in social insects, further make the distribution of sizes deviate from lognormality.

The assumption that linear size of biological specimens is normal (rather than lognormal) leads to a non-normal distribution of weight (since weight or volume is roughly proportional to the 2nd or 3rd power of length, and Gaussian distributions are only preserved by linear transformations), and conversely assuming that weight is normal leads to non-normal lengths.

This is a problem, because there is no *a priori* reason why one of length, or body mass, and not the other, should be normally distributed. Lognormal distributions, on the other hand, are preserved by powers so the "problem" goes away if lognormality is assumed. On the other hand, there are some biological measures where normality is assumed, such as blood pressure of adult humans. This is supposed to be normally distributed, but only after separating males and females into different populations (each of which is normally distributed).

FINANCIAL VARIABLES

Already in 1900 Louis Bachelier proposed representing price changes of stocks using the normal distribution. This approach has since been modified slightly. Because of the multiplicative nature of compounding of returns, financial indicators such as stock values and commodity prices exhibit "multiplicative behaviour". As such, their periodic changes (e.g., yearly changes) are not normal, but rather lognormal - i.e. *logarithmic returns* as opposed to values are normally distributed. This is still the most commonly used hypothesis in finance, in particular in option pricing in the Black–Scholes model.

However, in reality financial variables exhibit heavy tails, and thus the assumption of normality understates the probability of extreme events such as stock market crashes. Corrections to this model have been suggested by mathematicians such as Benoît Mandelbrot, who observed that the changes in logarithm over short periods (such as a day) are approximated well by distributions that do not have a finite variance, and therefore the central limit theorem does not apply. Rather, the sum of many such changes gives log-Levy distributions.

DISTRIBUTION IN STANDARDIZED TESTING AND INTELLIGENCE

In standardized testing, results can be scaled to have a normal distribution – for example, the SAT's traditional range of 200–800 is based on a normal distribution with a mean of 500 and a standard deviation of 100. As the entire population is known, this normalization can be done, and allows the use of the Z test in standardized testing.

Sometimes, the difficulty and number of questions on an IQ test is selected in order to yield normal distributed results. Or else, the raw test scores are converted to IQ values by fitting them to the normal distribution.

In either case, it is the deliberate result of test construction or score interpretation that leads to IQ scores being normally distributed for the majority of the population. However, the question whether *intelligence* itself is normally distributed is more involved, because intelligence is a latent variable, therefore its distribution cannot be observed directly.

DIFFUSION EQUATION

The probability density function of the normal distribution is closely related to the (homogeneous and isotropic) diffusion equation and therefore also to the heat equation. This partial differential equation describes the time evolution of a mass-density function under diffusion. In particular, the probability density function

$$\varphi_{0,t}(x) = \frac{1}{\sqrt{2\pi t}} \exp\left(-\frac{x^2}{2t}\right),$$

for the normal distribution with expected value 0 and variance t satisfies the diffusion equation:

$$\frac{\partial}{\partial t}\varphi_{0,t}(t)=\frac{1}{2}\frac{\partial^2}{\partial x^2}\varphi_{0,t}(x).$$

If the mass-density at time $t = 0$ is given by a Dirac delta, which essentially means that all mass is initially concentrated in a single point, then the mass-density function at time t will have the form of the normal probability density function with variance linearly growing with t.

This connection is no coincidence: diffusion is due to Brownian motion which is mathematically described by a Wiener process, and such a process at time t will also result in a normal distribution with variance linearly growing with t.

More generally, if the initial mass-density is given by a function $\Phi(x)$, then the mass-density at time t will be given by the convolution of Φ and a normal probability density function.

USE IN COMPUTATIONAL STATISTICS

The normal distribution arises in many areas of statistics. For example, for a random variable with finite variance, the sampling distribution of the sample mean is approximately normal, even if the distribution of the population from which the sample is taken is not normal. However, for distributions with infinite or undefined variance, such as the Cauchy distribution, the sampling distribution of the sample mean need not be approximately normal.

In addition, the normal distribution maximizes information entropy among all distributions with known mean and variance, which makes it the natural choice of underlying distribution for data summarized in terms of sample mean and variance. The normal distribution is the most widely used family of distributions in statistics and many statistical tests are based on the assumption of normality.

GENERATING VALUES FOR NORMAL RANDOM VARIABLES

For computer simulations, it is often useful to generate values that have a normal distribution. There are several methods and the most basic is to invert the standard normal cdf. More efficient methods are also known, one such method being the Box-Muller transform. An even faster algorithm is the ziggurat algorithm. These are discussed below. A simple approach that is easy to programme is as follows. Simply sum 12 uniform (0,1) deviates and subtract 6 (half of 12). This is quite usable in many applications.

The sum over these 12 values has an Irwin–Hall distribution; 12 is chosen to give the sum a variance of exactly one. The resulting random deviates are limited to the range ("6, 6) and have a density which is a 12-section eleventh-order polynomial approximation to the normal distribution. The Box-Muller method says that, if you have two independent random numbers U and V uniformly distributed on (0, 1], (e.g. the output from a random number generator), then two independent standard normally distributed random variables are X and Y, where:

$$X = \sqrt{-2\ln U}\ \cos(2\pi V),$$

$$Y = \sqrt{-2\ln U}\ \sin(2\pi V).$$

This formulation arises because the chi-square distribution with two degrees of freedom is an easily-generated exponential random variable (which corresponds to the quantity $\ln U$ in these equations). Thus an angle is chosen uniformly around the circle via the random variable V, a radius is chosen to be exponential and then transformed to (normally distributed) x and y coordinates.

A method that is much faster than the Box-Muller transform but which is still exact is the so-called Ziggurat algorithm developed by George Marsaglia. In about 97% of all cases it uses only two random numbers, one random integer and one random uniform, one multiplication and an if-test. Only in 3% of the cases where the combination of those two falls outside the "core of the ziggurat" a kind of rejection sampling using logarithms, exponentials and more uniform random numbers has to be employed.

There is also some investigation into the connection between the fast Hadamard transform and the normal distribution, since the transform employs just addition and subtraction and by the central limit theorem random numbers from almost any distribution will be transformed into the normal distribution. In this regard a series of Hadamard transforms can be combined with random permutations to turn arbitrary data sets into a normally-distributed data.

NUMERICAL APPROXIMATIONS OF THE NORMAL DISTRIBUTION AND ITS CDF

The normal distribution function is widely used in scientific and statistical computing. Therefore, it has been implemented in various ways. The GNU Scientific Library calculates values of the standard normal cdf using piecewise approximations by rational functions.

Another approximation method uses third-degree polynomials on intervals. The article on the bc programming language gives an example of how to compute the cdf in Gnu bc. For a more detailed discussion of how to calculate the normal distribution.

SKEW NESS AND KURTOSIS

A fundamental task in many statistical analyses is to characterize the *location* and *variability* of a data set. A further characterization of the data includes skewness and kurtosis.

Skewness is a measure of symmetry, or more precisely, the lack of symmetry. A distribution, or data set, is symmetric if it looks the same to the left and right of the centre point.

Kurtosis is a measure of whether the data are peaked or flat relative to a normal distribution. That is, data sets with high kurtosis tend to have a distinct peak near the mean, decline rather rapidly, and have heavy tails.

Data sets with low kurtosis tend to have a flat top near the mean rather than a sharp peak. A uniform distribution would be the extreme case.

The histogram is an effective graphical technique for showing both the skewness and kurtosis of data set.

Definition of Skewness For univariate data $Y_1, Y_2, ..., Y_N$, the formula for skewness is:

$$skewness = \frac{\sum_{i=1}^{N}(Y_i - Y)^3}{(N-1)s^3}$$

where Y is the mean, is the standard deviation, and N is the number of data points. The skewness for a normal distribution is zero, and any symmetric data should have a skewness near zero. Negative values for the skewness indicate data that are skewed left and positive values for the skewness indicate data that are skewed right.

By skewed left, we mean that the left tail is long relative to the right tail. Similarly, skewed right means that the right tail is long relative to the left tail. Some measurements have a lower bound and are skewed right. For example, in reliability studies, failure times cannot be negative. *Definition of Kurtosis* For univariate data $Y_1, Y_2, ..., Y_N$, the formula for kurtosis is:

$$kurtosis = \frac{\sum_{i=1}^{N}(Y_i - \bar{Y})^4}{(N-1)s^4}$$

where $\bar{Y}$ is the mean, is the standard deviation, and N is the number of data points.

The kurtosis for a standard normal distribution is three. For this reason, some sources use the following defition of kurtosis:

$$kurtosis = \frac{\sum_{i=1}^{N}(Y_i - \bar{Y})^4}{(N-1)s^4} - 3$$

This definition is used so that the standard normal distribution has a kurtosis of zero. In addition, with the second definition positive kurtosis indicates a "peaked" distribution and negative kurtosis indicates a "flat" distribution.

Which definition of kurtosis is used is a matter of convention. When using software to compute the sample kurtosis, you need to be aware of which convention is being followed.

Examples The following example shows histograms for 10,000 random numbers generated from a normal, a double exponential, a Cauchy, and a Weibull distribution.

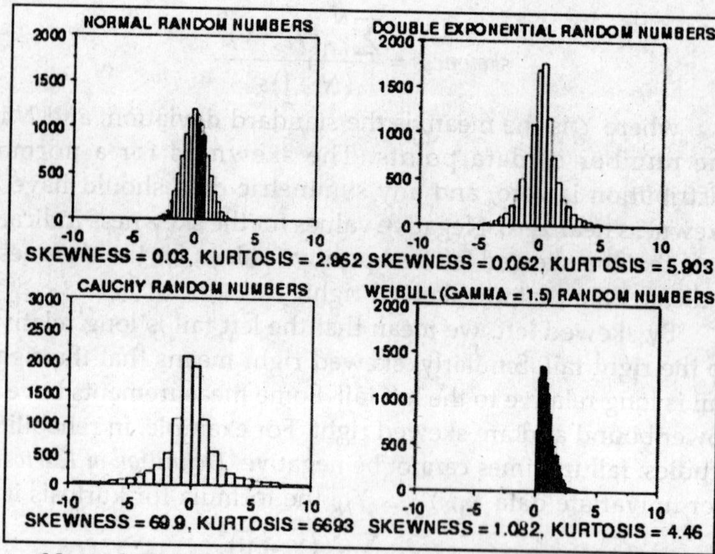

Normal Distribution The first histogram is a sample from a normal distribution. The normal distribution is a symmetric distribution with well-behaved tails. This is indicated by the skewness of 0.03. The kurtosis of 2.96 is near the expected value of 3. The histogram verifies the symmetry.

Double Exponential Distribution The second histogram is a sample from a double exponential distribution. The double exponential is a symmetric distribution. Compared to the normal, it has a stronger peak, more rapid decay, and heavier tails. That is, we would expect a skewness near zero and a kurtosis higher than 3. The skewness is 0.06 and the kurtosis is 5.9. *Cauchy Distribution* The third histogram is a sample from a Cauchy distribution.

For better visual comparison with the other data sets, we restricted the histogram of the Cauchy distribution to values between -10 and 10. The full data set for the Cauchy data in fact has a minimum of approximately -29,000 and a maximum of approximately 89,000.

The Cauchy distribution is a symmetric distribution with heavy tails and a single peak at the centre of the distribution. Since it is symmetric, we would expect a skewness near zero. Due to the heavier tails, we might expect the kurtosis to be larger than for a normal distribution. In fact the skewness is 69.99 and the kurtosis is 6,693. These extremely high values can be explained by the heavy tails. Just as the mean and standard deviation can be distorted by extreme values in the tails, so too can the skewness and kurtosis measures.

Weibull Distribution The fourth histogram is a sample from a Weibull distribution with shape parameter 1.5. The Weibull distribution is a skewed distribution with the amount of skewness depending on the value of the shape parameter.

The degree of decay as we move away from the centre also depends on the value of the shape parameter. For this data set, the skewness is 1.08 and the kurtosis is 4.46, which indicates moderate skewness and kurtosis.

Dealing with Skewness and Kurtosis Many classical statistical tests and intervals depend on normality assumptions. Significant skewness and kurtosis clearly indicate that data are not normal. If a data set exhibits significant skewness or kurtosis (as indicated by a histogram or the numerical measures), what can we do about it?

One approach is to apply some type of transformation to try to make the data normal, or more nearly normal. The Box-Cox transformation is a useful technique for trying to normalize a data set.

In particular, taking the log or square root of a data set is often useful for data that exhibit moderate right skewness. Another approach is to use techniques based on distributions other than the normal. For example, in reliability studies, the exponential, Weibull, and lognormal distributions are typically used as a basis for modeling rather than using the normal distribution. The probability plot correlation coefficient plot and the probability plot are useful tools for determining a good distributional model for the data.

THE SIGNIFICANCE OF STATISTICAL MEASURES – CONCEPT OF STANDARD ERROR AND ITS USES

Many times the outcome of a situation is difficult, maybe impossible, to predict. All we can say is that there is some range or distribution of possible outcomes. This is true for situations involving only inanimate objects, but is especially true for situations (like those you might find in an HCI environment) involving human beings. We might hope during these times to see some of the typical behaviors or events possible. This notion lies behind the statistical quantity of the *mean*.

It would also be nice to know something about the variety of events that are likely to occur. This corresponds to a quantity like *variance* or else *standard deviation*. Another problem is that we can only make a finite number of measurements on the real world, called a *sample*, as we seek to gain information about it.

It's possible that the sample we get may not actually represent what is typical in the real world. We would like to be able to get an idea of what level of *confidence* can we place on the ability of our measurements to represent what is really going on in the world. When we need to compare two samples or a sample to some required value, we can use the *t*-test to determine the how *significant* our sample is. If we have sample data that falls into categories, the *chi-square* analysis helps us determine the significance.

Two very good discussions of these topics, with different levels of depth of coverage, are listed below in the Links section. There are also other links to statistics-related information in that section. I have also provided a section on the Formulas relating to the above statistical measures.

LINKS

For a very basic overview of the field of statistics the Introduction To Statistics link from Arizona State is your best bet. A more moderate level discussion is in the UCLA Statistics Textbook.

A Short History of Probability:

The field of statistical analysis grew out of probability theory, and here is a brief history of that field. Notice how many famous mathematicians made contributions.

Introduction to Statistics:

From a course at Arizona State. Its for Education majors, so you know it can't be too complicated! It gives a brief, clear overview of the basic topics. Its not very good at showing how to make calculations, but it is good at describing the quantities and their properties. Some strong points are:

- Describing Centre and Spread of Distributions, especially the explanation and examples of *mode, median,* and *mean*. Also the discussion on the attributes of the *variance* and *standard deviation* of a distribution.
- Normal Distribution
- Introduction to Statistical Inference
- Inferential Tests of Means (Hypothesis Testing)
- Also (and this is very interesting to me) there is a link at the bottom of the page to the Statistics index page at the on-line Encyclopedia Britannica. The reason this is interesting is that if you go through the *Britannica* homepage (which is where my link above points), you have to either be a registered user or 7-day trial user (or still register). But the link off of the Arizona State page already seems to have registration information in the URI of the link, so you get right in (and since I am doubtful whether this was the intent of the *Encyclopedia Britannica,* I'm not going to reproduce that URI here). The *Britannica*'s coverage of the topic is more detailed than that of the Arizona State course, but is, as you would expect, excellent.

UCLA Statistics Textbook:

The discussion here is at a higher level than at the above site. This seems to be a work in progress (some links point nowhere), but I like the Introduction section, especially the sub-topics on:

- Variables
- Variance
- Sampling
- Inference

SurfStat *australia*:

From the Department of Mathematics at The University of Newcastle, Australia. An on-line statistics textbook, at least in theory. Some pages are missing and you get the dreaded 404 HTTP error code (which means it couldn't find the file). There are Java applets dealing with the Normal distribution, linear regression, and discrete probability distributions. There is also a choice of Java applet or text for computing or viewing tables of values for the Normal distribution, t-distribution, or chi-squared distribution.

Interesting Java Applets:

A listing from the Institute of Statistics & Decision Sciences at Duke.

FORMULAS

Our textbook also gives a good description of the basic elements of statistics. It is particularly strong in working out examples to show you how to use the formulas, except for the following error: on the top of page 242, on the first line, it mentions *10* degrees of freedom.

In problems where you are comparing two samples with N_1 and N_2 values, there are $N_1 + N_2 - 2$ degrees of freedom, which equals *9* for this problem. One thing that I thought would be nice here is a formula list as well as a brief synopsis of the *t*-test and the *chi-square* test.

The *mean* is the average value of a distribution.

$$\text{Mean} = \bar{X} = \frac{\sum_{i=1}^{N} X_i}{N}$$

The *standard deviation* of a distribution is a measure of how *spread out* it is. About two-thirds of a normal distibution (which is what approximates most large populations) lies within one standard deviation of the mean. Here is Figure from the text, which shows the percentages of a normally distributed population that lie some number of standard deviations from the mean:

The standard deviation can be calculated by first taking the sum of the squares of the differences between the sample values and the mean, which is labeled *SS* below. From this the *variance* is calculated, and then the standard deviation.

Sum of Squares of Differences from the Mean

$$= SS = \sum_{i=1}^{N}(X_1 - X)^2 = \sum_{i=1}^{N}(X_i^2) - \frac{\overline{X}^2}{N}$$

$$\text{Variance} = s^2 = \frac{SS}{N-1}$$

$$\text{Standard Deviation} = s = \sqrt{(s^2)}$$

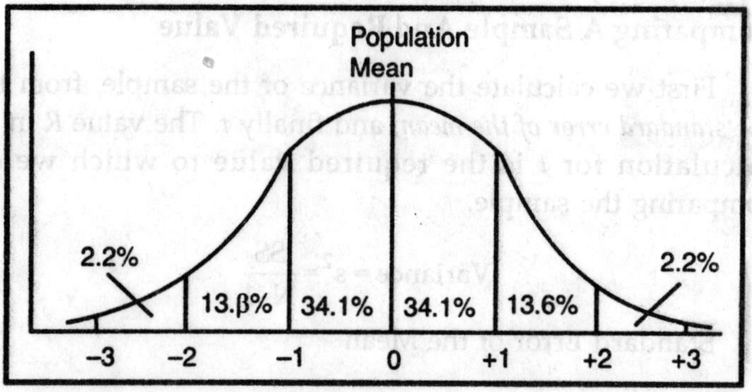

t-test

- Null hypothesis

Our deliberate change in the experimental conditions has had no effect; any difference in sample means or a sample mean and a required value is due entirely to variations among the population.

- Experimental hypothesis

Our change in the experimental conditions has had an effect on scores, which is reflected in the difference in sample means or the sample mean and a required value.

We want to set an upper bound on the probability that the null hypothesis is true. This significance value is represented by the greek letter alpha, and a typical value to shoot for is 0.05. First we must compute a value for *t*.

COMPARING TWO SAMPLES

First we calculate the variance of the two samples, from this the *standard error of difference,* and finally *t*.

$$\text{Variance} = s^2 = \frac{SS_1 + SS_2}{N_1 + N_2 - 2}$$

Standard Error of Difference

The text can be consulted to find the critical value of *t* given the number of degrees of freedom ($N_1 + N_2 - 2$) and a *two-tailed* significance value. If the computed *t* lies above this critical value, we can reject the null hypothesis with a level of probability less than the significance value (given by alpha).

Comparing A Sample And Required Value

First we calculate the variance of the sample, from this the *standard error of the mean,* and finally *t*. The value *R* in the calculation for *t* is the required value to which we are comparing the sample.

$$\text{Variance} = s^2 = \frac{SS}{N-1}$$

Standard Error of the Mean

$$= s_{em} = \sqrt{\frac{s^2}{N}}$$

$$t = \frac{(\bar{X} - R)}{s_{em}}$$

CHI-SQUARE TEST

Given *N* categories of data, each with observed and expected frequencies f_{oi} and f_{ei}, we have

$$\chi^2 = \sum_{i=1}^{N} \left[\frac{(f_{oi} - f_{ei})^2}{f_{ei}} \right]$$

We compare the calculated value of chi-squared with values in a table of critical values. There are N - 1 degrees of freedom. If the value in the table is *less* than our calculated value, we can reject the null hypothesis.

TESTING OF DIFFERENCE BETWEEN TWO MEANS – TEST FOR SMALL AND LARGE SAMPLES

Learning Objectives:

- State the assumptions for testing the difference between two means
- Estimate the population variance assuming homogeneity of variance
- Compute the standard error of the difference between means
- Compute t and p for the difference between means.

It is much more common for a researcher to be interested in the difference between means than in the specific values of the means themselves. This section covers how to test for differences between means from two separate groups of subjects. A later section describes how to test for differences between the means of two conditions in designs where only one group of subjects is used and each subject is tested in each condition.

We take as an example the data from the "Animal Research " case study. In this experiment, students rated (on a 7-point scale) whether they thought animal research is wrong. The sample sizes, means, and variances are shown separately for males and females.

Table. Means and Variances in Animal Research study.

Condition	*n*	*Mean*	*Variance*
Females	17	5.353	2.743
Males	17	3.882	2.985

As you can see, the females rated animal research as more wrong than did the males. This sample difference between the female mean of 5.35 and the male mean of 3.88 is 1.47. However, the gender difference in this particular sample is not very important. What is important is whether there is a difference in the population means.

In order to test whether there is a difference between population means, we are going to make three assumptions:

- The two populations have the same variance. This

assumption is called the assumption of homogeneity of variance.

- The populations are normally distributed.
- Each value is sampled independently from each other value. This assumption requires that each subject provide only one value. If a subject provides two scores, then the scores are not independent. The analysis of data with two scores per subject is shown in the section on the correlated t test later in this chapter.

The consequences of violating the former two assumptions are investigated in the simulation in the next section. For now, suffice it to say that small-to-moderate violations of assumptions 1 and 2 do not make much difference. It is important not to violate assumption 3.

We saw the following general formula for significance testing in the section on testing a single mean:

$$t = \frac{\text{statistic-hypothesized value}}{\text{estimated standard error of the statistic}}$$

In this case, our statistic is the difference between sample means and our hypothesized value is 0. The hypothesized value is the null hypothesis that the difference between population means is 0.

We continue to use the data from the "Animal Research" case study and will compute a significance test on the difference between the mean score of the males and the mean score of the females. For this calculation, we will make the three assumptions specified above.

The first step is to compute the statistic, which is simply the difference between means.

M1 - M2 = 5.3523 - 3.8824 = 1.470

Since the hypothesized value is 0, we do not need to subtract it from the statistic.

The next step is to compute the estimate of the standard error of the statistic. In this case, the statistic is the difference between means so the estimated standard error of the statistic is $\left(S_{M_1-M_2}\right)$. Recall from the relevant section in the chapter on sampling distributions that the formula for the standard error of the difference in means in the population is:

$$\sigma_{M_1-M_2} = \sqrt{\frac{\sigma_1^2}{n_1}+\frac{\sigma_2^2}{n_2}} = \sqrt{\frac{\sigma^2}{n}+\frac{\sigma^2}{n}} = \sqrt{\frac{2\sigma^2}{n}}$$

In order to estimate this quantity, we estimate σ2 and use that estimate in place of σ2. Since we are assuming the population variances are the same, we estimate this variance by averaging our two sample variances. Thus, our estimate of variance is computed using the following formula:

$$\text{MSE} = \frac{s_1^2 + s_2^2}{2}$$

where MSE is our estimate of σ2. In this example, MSE = (2.743 + 2.985)/2 = 2.864.
Since n (the number of scores in each condition) is 17,

$$s_{M_1-M_2} = \sqrt{\frac{2MSE}{n}} = \sqrt{\frac{(2)(2.864)}{17}} = 0.5805.$$

The next step is to compute t by plugging these values into the formula:
t = 1.47/.5805 = 2.533.

Finally, we compute the probability of getting a t as large or larger than 2.53 or as small or smaller than -2.53. To do this, we need to know the degrees of freedom. The degrees of freedom are the number of independent estimates of variance on which MSE is based. This is equal to (n1 -1) + (n2 -1) where n1 is the sample size for the first group and n2 is the sample size of the second group. For this example, n1 = n2 = 17. When n1= n2, it is conventional to use "n" to refer to the sample size of each group. Therefore the degrees for freedom are 16 + 16 = 32.

Once we have the degrees of freedom, we can use the t distribution calculator to find the probability. Figure shows that the probability value for a two-tailed test is 0.0164. The two-tailed test is used when the null hypothesis can be rejected regardless of the direction of the effect. It is the probability of a t < -2.533 or > 2.533.

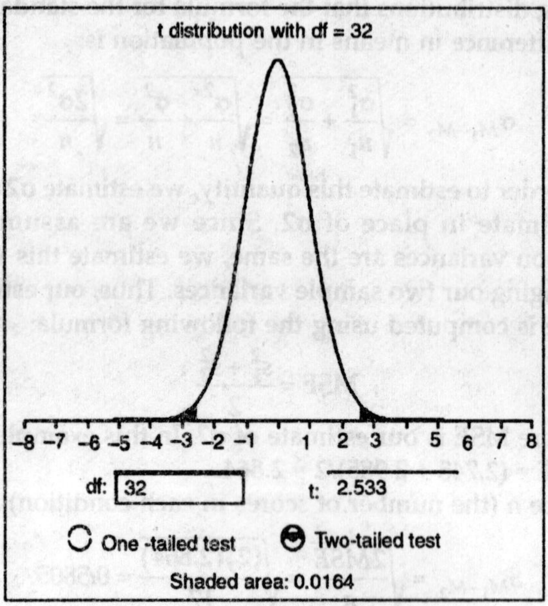

Fig. The Two-tailed Probability.

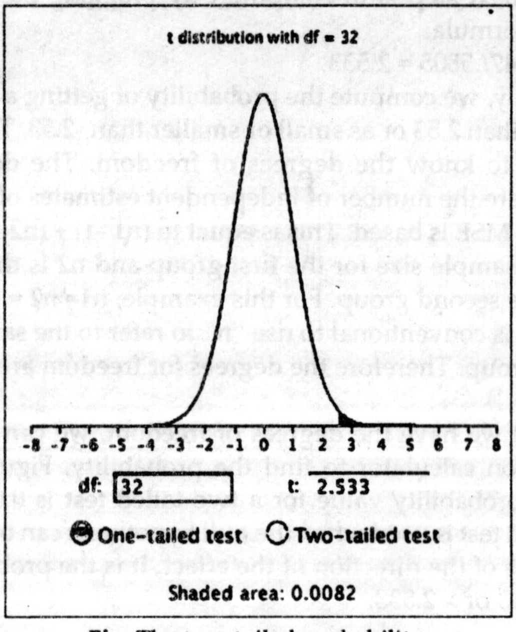

Fig. The two-tailed probability.

As you can see, the probability value of 0.0082 is half the value for the two-tailed test.

ONLINE CALCULATOR: T DISTRIBUTION

Formatting Data for Computer Analysis

Most computer programs that compute t tests require your data be in a specific form. Consider the data in Table.

Table. Example Data

Group 1	*Group 2*
3	2
4	4
5	6

Here there are two groups, each with three observations. To format these data for a computer programme, you normally have to use two variables: the first specifies the group the subject is in and the second is the score itself. For the data in Table, the reformatted data look as follows.

Table. Reformatted Data

G	Y
1	3
1	4
1	5
2	2
2	4
2	6

To use Analysis Lab to do the calculations, you would copy the data and then

- Click the "Enter/Edit User Data" button (You may be warned that for security reasons you must use the keyboard shortcut for pasting data).
- Paste your data.
- Click "Accept Data"
- Set the Dependent Variable to Y
- Set the Grouping Variable to G
- Click the t-test confidence interval button.

The t value is -2.4495, the df = 4, and p = 0.0705.

Computations for Unequal Sample Sizes (optional)

The calculations are somewhat more complicated when the sample sizes are not equal. One consideration is that MSE, the estimate of variance, counts the sample with the larger sample size more than the sample with the smaller sample size. Computationally this is done by computing the sum of squares error (SSE) as follows:

$$SSE = \sum(X - M_1)^2 + \sum(X - M_2)^2$$

where M1 is the mean for group 1 and M2 is the mean for group 2. Consider the following small example:

Table. Unequal n

Group 1	Group 2
3	2
4	4
5	

M1 = 4 and M2 = 3.

SSE = (3-4)2 + (4-4)2 + (5-4)2 + (2-3)2 + (4-3)2 = 4

Then, MSE is computed by: MSE = SSE/df

where the degrees of freedom (df) are computed as before:

df = (n1 -1) + (n2 -1) = (3-1) + (2-1) = 3.

MSE = SSE/df = 4/3 = 1.333.

The formula

$$S_{M_1 - M_2} = \sqrt{\frac{2MSE}{n}}$$

is replaced by

$$S_{M_1 - M_2} = \sqrt{\frac{2MSE}{n_h}}$$

where nh is the harmonic mean of the sample sizes and is computed as follows:

$$nh = \frac{2}{1/n_1 + 1/n2} = \frac{2}{1/3 + 1/2} = 2.4 \quad \text{and}$$

$$S_{M_1 - M_2} = \sqrt{\frac{(2)(1.333)}{2.4}} = 1.054.$$

Therefore,

t = (4-3)/1.054 = 0.949 and the two-tailed p = 0.413.

ELEMENTARY IDEAS ABOUT F-TEST ONE-WAY ANALYSIS OF VARIANCE

In statistics, analysis of variance (ANOVA) is a collection of statistical models, and their associated procedures, in which the observed variance is partitioned into components due to different explanatory variables. In its simplest form ANOVA gives a statistical test of whether the means of several groups are all equal, and therefore generalizes Student's two-sample *t*-test to more than two groups.There are three conceptual classes of such models:

- Fixed-effects models assumes that the data came from normal populations which may differ only in their means. (Model 1)
- Random effects models assume that the data describe a hierarchy of different populations whose differences are constrained by the hierarchy. (Model 2)
- Mixed-effect models describe situations where both fixed and random effects are present. (Model 3)

In practice, there are several types of ANOVA depending on the number of treatments and the way they are applied to the subjects in the experiment:

- One-way ANOVA is used to test for differences among two or more independent groups. Typically, however, the one-way ANOVA is used to test for differences among at least three groups, since the two-group case can be covered by a T-test. When there are only two means to compare, the T-test and the F-test are equivalent; the relation between ANOVA and *t* is given by $F = t^2$.
- One-way ANOVA for repeated measures is used when the subjects are subjected to repeated measures; this means that the same subjects are used for each treatment. Note that this method can be subject to carryover effects.
- Factorial ANOVA is used when the experimenter wants to study the effects of two or more treatment variables. The most commonly used type of factorial ANOVA is the 2×2 (read as "two by two", as you

would a matrix) design, where there are two independent variables and each variable has two levels or distinct values. Factorial ANOVA can also be multi-level such as 3×3, etc. or higher order such as 2×2×2, etc. but analyses with higher numbers of factors are rarely done by hand because the calculations are lengthy. However, since the introduction of data analytic software, the utilization of higher order designs and analyses has become quite common.

- When one wishes to test two or more independent groups subjecting the subjects to repeated measures, one may perform a factorial mixed-design ANOVA, in which one factor is a between-subjects variable and the other is within-subjects variable. This is a type of mixed-effect model.
- Multivariate analysis of variance (MANOVA) is used when there is more than one dependent variable.

MODELS

Fixed-Effects Models

The fixed-effects model of analysis of variance applies to situations in which the experimenter applies several treatments to the subjects of the experiment to see if the response variable values change. This allows the experimenter to estimate the ranges of response variable values that the treatment would generate in the population as a whole.

Random-Effects Models

Random effects models are used when the treatments are not fixed. This occurs when the various treatments (also known as factor levels) are sampled from a larger population. Because the treatments themselves are random variables, some assumptions and the method of contrasting the treatments differ from ANOVA model 1.

Most random-effects or mixed-effects models are not concerned with making inferences concerning the particular sampled factors. For example, consider a large manufacturing plant in which many machines produce the same product. The statistician studying this plant would have very little interest in comparing the three particular machines to each other. Rather, inferences that can be made for *all* machines are of interest, such as their variability and the overall mean.

Assumptions:

- Independence of cases - this is a requirement of the design.
- Normality - the distributions in each of the groups are normal.
- Equality (or "homogeneity") of variances, called homoscedasticity — the variance of data in groups should be the same.

Levene's test for homogeneity of variances is typically used to confirm homoscedasticity. The Kolmogorov-Smirnov or the Shapiro-Wilk test may be used to confirm normality. Some authors claim that the F-test is unreliable if there are deviations from normality (Lindman, 1974) while others claim that the F-test is robust (Ferguson & Takane, 2005, pp.261-2). The Kruskal-Wallis test is a nonparametric alternative which does not rely on an assumption of normality.

These together form the common assumption that the errors are independently, identically, and normally distributed for fixed effects models, or:

$$\varepsilon \sim N\left(0.\sigma^2\right).$$

LOGIC OF ANOVA

Partitioning of the sum of squares

The fundamental technique is a partitioning of the total sum of squares (abbreviated *SS*) into components related to the effects used in the model. For example, we show the model for a simplified ANOVA with one type of treatment at different levels.

$$SS_{\text{Total}} = SS_{\text{Error}} + SS_{\text{Treatments}}$$

The number of degrees of freedom (abbreviated *df*) can

be partitioned in a similar way and specifies the chi-square distribution which describes the associated sums of squares.

$$df_{\text{Total}} = df_{\text{Error}} + df_{\text{Treatments}}$$

The F-test

The F-test is used for comparisons of the components of the total deviation. For example, in one-way, or single-factor ANOVA, statistical significance is tested for by comparing the F test statistic

$$F = \frac{\text{variance of the group means}}{\text{Mean of the within-group variances}}$$

$$F^* = \frac{\text{MSTR}}{\text{MSE}}$$

where:

$$\text{MSTR} = \frac{\text{SSTR}}{I = 1}, I = \text{number of treatments}$$

and

$$\text{MSE} = \frac{\text{SSE}}{n_T - I}, nr = \text{total number of cases}$$

to the F-distribution with I-$1, n_T$-I degrees of freedom. Using the F-distribution is a natural candidate because the test statistic is the quotient of two mean sums of squares which have a chi-square distribution.

ANOVA ON RANKS

As first suggested by Conover and Iman in 1981, in many cases when the data do not meet the assumptions of ANOVA, one can replace each original data value by its rank from 1 for the smallest to N for the largest, then run a standard ANOVA calculation on the rank-transformed data. "Where no equivalent nonparametric methods have yet been developed such as for the two-way design, rank transformation results in tests which are more robust to non-normality, and resistant to outliers and non-constant variance, than is ANOVA without the transformation."

However Seaman *et al.* (1994) noticed that the rank transformation of Conover and Iman (1981) is not appropriate for testing interactions among effects in a factorial design as it can cause an increase in Type I error (alpha error). Furthermore, if both main factors are significant there is little power to detect interactions.

A variant of rank-transformation is 'quantile normalization' in which a further transformation is applied to the ranks such that the resulting values have some defined distribution (often a normal distribution with a specified mean and variance).

Further analyses of quantile-normalized data may then assume that distribution to compute significance values.

- Conover, W. J. & Iman, R. L. (1981). Rank transformations as a bridge between parametric and nonparametric statistics. *American Statistician, 35,* 124-129.
- Helsel, D. R., & Hirsch, R. M. (2002). *Statistical Methods in Water Resources: Techniques of Water Resourses Investigations, Book 4, chapter* A3. U.S. Geological Survey. 522 pages.
- Seaman, J. W., Walls, S. C., Wide, S. E., & Jaeger, R. G. (1994). Caveat emptor: Rank transform methods and interactions. *Trends Ecol. Evol., 9,* 261-263.

EFFECT SIZE MEASURES

Several standardised measures of effect are used within the context of ANOVA to describe the degree of relationship between a predictor or set of predictors and the dependent variable. Partial ç² (*Partial eta-squared*): Partial eta-squared describes the percentage of variance explained in the dependent variable by a predictor controlling for other predictors. Eta squared is generally considered to be a biased estimator of treatment effect, usually overestimating the value of the treatment effect by a significant amount.

It is, however, an easily calculated estimator the proportion of the variance in a population explained by the treatment.

$$\eta^2 = \frac{SS_{treatment}}{SS_{total}}$$

The following rules of thumb have emerged: small = 0.01; medium = 0.06; large = 0.14 These rules were taken from: Kittler, J. E., Menard, W., & Phillips, K., A. (2007). Weight concerns in individuals with body dysmorphic disorder. Since this ranking of effect size has been repeated from Cohen, J. (1988).

Statistical power analysis for the behavioral sciences. Hillsdale, NJ: Lawrence Earlbaum Associates with no change or comment over the years their validity is questionable outside of psychological/behavioral studies and questionable even then without a full understanding of the limitations ascribed by Cohen. The use of specific partial eta-square values for large medium or small as a "rule of thumb" should be avoided.

Omega Squared

Omega squared provides a relatively unbiased estimate of the variance explained in the population by a predictor variable. It takes random error into account more so than eta squared, which is incredibly biased to be too large. The calculations for omega squared differ depending on the experimental design. For a fixed experimental design (in which the categories are explicitly set), omega squared is calculated as follows:

$$\hat{\omega}^2 = \frac{SS_{treat} - df_{treat} MS_{error}}{SS_{total} + MS_{error}}$$

Cohen's *f* This measure of effect size is frequently encountered when performing power analysis calculations. Conceptually it represents the square root of variance explained over variance not explained.

FOLLOW UP TESTS

A statistically significant effect in ANOVA is often followed up with one or more different follow-up tests. This can be done in order to assess which groups are different from which other groups or to test various other focused hypotheses. Follow up tests are often distinguished in terms of whether they are planned (a priori) or post hoc. Planned tests are determined before looking at the data and post hoc tests are performed after looking at the data. Post hoc tests such as Tukey's test most commonly compare every group mean with every other group mean and typically incorporate some method of controlling of Type I errors.

Comparisons, which are most commonly planned, can be either simple or compound. Simple comparisons compare one group mean with one other group mean. Compound comparisons typically compare two sets of groups means where one set has at two or more groups (e.g., compare average group means of group A, B and C with group D). Comparisons can also look at tests of trend, such as linear and quadratic relationships, when the independent variable involves ordered levels.

POWER ANALYSIS

Power analysis is often applied in the context of ANOVA in order to assess the probability of successfully rejecting the null hypothesis if we assume a certain ANOVA design, effect size in the population, sample size and alpha level. Power analysis can assist in study design by determining what sample size would be required in order to have a reasonable chance of rejecting the null hypothesis.

Examples

Group A is given vodka, Group B is given gin, and Group C is given a placebo. All groups are then tested with a memory task. A one-way ANOVA can be used to assess the effect of the various treatments (that is, the vodka, gin, and placebo). Group A is given vodka and tested on a memory task. The same group is allowed a rest period of five days and then the experiment is repeated with gin. The procedure is repeated using a placebo. A one-way ANOVA with repeated measures can be used to assess the effect of the vodka versus the impact of the placebo.

In an experiment testing the effects of expectations, subjects are randomly assigned to four groups:

- Expect vodka—receive vodka
- Expect vodka—receive placebo
- Expect placebo—receive vodka
- Expect placebo—receive placebo (the last group is used as the control group)

Each group is then tested on a memory task. The advantage of this design is that multiple variables can be tested at the same time instead of running two different experiments. Also, the experiment can determine whether one variable affects the other variable (known as interaction effects). A factorial ANOVA (2×2) can be used to assess the effect of expecting vodka or the placebo and the actual reception of either.

Ronald Fisher first used variance in his 1918 paper The Correlation Between Relatives on the Supposition of Mendelian Inheritance. His first application of the analysis of variance was published in 1921. Analysis of variance became widely known after being included in Fisher's 1925 book *Statistical Methods for Research Workers.*

Bibliography

Barratt-Peacock, John. (2003). Australian home education : A model. *Evaluation and Research in Education, 17*(2 & 3), 101-111. [Australia]

Barson, Leslie Safran. (2006). *Learner-managed learning and home education: A European perspective.* Bramcote, Nottingham, United Kingdom: [United Kingdom, Britain]

Budajczak, Marek. (2004). *Edukacja domowa.* Gdansk, Poland: Gdanskie Wydawnictwo Psychologiczne. (On home education in Polish; an academic treatise by Polandís leading academic scholar on the topic of homeschooling.) [Poland].

Burkard, Tom & OíKeeffe, Dennis. (2005) Homeschooling: The case against compulsory school attendance laws. In Bruce S. Cooper (Ed.), *Home schooling in full view: A reader,* p. 229-249. Greenwich, CT: [United Kingdom, Britain, and international]

Cizek, Gregory J. (1993). The mismeasure of home schooling effectiveness: A commentary. *Home School Researcher, 9*(3), 1-4.

Cooper, Bruce S. (Ed.). (2005). *Home schooling in full view: A reader.* Greenwich, CT.

Duvall, Steven F. (2005). The effectiveness of home schooling students with special needs. In Bruce S. Cooper (Ed.), *Home schooling in full view: A reader,* p. 151-166. Greenwich, CT.

Duvall, Steven F., Ward, D. Lawrence, Delquadri, Joseph C., & Greenwood, Charles R. (1997). An exploratory study of home school instructional environments and their effects on the basic skills of students with learning disabilities. *Education and Treatment of Children,* 20(2), 150-172.

Gabb, Sean. (2005). Home schooling: A British perspective. In Bruce S. Cooper (Ed.), *Home schooling in full view: A reader*, p. 99-227. Greenwich, CT: [United Kingdom, Britain]

Howell, Charles. (2005). Parental duty and the shape of the future. *Home School Researcher, 16*(3), 1-14.

Ray, Brian D. (1990). *A nationwide study of home education: Family characteristics, legal matters, and student achievement*. Salem, OR: National Home Education Research Institute.**

Ray, Brian D. (1994). *A nationwide study of home education in Canada: Family characteristics, student achievement, and other topics*. Salem, OR: National Home Education Research Institute.

Ray, Brian D. (1997). *Strengths of their own—Home schoolers across America: Academic achievement, family characteristics, and longitudinal traits*. Salem, OR: National Home Education Research Institute.

Ray, Brian D. (2000). Home schooling for individualsí gain and societyís common good. *75* (1 & 2), 272-293.

Ray, Brian D. (2000). Home schooling: The ameliorator of negative influences on learning? *75*(1 & 2), 71-106.

Ray, Brian D. (2004). *Home educated and now adults: Their community and civic involvement, views about homeschooling, and other traits*. Salem, OR: National Home Education Research Institute.

Ray, Brian D., & Eagleson, Bruce K. (2008, August 14). State regulation of homeschooling and homeschoolersí SAT scores. *Journal of Academic Leadership, 6*(3). Retrieved August 25, 2008.

Rudner, Lawrence M. (1999). Scholastic achievement and demographic characteristics of home school students in 1998. *Educational Policy Analysis Archives, 7*(8); Retrieved 5/28/07.

Shyers, Larry E. (1992). A comparison of social adjustment between home and traditionally schooled students. *Home School Researcher, 8*(3), 1-8.

Somerville, Scott W. (2005). Legal rights for homeschool families. In Bruce S. Cooper (Ed.), *Home schooling in full view: A reader*, p. 135-149. Greenwich, CT.

Index

D

E

F

G

H

I

K

L

M

N

O

U

V